Life Without Limits

Life
Without
Limits

The Message of Mark's Gospel

Lloyd J. Ogilvie

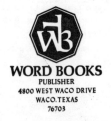

WORD BOOKS
PUBLISHER
4800 WEST WACO DRIVE
WACO, TEXAS
76703

LIFE WITHOUT LIMITS
Copyright © 1975 by
Word, Incorporated, Waco, Texas

Printed in the United States of America.

Library of Congress catalog card number: 75–24829

ISBN 0–8499–2861–3

Except where otherwise marked, Scripture quotations are
from the Revised Standard Version of the Bible, copyrighted
1946 (renewed 1973), 1956 and © 1971 by the Division of
Christian Education of the National Council of the Churches of
Christ in the U.S.A., and are used by permission.

First Printing, December 1976
Second Printing, May 1977
First Paperback Printing, February 1979
Second Paperback Printing, May 1979

To Scott

A wonderful son, a trusted friend,
with limitless gusto and enthusiasm

CONTENTS

PREFACE

I can remember the anticipation I felt as the Flying Scotsman pulled into the Edinburgh railroad station. It was good to be in the city I have grown to love ever since I did graduate studies there some years before. My expectancy, however, was more than just being in that lovely, history-filled city. It was the delicious knowledge that I had a month ahead for study, quiet and prayer.

My room was in the University Staff Club near the New College Library of the University of Edinburgh. Through the graciousness of Principal John MacIntyre, I was given full use of the library. I can remember the delight I felt at being able to be alone with my Lord to refill the wells of my mind and spirit after a year of exhausting, exhilarating and challenging ministry as pastor of the Hollywood Presbyterian Church.

My one task was to renew my relationship with the Savior through a comprehensive study of the Gospel of Mark. I was convinced that the person of Christ alone could be the source of new vision and power for me and the people to whom I would return to preach and lead. Zinzendorf was right and expressed my feelings that August. "I have a great need for Christ; I have a great Christ for my needs."

At home my country was passing through the last stages of the Watergate crisis. The impeachment of the President was imminent and the economic conditions were tedious. The Church in America was floundering for direction. My own congregation was grappling with the implications of what was to be God's strategy for the next stages of the emerging ministry of that great church as an equipping center for the ministry of the laity in the world.

My study of history had convinced me that any period of revival had been preceded by a rediscovery of Jesus Christ. He alone had been able to revitalize the sagging spirit of depleted Christians; he alone had been able to invigorate a passion for the needs of people; and he alone had energized the Church with new fire and contagion. I knew that I was living in one of those times that needed Christ more than anything else.

That was the conviction which led me to a fresh study of our Lord as he was so impellingly presented in the first Gospel to be

9

written. I began with the Greek text, lingering in every verse and around every word, writing my own translation. Then I read and reread the many English translations. That was followed by an exercise of what I call sanctified imagination. I tried to picture myself in each incident of the fast-moving account of Mark's tabulation of the triumphant adequacy of Christ. Then I pictured people and their needs being met in the way Christ ministered to people. The result of the prolonged study was a freshness in my own relationship with Christ.

In each of the chapters of this book, I have tried to capture what actually took place and then have related it to the problems and frustrations we all face in living. The exposition of the text of Mark is to expose the deeper meaning of what Jesus said and did. The contemporary, life-oriented application is to help all of us catch the drumbeat of the Master for today's adventure in discipleship.

The next phase of preparation for writing was to preach through Mark using the insights and ideas my time of study had revealed. The necessity of being articulate and relevant to people forced me to make the research more than facts or intellectual exercise. What was effective and meaningful to my people in the year's preaching of Mark greatly affected what I eventually wrote. What I had suspected to be true was validated: a year's focus on the person of Christ brought new life for preacher and people. I am not the same man I was when I began my study.

Mark had one purpose: to present Jesus of Nazareth as the Messiah, the Son of God, the Savior of all people. He wanted to impress his readers with the fact that the limitless power of God had been incarnated in Jesus' life, message, death, and resurrection. But he also wanted to communicate that God's limitless power was still available through the living Christ. The life Jesus lived was now offered to those who accepted him as Savior and Lord. Mark really believed that a personal relationship with Christ would result in the same power as he dramatized so vividly in the lives of people who met him during his ministry. The same is true for us.

Each chapter of this study of Mark is an exposition of a portion of the Gospel. Some deal with a few verses, while others catch the sweep of Mark's thought covering larger portions of the Gospel. I have designated the portions of Scripture to be covered so that what I wrote could be helpful for personal, daily devotions as well as resource material for small groups. I encourage you to read the

Scripture in preparation for each chapter. My aim is to communicate Mark's message with contemporary application and illustrations of real people who are living the adventure of the new life in Christ today.

When I had finished all the phases of preparation described here, I leaned back from my desk one day with an intriguing question, "If I had been a copy editor of the New Testament and had to write a title for Mark's Gospel, what would I write?" A title flashed into my mind. "Life without Limits." That's exactly what I had observed in the Savior and the life he makes available and precisely what I feel I have been guided to communicate here. Hence, the title of this book. My prayer is that life in Christ will be nothing less for you.

CHAPTER 1

THE GOSPEL ACCORDING TO YOU

There is a gospel according to you. A gospel is the good news of what God has done in and through Jesus Christ. What that means to us and how it is expressed through what we say and do is our gospel. It is being written in our attitudes, values, actions, and relationships. The people around us are reading our gospel every day.

The gospel according to us is the life, message, death, resurrection, and present power of Christ as each is ingrained, infused, and imputed in our character, convictions, and countenance. Our gospel is however much of the biblical Gospels and the influence of the living Christ that has become the settled truth by which we live. It is our credo, our stance and stature. The hope we expose in difficulty; the way we respond to life's opportunities.

The final test of the quality of our gospel is what the people around us would say are our basic convictions about life, death, and purpose. Our families, the people with whom we work, our friends, and the people whose lives we touch in pressure or tragedy can tell whether our gospel has given us vitality and viability. They know from the laboratory of life the result the historic gospel has had on us intellectually, emotionally, volitionally, and interpersonally.

Perhaps the greatest challenge of our period of history is for Christians to shape their own gospel more consistently around the essence of the true gospel. It is disturbing that so much of the gospel we are writing in our daily lives is a contradiction to the historic gospel. Many of us who believe in Jesus Christ as Messiah and Savior have difficulty shaping our lives around his Lordship. Our lack of freedom and joy betrays the ideas of the faith we portray. Often our fears and frustrations proclaim a very different gospel. Our personal, political and professional presuppositions actually communicate what's important to us, and the securities by which we live. If we were to pick three people and ask them to write a gospel according to us—an explanation of what they believe is our reason for being·and our strategy for life—what would they write?

The purpose of this book is to enable us to reconsider our gospel. I want to relive with you the life of Jesus Christ as seen through the eyes and experience of Mark. My hope is that everything he said and did will reorient our total life We will linger at each event, contemplate each saying, behold each miracle, feel each healing, experience each tragedy and triumph, and receive each benefit of the amazing life of Jesus. The result can be that Mark's Gospel will become our gospel. We will be able to say, "Christ is my Lord, my hope, my life!" Only what is dramatically rediscovered can be dynamically reproduced as our own gospel.

That's what happened to Mark. It took years of observation and learning before he had a Gospel to write. What he observed of Jesus as an eyewitness, learned from the disciples about him, and then was forced to go through in his own life hammered out his gospel.

We first meet Mark during the last week of Jesus' ministry. His mother, Mary, owned the house which was the site of the Upper Room. He was part of an underground fellowship which helped stage the triumphal entry of Jesus as Messiah. He made the arrangements for the Last Supper in his home and was an observer of the tragic events of Jesus' betrayal, trial, and crucifixion. It was that same upper room which continued as the meeting place of the disciples during the excruciating days of frightened waiting after the crucifixion. His mother had been one of the first witnesses to the resurrection. As the host of the disciples, Mark must have been one of the participants in the joy of the good news that Jesus was alive. And it was to his home that the disciples returned to wait for the power Jesus promised. I believe that he was with the apostolic fellowship when Jesus returned in the power of the Holy Spirit and the Church was born.

Mark was a part of the infant Church that began to grow in Jerusalem. He gave not only his home but his heart to the living Christ. Perhaps he was one of those who influenced the conversion of his cousin, Barnabas, who became distinguished for selling his lands and possessions and giving the proceeds to the apostles. As a part of a wealthy family, young Mark used his influence and financial resources to aid the fellowship of the Church. He shared the joyous adventure of the post-Pentecost expansion of the Church throughout Jerusalem and experienced the dynamic sessions of prayer and praise the Book of Acts vividly describes.

The more I study the life of Mark, the more I believe it must have been during those early months of the growth of the Church that Mark came under the influence of Peter. Peter became Mark's hero, friend, and teacher. From him Mark learned what Christ could do for a man who trusted his Lordship unreservedly. Mark knew of Peter's denial and repeated failures. But he also knew the new Peter in whom Christ lived. This Peter was the manly exposure of what happens when a person loves Christ with all his heart and courageously lives for him regardless of opposition.

We can imagine what Mark felt when he shared the Church's prayers for Peter when he was imprisoned for proclaiming Christ as Messiah and Lord. Acts 12:12 clearly indicates that the prayer meeting for Peter was held in Mark's home. He must have been amazed and delighted when the prayers for his friend were answered and Peter was released by God. The friendship he had with Peter was to become one of the most redeeming factors in his life.

It was in the next chapters of Mark's life that the gospel which he had heard and observed was to become his own. As is often the case, it happened through weakness, failure and discouragement.

Mark became an assistant of Paul on the first missionary journey with his cousin Barnabas. It was at Perga of Pamphylia that Mark deserted them. The reason for his defection is not known. Fear, hardship, and persecution must have been part of it. We can only imagine how difficult it was to measure up to Paul's standards of obedience to Christ. Perhaps, in addition to Mark's loneliness for Jerusalem and the warm fellowship with Peter and the others he had known, there was conflict between them. Up to this time Mark had been on the receiving end of the dynamic of the early Church. Now he was called upon to give what had not yet become his own. I think it was integrity which made him desert the evangelistic mission of Paul and Barnabas. He knew he did not have what it took, and honesty enabled him to return to Jerusalem. But that didn't ease the smarting wound of failure. Imagine what it must

have been like to go home to Jerusalem! How could he explain?
What excuse could he give? Weakness, lack of courage, cowardice?
All those must have become his second name back in Jerusalem.
But beneath it all, Mark must have known that the gospel was
not yet a part of his character. That's why he lacked courage.

Barnabas was not as severe with Mark as Paul. When it was
time to take the second missionary journey, he petitioned Paul to
take Mark with them. Luke records the conflict which resulted.
"And Barnabas wanted to take with them John called Mark. But
Paul thought best not to take with them one who had withdrawn
from them in Pamphylia, and had not gone with them to the work.
And there arose a sharp contention, so that they separated from
each other; Barnabas took Mark with him and sailed away to
Cyprus" (Acts 15:37–39). How very honest the Scriptures are! We
need not sentimentalize the early Church as sweetness and light.
The first-century Christians had the same squabbles we have today.
But the Scriptures are just as accurate and authentic about the
resolution of those problems.

We can see that as we follow the remedial path of Mark in later
years. We are sure that Barnabas, the one called the son of encouragement, was able to encourage Mark. Mark didn't need condemnation but conviction. He needed help to make the gospel his
own. And that's exactly what happened.

Mark's hero and friend Peter was the one who made a man out
of a vacillating, frightened defector. In his own epistle Peter calls
him "Mark, my son" (1 Pet. 5:13), a phrase which indicates not
only difference in their ages but the depth of their affection. Mark
became Peter's disciple and interpreter. To hurt deeply is to be
able to help deliberately. Mark listened to Peter's preaching
tempered by the fires of experience. He shared long hours of companionship which imprinted Peter's character on Mark. Most of all
Peter's forgiveness and compassion enabled Mark to accept Christ's
forgiveness and make a new beginning. Peter knew about failure. He was a rock that had cracked in denial and resistance to
his Lord. People who have known the anguish of failure can help
those of us who fail.

The crucial thing for us as we begin a study of Mark's Gospel is
to see the influence of Peter's life and message on Mark. It was
from Peter that Mark learned the intimate details of what Christ
had said and done. That's what makes this Gospel so exciting. It

is vivid, firsthand, authentic. A. M. Hunter says, "We shall not go far astray if we find in the gospel according to Mark the 'reminiscences of Jesus as told by Peter to his friend John Mark.' "[1]

Irrespective as to what happened while Mark was with Peter, the result was amazing. The reconciliation for which Christ died was experienced between Paul and Mark. The power of the gospel became his realized experience. And Paul mentions him with loving care in several of his letters: He commends him to the church at Colossia (Col. 4:10–11); Timothy is instructed to bring Mark to him, "Get Mark and bring him with you; for he is very useful in serving me" (2 Tim. 4:11)—not a bad commendation for a rehabilitated failure! Mark shares Paul's apostolic greeting to Philemon (Philem. 24), and it is he who gives comfort and strength in prison to Paul, whom he had failed less than ten years before. Now Mark became, lived, and communicated the gospel which had been so difficult to make his own.

That's why I love Mark and his Gospel so much. He went through what we all experience in seeking to be faithful and obedient to Christ. What he wrote down was more than church rhetoric or lifeless conceptualism. His Gospel was a Person, Jesus Christ himself. He wanted everyone to know Christ and experience the new life he had found.

That gives meaning and purpose to the difficulties and failures of our lives as we seek to make the gospel our own. Everything that happens—every experience we have which illuminates our inadequacy and God's sufficiency—is to hammer out the gospel according to us. It is all in preparation for us to be able to say, "I know this to be true; it has *happened* to me!"

It was after Paul and Peter had been martyred that Mark realized the need for a terse, brief and fast-moving account of the life and message of Jesus. The early church at Rome needed a written record of the sayings of Jesus along with a chronology of his acts and deeds. Persecution of the Christians necessitated it. The pressures for denial and defection were horrendous. Mark knew the only solution to difficulty which had worked in his own life: the Person of Christ! Meditation on him as the Messiah had broken the binds of defeat and failure in his own experience. He knew that

---

[1] A. M. Hunter, *The Gospel According to Mark* (London: S.M.C. Press Ltd., 1949), p. 17.

the church at Rome did not need the frills of theological reflection. They needed the greatest story ever told about the most triumphant life ever lived. That's why he wrote the first recorded Gospel.

Mark took the sayings of Jesus which had been retold again and again among the early Christians, the account of his life as related by Peter, his own experiences of Jesus as an eyewitness, and developed his Gospel under the guidance of the Holy Spirit. With breathless urgency and rapid-fire movement, he wrote the good news which had become the hope of his own life. His words are like a fast-moving river of thought, and we find ourselves caught up in the currents and are moved along swiftly from event to event.

Mark's purpose in writing is clear from the beginning. He wanted to expose Jesus of Nazareth as the Son of Man, Messiah, the life and power of God. But he also wanted to show life as it was meant to be for us. He wanted his reader to find himself in every passage with "you are there" realism. The hoped for response from us is that we will make Jesus our Lord and begin to live the startlingly exciting adventure he came to offer.

The result will be our own gospel. The word *gospel* meaning "good news" had three stages in its development. It meant the bearer of good news, the good news itself, and finally it was used for the reward given to someone who carried the good news. Jesus is all three for us. He brought the good news of God's love and forgiveness. He was that incarnate in himself. Now he is himself the reward of those who accept him. Mark did not give the church at Rome advice or analysis about the problems of persecution—he gave them Christ. That's our greatest need today. Luther was right. "Man only needs Jesus Christ!"

But to make him our own, to live in him, to learn from him, to experience his power, to receive his indwelling life-Spirit is the only way to be the gospel for our times. When we are Christ-captivated and Christ-conditioned we will be good news in a world filled with bad news of human inability and inadequacy. Life without limits is offered to us in Mark's Gospel. Christ is the limitless power of God incarnate in history. All power in heaven and earth is released through him. Once it becomes our own good news, we will model life without limits to the people around us.

CHAPTER 2

THREE TO GET READY

Mark 1:1-11

I have found that there are several crucial elements in creative communication of truth. The first is the content itself. It must be authentic in every way and stand the test of careful examination and experimentation. Then it must be made clear by the communicator in all its meaning and ramifications. The second is the communicator himself. Is he convinced about the truth he is communicating? Has it happened to him? Has he tested it in the laboratory of his own life? The third is the recipient of the communication as reader or listener. Does the communicator understand where he is and is he sensitive to what he has experienced and believed? Has he been listened to prior to the communication? What are his problems, hopes, and expectations? What are the full implications of the content for him if he accepted it? Is it understandable to him in language he can assimilate? Are there gripping illustrations which give him windows through which to look at the truth and consider its dynamics? The last element is the action which the truth dictates. If the recipient accepts it, what should he do about it? What behavioral changes would indicate that he has made the truth his own?

Mark is an excellent communicator. He includes all these elements in the prologue to his Gospel. He states his content forthrightly and impellingly. The purpose of his Gospel is Jesus Christ, the Son of God. He clarifies this purpose with great care. He wants to establish beyond question that Jesus is the long awaited Messiah, and the limitless resources of God revealed in him. His message, life, death and resurrection are to defeat all the enemies which frustrate and debilitate us. And he is alive now to continue in us as Savior and Lord what he began in his earthly ministry.

From the very beginning of the Gospel we feel the intimacy and intensity of the author. He is convincing because he is convinced. Mark knows his central character personally and has tried out every idea he writes about him.

But also, he knew his readers. He felt their need, empathizing with their plight and problem. He had listened intently to the early church at Rome. His heart beat with theirs. He knew that they did not need more advice about obedience. They needed to be loved. And Mark knew how to do that. He didn't want to answer unasked questions nor give dissertations which were not immediately applicable to their needs. The Church needed to be sure of Christ. In describing what he accomplished Mark could dramatize the limitless life available to them. He was convinced that Christ himself was the only liberating and lasting motivation of the Christian life.

When I was privileged to share the exciting days of the birth and growth of the Winnetka Presbyterian Church some years ago, I was amazed at the hunger for Jesus Christ in that affluent, sophisticated suburb of Chicago. The more we preached Christ, studied his life and message, claimed the contemporary power of his presence, and modeled the new life made possible by his indwelling Spirit, the more people flocked to the church. The hunger for Jesus Christ was vividly communicated to me on the day we finished the new building to house the life of the emerging congregation. The night before we all had worked to finish up the preparations of the building for dedication. The next day when I mounted into the beautifully carved, new pulpit, I looked down at the Bible to read my text. There boldly staring up at me was a plaque placed over the open Scriptures. It quoted the words of the Greeks who came seeking Jesus. "Sir, we wish to see Jesus!" That not only expressed the deepest need of the congregation but its fondest hope. I later learned that the man who had slipped into the sanctuary late at night to put the startling and undeniable challenge before me was a highly educated, polished, and cultured Christian who recently had found new life in Christ. He knew his greatest need was shared by the whole congregation.

Mark knew from his own experience that only Christ could satisfy, sustain, and strengthen the struggling, infant church at

Rome. From his hero Peter he had learned what to do in trouble. Mark heard Peter say, "Beloved, do not be surprised at the fiery ordeal which comes upon you to prove you, as though something strange were happening to you. But rejoice in so far as you share Christ's sufferings" (1 Pet. 4:12–13). And from Paul he had learned the triumphant adequacy of Christ. "For all things are yours, whether Paul or Apollos or Cephas or the world or life or death or the present or the future, all are yours; and you are Christ's and Christ is God's" (1 Cor. 3:21–23).

But as the years rolled by, separating the early Church from the historic Jesus, questions arose and conviction about the gospel was needed. The first-century Christians were constantly harassed not only by painful rejection and persecution but by challenges of the authenticity of Jesus as Messiah.

That's why Mark began his Gospel with the prophetic promises of the Old Testament and dramatized how Jesus fulfilled each impeccably. He did not present Jesus as an historical figure in a vacuum, but rather as the one to whom all history had been leading. Even in his introduction to the Gospel the truth Mark revealed had personal implications for the reader. The response given by the people to the prophetic ministry of John the Baptist was the response he wanted from his friends at Rome. Expressing the need of Israel for God, he is very inclusive: "All of Judea and all of the people of Jerusalem went out to hear John." The people longed for revival, for something more than the rites and rituals of formalized religion. They were tired of drab obligations and guilt-inducing rules—heritage and history had been substituted for God himself. Now, out in the wasteland where the Jordan River empties into the Dead Sea was one who had a compelling word from God. No wonder "all" of the people surged out to hear him. They had a hunger for God.

So did the Christians at Rome. And so do we. It is a great gift from God to realize our hunger for him. The church at Rome could not substitute its new customs for God. Today, one of the greatest needs in the Church is to recover our appetite for him. It is tragic how the church with its endless committee meetings and purposeless customs can make us think we are fed.

We get fed up, but not satisfied. Mark wants all of us to feel the need expressed by those persistent pilgrims who heard John gladly. They recognized the despair of the time, the disparity of Israel's impotent nationalism, and the discouragement of their own lives. From the villages, cities, and countryside they came, saying, "We need God!"

There was a belief that Elijah would return just before the Messiah was to arrive on the scene. John was the Elijah-figure for Mark, preparing the way so the Messiah could not only enter history but into the hearts of a prepared people.

In preparing the way for the coming Messiah, John proclaimed three things the world needed before the Messiah came.

The same preparation is needed today for Christ to come in power to each of us, the church, and our nation.

The first is confession of sin. Not just sins, but Sin. That means separation from the God for whom we were created. All the subtle sins come from that. We were fashioned for relationship with God and others. Anything which debilitates that is sin.

John proclaimed the judgment of God: a crucial ingredient of his love. God cares profoundly. He will not let us go. The way he wants us to live in fellowship with him had been delineated clearly in the commandments. John's preaching was not angry condemnation, but an urgent recall to God's objective guide for living.

Here at last was a word from God! In it they could see themselves as they were and admit what they had done with the gift of life. They could admit how they had drifted from God and how their nation had rebelled against him.

There's something very refreshing about confession. It is tonic for the soul; not a rearrangement of ideas, but a flushing out of the heart. Only a sinner needs a Savior. And when we admit our need for someone to heal our soul sickness, we can acknowledge and receive what Mark has to say about the one who came to do just that.

The second aspect of John's message is repentance. The Greek word for repentance is *metanoia,* meaning a radical turn to God. That's what Isaiah had in mind, "Return to the Lord" (55:7), and Hosea, "Come, let us return to the Lord" (6:1). Like the Prodigal Son, it means humbly returning home after the squandering of life. This is far more than a mere change of mind; it involves a new direction—toward God.

I believe that's the greatest need in America. The past few years have shocked us into a realization that though we pledge our allegiance to a nation under God, we are way *under.* And the distance is growing. The moral and political condition across our land screams out the truth. We had a unique place in God's strategy for history, but our vision of it has faded.

What can be done? We can do what the people who went to hear John did. Admit it and repent. God's new age is just a repentance away. Recently I saw a poster which read, "If you feel separated from God, who moved?" Not God! John's listeners discovered that, and so must we.

The third dynamic of John's preparatory ministry is baptism. That may be more difficult to identify with readily. Many of us have been baptized with varying degrees of meaning. But the spiritual implications of baptism should be fresh every day. For John, baptism was a tangible sign of dedication, cleansing, and commitment. It was practiced by him to give people a physical experience of the spiritual reality of their confession and repentance. Israel needed to be cleansed and any Jew who wanted to join his purification movement was baptized. Baptism had profound psychological effects on people and was a vivid witness to others of their commitment. It symbolized the drowning of an old self and a raising up of a new person. John distinguished clearly between his baptism of water and the baptism of the Holy Spirit which would be done by the one for whose ministry he was preparing. "I have baptized you with water, but he will baptize you with the Holy Spirit."

Our post-resurrection understanding of baptism gives it further meaning. For us baptism is to die with Christ in a death like his and be raised up in a resurrection like his (Rom. 6). The result of that is the confirmation of God. That's the impact of Mark's account of Jesus' baptism. Why did he record that? Surely to give further proof that Jesus was the Messiah, but also to communicate the assurance of God on Jesus and anyone who believes in him. What God said to Jesus at his baptism he now says to us. Preparation for Mark's Gospel is in the realization that through Christ we are God's beloved sons and daughters in whom he is well pleased.

Mark tells us that the heavens opened after Jesus' baptism and the Spirit descended on him. This was not just a parting of the clouds. "The heavens" is Hebrewism for God and his power. The voice which declared Jesus God's beloved Son is still speaking in our souls. "You're mine. You're unique and special. I am pleased with you! I love you. Through my beloved Son you are my beloved person."

I need the heavens to open like that every day. Without God's assurance I am left to compulsive self-justification. But without the dove of the Spirit, God's invigorating, infusing, and inspiring power I cannot live the limitless life I was loved and forgiven to know.

Mark's prologue to this Gospel has fulfilled his intention. The Messiah about whom we will read accomplished what he did because he was anointed with power at his baptism. Jesus was not the best of good men but the long awaited Son of God. Mark's prologue says, really, "Listen to what I have to say. The one I want to tell you about is the authentic Messiah. What I will tell you about him is a matter of life and death!"

Three things to get ready: confession of our need, return to the only one who can meet those needs, and a dedication to receive what he has to offer. The result is the realization that the Lord portrayed on the pages of this Gospel lived and died for each of us.

CHAPTER 3

HOW TO STAY ALIVE

Mark 1:12–15

Why is it so few Christians act like Christ? Why is it difficult to maintain the enthusiasm and joy of our initial commitment and grow in Christ's love and power? When we give our problems to Christ, why do we still have problems? Why, after the experience of Christ's victory, do we find it so hard to live a victorious life? How can it be that so many Christians are tired out, uptight, out of power, without vision, and unable to communicate their faith to other people? Why is it that after we come alive in Christ it's so difficult to stay alive?

If the personal is too painful, let's shift to the Church. Why is it that the Church finds it difficult to be the new creation of God's people? Why, with all we believe, is there so little love and freedom in most churches? Why do we wring our hands in anxious anguish over human need all around us when the same power revealed in Jesus is given to his people? Why has the Church historically been the bastion of resistance rather than the adventuresome leaders of renewal in society? So often our economic and political convictions are more important than Christ and the gospel. Why is that?

These questions are not new! The early Church faced them and the church at Rome for which Mark wrote his Gospel grappled with them in particular. How can a new Christian stay alive in persecution and temptation? Will the power of Christ stand the test of reality? Mark's answer was no trite treatise on growing spirituality. Rather he brought the Church back to Christ. He wanted them to be sure that the Lord in whom they had placed their trust was truly the Messiah. What happened to Christ would happen to them, only now, because of what happened to him, they could face temptation and grow through it.

Our exposition of Mark brings us to the temptation of Jesus. After the assurance of the baptism, he was driven by the Spirit into the wilderness to be tempted by Satan, to be ministered to by angels, and to win the battle which gives us the secret of how to stay alive spiritually.

Note that Jesus' temptation was punctuated by two powerful parentheses. In the baptism was the affirmation of his Messiahship. "This is my beloved Son in whom I am well pleased." Then followed the temptation in the wilderness. After that we see Jesus striding out with tempered triumph proclaiming that the Kingdom of God is at hand. There was only one adequate response to that: repent, believe the gospel!

The same is true for us. We begin the Christian life with the liberating experience of God's grace penetrating to the depth of our souls. But he does not leave us there. The wilderness temptation follows as surely as night follows day. Like Jesus, the assurance of the anointing is followed by the tempering of testing temptation. He will not leave us half-healed; excited but unchanged. He knows that unless we are liberated at the core we cannot stay alive. We cannot live a new life with old values, motives and attitudes. God wants more than a foot in the door of our hearts; he wants to come live in us and take complete control of our total being.

We all know about temptations, but I want to talk about *the* temptation. There is an essential temptation through which we must pass which makes all others easier to face and overcome. Once we have victory in this temptation we are really ready to live. This temptation prepares us to face all others. What do you think it is? Jesus passed through it and so must we.

He knew he was the Messiah. All power in heaven and earth was at his disposal, but he had to decide how he was to do his work. He was conscious of a tremendous task and of his limitless powers.

Jesus faced the same challenge we all face, only to a greater degree. What resources did he possess? He had to evaluate his gifts, decide how he would use them in his strategy to establish the Kingdom—the rule of God in men's minds and hearts in their relationships, and through them in every area of society. In a way, every person who thinks at all is faced with the same questions: What are my gifts, how can I use them for others and a better world, and how shall I go about it? Shall we live for ourselves or for others as a fulfillment of God's will? That's the challenge . . . and life's greatest temptation.

The word *temptation* really means trial or testing. Jesus passed through this experience, not to be Messiah, but because he was! He had to begin his battle. We are also tempted or tested, not in order to be God's people, but because we already are and must become prepared to live victoriously over beguiling distractions. Just as Jesus was tempted after the confirmation of the Holy Spirit at baptism, so it is as we begin to realize that as God's people with some sense of his love and power, we, too, must be tested and prepared. Anyone who has not had this experience of God's call doesn't know real temptation. He just drifts through life, doing what's expected, without knowing the issues.

Jesus' tempter was called Satan. Satan means adversary—or one who presents a case against us. He gets the goods on us and holds it against us. In Jesus' temptation as in ours, the power of evil tries to wage his battle with the good, the subtle, the admired, the accepted.

Note the progression in our text: "The Spirit immediately drove him out into the wilderness. And he was in the wilderness forty days, tempted by Satan; and he was with the wild beasts; and the angels ministered to him" (Mark 1:12-13).

There are the three phases of our greatest experience of preparation to live. Like Jesus, we are:

1. Driven by the Spirit.
2. Tempted by Satan.
3. Ministered to by angels.

Why would Jesus be driven by the Spirit? The Spirit is to protect us, not drive us to temptation. How strange! The verb is a strong one. It really means "thrust" or "cast" or "under control of." Under the strong motivating, pressing control of the Spirit, we see Jesus leaving the beautiful solemnity of his baptism beside the Jordan River with measured, determined steps. It was no leisurely, meditative walk, but swift, impetuous movement, as one driven irresistibly by the knowledge that there was something which must be done, a battle that must be fought.

The Spirit drove Jesus to the wilderness in order to engage in battle with the power of evil. As the first fully obedient man in the midst of disobedience, Jesus had a battle to fight with evil at every turn of his life. The essential battle, however, was to be fought and won now at the beginning of his ministry. Here in absolute solitude, alone without the distraction or help of family or friend, he wrestled with the basic temptation.

The wilderness stretches between Jerusalem on the central plateau and the Dead Sea. In the Old Testament we find this area referred to as the "Devastation." It is an area of thirty-five by fifteen miles. Sand, crumbling limestone and scattered shingle combine to establish a desolate mood. The hills of sand are like dust heaps; the limestone is blistered and peeling, rocks are bare and jagged. Under the heat of the sun it becomes like a furnace. It was here that Jesus had to sort things out.

God put him through it to defeat the power of evil and to enable him to strengthen those who were tempted. The author of Hebrews observed the truth, "For we have not a high priest who is unable to sympathize with our weaknesses, but one who in every respect has been tempted as we are, yet without sinning" (Heb. 4:15).

How does this fit in with Jesus' prayer, "Lead us not into temptation," or James' thought, "Let no one say when he is tempted, 'I am tempted by God,' for God cannot be tempted with evil and he himself tempts no one"? Is there a disunity in Scripture exposed here? No. Here are two different aspects of one truth. Does God tempt us or not? Note that our text says that Jesus was driven by the Spirit and tempted by Satan. God pressed Jesus into battle with evil so that the crucial, central issue of life could be faced, battled through, and won by his power. Jesus had to decide between the world's good and God's best.

If you were the devil's helper and had to figure out a strategy for defeating Jesus early in his ministry, what would you do? A frontal attack with the obvious temptations would be rejected. Somehow you would have to work out temptations which looked creative, righteous, beneficial. They would have to be attractive enough to tempt him to take an easy way to accomplish the ultimate. That's just what the evil one tried to do! The Matthew account of the same event gives us a clear picture of the specifics (Matt. 4:1–11).

The three temptations for Jesus—to change stones into bread, to cast himself down from the Temple, and to accept the kingdom of the world for worshiping Satan—are the ones we all must face in order to be free to conquer the lesser, subtler manifestations of

these three temptations. They are the tempting troika, the tantaliz-
ing trinity of the immediate, the expedient, the temporary.

The immediate is always a tender trap. We want everything
yesterday! The hardest cruelest word is wait. Wait until you are
older, wait until you get to college, wait until you deserve it, wait
until you can afford it. Wait . . . wait!

Satan challenged Jesus to turn the stones into bread. The wilderness area had thin slabs of stone strewn by the erosion of nature
along the pathway. After many days without food and water, Jesus
was famished. The hungrier he became, the more he empathized
with the hungry masses he had seen everywhere in Palestine. The
tempter played upon this physical hunger. How easy it would be
for Jesus to use his Messianic powers to produce bread for people's
physical hunger rather than be the Bread of Life for the deep
spiritual hunger for God's love and power. Jesus was tempted by
the intriguingly immediate. And so are we. How shall we use our
gifts? To satisfy the desires within: hunger, security, sex, popularity, power? The first temptation, then, was to try to accomplish
God's purposes with man's provision. That would have been
enough for Jesus or any of us in the wilderness.

But it is nothing in comparison to the temptation of expediency.
Jesus was tempted to cast himself down from the pinnacle of the
Temple. Two images converge to make a treacherous, attention-
getting gimmick. The pinnacle of the Temple perhaps really
meant the corner of the plateau where Solomon's porch and the
Royal Porch met at Mt. Zion. Here there is a sheer drop of 450
feet into the Kidron Valley. Jesus could shortcut the long process
of getting a following by testing the Scripture of Psalm 91:11-12.
If, indeed, angels protected him, he would be the hero of Israel and
recognized immediately as the Messiah.

The lingering question raised by this temptation is how shall we
affect and influence the lives of people? How shall we lead? How
can we get people to do what we want? Every person, young and
old, is faced with this question and is tempted with easy answers.

We are tempted to manipulate, arrange, and coerce to get our
way. And in the process we often negate, hurt, or even destroy the
people around us. There is a kind of gamesmanship we learn in our
society which uses compliments, guilt, fear, anger, and frustration
to get people to do what we want. And we can use the elements of

our religious and cultural heritage to do it legitimately, just as Satan used Scripture to tempt Jesus. The time-honored prejudices of our society, our "values," can be used to segregate, negate, castigate, and mitigate—and all in honor of the good! The challenge of the second temptation was to accomplish our purposes by God's power.

But give most care to the intent of the third temptation—the temporary and its bedfellow, compromise. The tempter took Jesus to see the kingdoms of the world. There is a plateau in the wilderness which overlooks the Jordan Valley. Here is a panorama which includes plush, green Jericho; Mount Nebo, from which Moses dreamed of fulfillment in the Promised Land; and the Dead Sea and beyond toward Egypt and the Nile Valley; and Jerusalem with its memories of bygone splendor and glory. The whole checkered tapestry of Israel's history was displayed before his eyes.

What was the future of his nation? Once great, now she was one of hundreds of little servant nations under the heel of Rome. What would God do with his people? Conquer the world? Save the world? Again and again Israel had to be broken and brought to realize that its purpose was to love, not subdue.

At this vulnerable moment in Jesus' struggle with evil, Satan promised him dominion over the kingdoms of this world by military might. The question would come to dog his steps right to the end when he entered Jerusalem in the last week of his life. And then he was able to choose the simple, humble way upon a donkey because he had won the battle long before in the wilderness.

The temptation is ours also. We are tempted with the temporary. How very easy it is to live a "peace at any price" or "war for any victory" kind of life. We are challenged to compromise our values in order to get what looks well, satisfies people, puts off conflict, or placates issues. Jesus could have led Israel to political victory, lived to a ripe old age, and been honored as a great hero or Nazareth's greatest Rabbi, but he would not have saved the world. He chose, instead, the way of the suffering servant in order to show men the way of humility and service. Nations and empires have come and gone, but the suffering Galilean remains supreme. Anything but Jesus Christ and life in him is a temporary solution to any problem.

We are being tempted today by the good of the temporary. We are easily beguiled because the alternatives seem so righteous. It is necessary that we seriously participate in the war on poverty, integration of society, changing of decadent structures. But let's be clear about it: People alone can change the world, and only what happens to people is permanent and lasting. And when the things which distort and debilitate people become God's agenda for us, he will give us his power to accomplish his purpose.

Everywhere we look in the Gospel records we see Jesus in conflict with evil. He met it in the resistance of the Pharisees as well as in the unclean spirits of the sick and confused. At the same time, we see the solicitous desires and efforts of his friends to keep him safe without conflict. Again and again he had to say, "Get behind me Satan!" He could say this because he had won! Now evil staggered before him. This shall be true for us also.

The third temptation, then, was to accomplish God's purposes with Satan's power. The price was high. All that was necessary was to worship Satan. For us that means the temporary, spectacular, manipulative devices we develop to shortcut our dependence on the Lord. Satan is concerned only with those who begin the new life in Christ. He will try anything to negate that. His most clever strategy is to get us to depend on him to do God's work. In the name of righteousness we coerce, haggle over doctrine, judge and negate people, use military might to subdue our enemies, and, finally, use people as things.

As Jesus was tempted in order to live, so are we. The source of our hope and help is the same. As Jesus was ministered to by angels, so are we. Paul discovered this and reminded the Corinthians: "No temptation has overtaken you that is not common to man. God is faithful, and he will not let you be tempted beyond your strength, but with the temptation will also provide the way of escape, that you may be able to endure it" (1 Cor. 10:13).

God is with us in our temptation. He sends his angels to sustain us through it. The word *angel* means "messenger" and is used in the Bible for spiritual and human agents who carry out God's will. Here in the temptation, "the angels" implies emissaries from God, particularized manifestations of his Spirit for the battle with evil. The result was inward peace and strength which came in the prolonged struggle for a clear understanding of the Father's will for Jesus' ministry. The same is true for us. Special messengers of his Spirit, along with people he deploys to help us, will be given in our times of temptation.

Browning was right, "When the fight begins within himself, a man's worth something."[1]

But the God who allows the fight never lets us go through it alone. Once we have had this time of essential testing we will be able to face and conquer all lesser temptations. Instead of the immediate, the expedient, and the temporary, we will have discovered our true resource, our true purpose, and our only source of power. Then we can live!

After the temptations, we see Jesus filled with the Spirit beginning his ministry. It was then that he found what I like to call the fourth temptation. It was not in the wilderness, but back in Galilee. He was told that his cousin John the Baptist had been arrested by Herod. That would have been a signal for retreat and withdrawal for anyone else. He could have been tempted to give up the vision of the Kingdom of God he had been anointed by God to proclaim. Instead he saw in John's arrest the completion of the preface of preparation for his Messiahship. He was able to face the temptation of discouragement. Why try? Will it make any difference? Will they do to me what they did to John? What other men would have interpreted as despair, Jesus could discern as God's timing to begin.

That's the way it works for us too. Once we have been in the wilderness and faced the ultimate temptation, the temptation to be discouraged is past. God is in charge. The signs which others read as hopelessness are the signal that our Lord is about to intervene to move us on to fulfill his plan for us. When things are bleak, Jesus strides forth with the good news of the Kingdom. When there is no human hope left, he reminds us that the Kingdom is at hand. And what else can we do in response than obey his command to repent and believe the gospel? We turn from despair and give our lives to the only way left: the gospel which for us now incorporates his message, life, Cross, resurrection and powerful presence.

I talked to a woman recently who had been brought to the end of herself. There was just not enough energy, time, love and patience in her to meet persistent demands of her husband and large family. She was trying to do it all herself and had run out of steam. She began to resent the relentless pressure, the feeling of

---

[1] Robert Browning, "Bishop Blougram's Apology."

being used, and the hopelessness of it ever being any different. A Christian counselor insisted that she get away for a few days. She took a personal retreat. In the quiet alone, she realized she had lost her only reliable source of power: Christ himself. She had been trying to be his person on her power. Discouragement had resulted. As she became rested, she started to pray again. Then she was led to the temptation passages in Mark and Matthew. She was amazed at how close she had come to a nervous breakdown by depending on her own strength. The woman she had become was a shrewlike extension of Satan. Then the Lord gave her the secret: "Do all you do as for me; thank me constantly for the challenges; trust me for the results; open yourself to my Spirit for the power to make your home my Kingdom. When things get tough, see it as a sign of a new incident of my intervention." The despair and discouragement lifted, and she was a new woman when she returned home.

It may not be possible for each of us to become involved in this kind of retreat, but there is one thing we can do right now. We can finish reading this chapter realizing the wilderness inside and the need to go through the temptations ourselves. Having done that we will be able to face anything!

CHAPTER 4

TAKING MEN ALIVE

Mark 1:16–20

This passage of Mark could change our lives. It contains a secret which could transform the Church. If believed and practiced by us, it would enrich and liberate the lives of the people around us. But most of all, each of us would discover our essential reason for being alive, and our lives would be enlivened and empowered by an exciting purpose which would release our unused potential.

I am convinced that we are all looking for a challenge which is demanding enough to stretch us and tap the best within us. We want to be involved in something which will make a difference to our time of history. The thing we fear most is having lived our lives pleasantly, but to have made no measurable difference whatever. We abhor irrelevance, insignificance, and ineffectiveness. What this passage has to say could radically change all that.

Each of us is the indispensable link in God's continuing creation. We were born, not only to know him, experience his love focused in Jesus Christ, respond by faith and live in obedience to his indwelling Holy Spirit, but also to become reproducers of our faith. The pervading purpose of our lives is to become involved in creative relationships to mediate grace to others. Communication of hope to individuals is the calling given to every Christian. We need not, dare not, look for the grand and spectacular as the underlying challenge of our lives. God's most important work is with individuals. And we are the link. We have been given the tremendous gift of words and the context of creative conversation as the basic expression of our ministry. Whatever else we do, if this element of personal work is lacking, we will live and die having missed our real purpose and life's most thrilling experience. My basic thesis then is this: Reaching one person at a time is still the best way to reach the world.

Jesus came out of the wilderness after his battle with Satan to declare that the Kingdom of God was at hand. Mark wanted his readers to recognize that Jesus was the Messiah. But the Kingdom of God, his rule in all of life, does not operate in a vacuum. It calls for people to live in its reality and power. Now Mark shows how the Messiah called the Kingdom people, the new Israel, the Church. He began by calling his disciples. How he did that and what he said to them is repeated in the life of every Christian. There can be no effectiveness or power for any Christian until he hears and responds to the same call.

Jesus passed along by the Sea of Galilee. There he saw Simon and Andrew, James and John casting their nets into the sea. The other Gospels indicate that the fishermen had previous contact with Jesus. They had been fascinated by John the Baptist's ministry and had witnessed the transfer of allegiance to Jesus when John boldly announced, "Behold the Lamb of God!"

We are sure that Jesus had attracted them and they had talked about his message and deeds. He too had noticed them and singled them out as potential disciples. Now the time was right for them to hear his challenging call. This would explain his imperious summons: "Come, follow me and I will make you fishers of men." He used a common fishing term to explain their new calling. In Greek it is zōgréō, to take alive. It meant to catch fish in such a way that they were still alive when brought to shore for sale.

Now the fishermen were going to become fishers of men in the same way. They were called to take men alive! But to do that would necessitate discipleship and training. For that Jesus offered the "follow me" of companionship—to walk the same road is the meaning. It is used in the associative-instrumental case, the idea communicated being, "to join with him." Fellowship, joint participation, a side by side communion with one another. That means accepting Jesus as Master and conforming wholly to his example. Out of that they would become what Jesus intended—fishers of men. God's eternal purpose of calling, loving and caring for people was now to be the reason the disciples were alive. The Messiah was the Master Fisher of men and the disciples were to learn from him how to do it. The brief years of Jesus' ministry were to be given to discipling these men in their essential calling of taking men alive.

That is the calling of every Christian. To be in Christ is to be in ministry and to be in ministry is to communicate to people the joy and power of the new life in Christ. Our relationships, conversation, remedial caring, costly involvement and supportive affirmation are to lead toward the opportunity of introducing people to the living Christ. To take men alive is to reproduce our faith in them in such a way that they stay alive. So often evangelism kills people off with conceptualisms or by binding people to a rigid set of rules. We introduce them to a cosmic policeman instead of a liberating Lord. We suffocate people with doctrine or churchmanship before they are out of the womb of birth. Denominationalism is strapped on people before the dynamic of Christ is communicated, and before they have heard the story of Christ's love. Could that be why so few Christians are able to reproduce their faith? Paul Tournier once said, "Our task as laymen is to live our personal communion with Christ with such intensity as to make it contagious."

It's amazing, isn't it, that so few contemporary Christians are fishers of men. Why is it that contagious Christians are such a rarity? All power in heaven and earth has been released for us to be communicators, and still we find it so difficult to talk to others about what has happened to us. Yet the intended fruit of one Christian is another. Jesus put it all too clearly later in his ministry: "I am the true vine and my Father is the vinedresser. Every branch of mine that bears no fruit, he takes away, and every branch that does bear fruit he prunes that it may bear more fruit. . . . I am the vine, you are the branches. He who abides in me, and I in him, he it is that bears much fruit . . ." (John 15:1,2,5). Fruitfulness is not a luxury; it is a requirement. The qualification is not just believing in Christ, but it is in being reproductive.

Yet many of us are not reproductive. Why? Some are embarrassed; to talk about our faith is too personal. We give advice, try to be helpful, escape in the evasion of being the "Christian presence." We seldom get around to sharing what Christ means to us and could mean to another person. Every age has had to discover its own language of communicating the faith. So, too, every Christian must find his own method of developing deep relationships with people in which he can share his hope in Christ.

Others of us are not reproductive because we don't want to get involved. It takes time, energy, and vulnerability to care about people. We would rather have a pipe line of grace for our individualistic personal faith and let the rest of the world go to hell. And that's just what happens to people who have never heard and accepted the love and forgiveness of Christ mediated through us. The keys of the kingdom were given to those fishers of men called by Jesus, and to us. But the frightening words that follow that gift are that "Whatever we bind on earth will be bound in heaven and what we loose on earth will be loosed in heaven." The bold truth is that God has entrusted person-centric expansion of the kingdom to us! Anyone who says "yes" to Christ and becomes a believer is given the keys. And in order to stay alive in Christ we must use the keys. The reason there are so many uptight, frustrated Christians is that we have clogged the channel of grace.

Jesus persisted in the training of his disciples all through his ministry. He knew that they could not become the men God intended them to be without being personal communicators to others. When he returned after the resurrection, he found the disciples back on the Sea of Galilee from which he had called them. His recall was piercing. He asked them a question: "Do you have any fish?" He was not concerned about their catch from the sea, but about the ministry with people for which he had died.

Let's look at Jesus' call to be fishers of men from a very selfish vantage. We can't grow in him unless we are sharing our faith. I don't know of any single Christian who is alive and vital in his faith who is dumb when it comes to communicating Christ's love with others. I have never found a negative, cantankerous Christian who is serious about sharing his faith. Once a person gets a taste of the delight of introducing people to Christ, he is never satisfied with a dull, bland, self-centered Christianity again. There is excitement and adventure in reproductive Christians. People and their needs are the passion of their lives. If the faith has become routine for you, a stopped-up channel is probably the reason.

But taking men alive does not require a superior spirituality. Our own needs and the discovery of what God can do with them is the point of contact with others. We all face the same problems. When we share what God is doing with ours and point to Christ as our answer, there is immediate identification. We often ask, "How can I become a fisher of men? With all the problems I've got, how can I help anyone else?" That's to miss the secret of the communication. If we wait until we have it all together (which will never be!), we will never get started. The difficulties and the dynamics of our lives and what Christ is teaching us is the bait for a fisher of men. We are to live out our faith in a way that our lives cannot be explained except for the presence of Christ as the Lord of our lives.

I don't trust Christians who refuse to reproduce their faith. Their security will be inverted on themselves. And it is quite likely they will be more involved with church work than the true work of the church. Divisive or nit-picking churchmen seldom are involved in the real Kingdom business. That's why they have so much time to argue about subtle details of church architecture, finances, or organization. There is no sickness in a church quite like the infectious infamy of nonreproductive ecclesiastics. John R. Mott, one of history's most capable fishers of men, said, "A multitude of laymen are in serious danger. It is positively perilous for them to hear more sermons, attend more Bible classes and read more religious and ethical works, unless accompanying it all there be afforded day by day an adequate outlet for their newfound truth."[1]

An architect will want to know what a building will be used for. He knows that form follows function. The church has often turned that around: function is dictated by form. The basic function of the church is evangelism. All of its forms must follow that. We exist to deploy fishers of men to take men alive. The training program of the church as an equipping station is to produce fishermen with the following qualities.

A *fisher of men is aware*. We are the link between God and men. An awareness of our calling makes us sensitive to the people around us who need Christ. I have a salesman friend who always keeps a list of prospects. From that he also knows how to keep a "prospective Christian list." He prays for these people, asks God to create an openness in their lives and looks for his appointed time to talk with them.

A *fisher of men is alert*. He knows how to listen. Once he has asked to be made ready for those whom God has made ready, he is alert to opportunities. The other day I asked a man how he was feeling. He replied, "Just fine, physically."

What an opening! I said, "Oh, is something wrong with the rest of you?" And to that he responded, "Well, as a matter of fact, yes.

---

[1] Quoted in Sherwood Wirt and Kersten Beckstrom, *Living Quotes for Christians* (New York: Harper & Row, 1974), p. 256.

I never thought you would ask!" And as we talked, he shared a problem with me which had him tied in knots. His earlier sub-verbal comment had been a nibble at the bait of the personal sharing of my faith which I had tried to do for months. But he also knew that I cared deeply about him. Now he wanted me to penetrate personally.

A fisher of men is available. The only way to fish for men and women is to be where they are! Our schedules are to be interrupted. I remember a woman in my congregation who said, "I don't have anyone to share my faith with. All my friends are Christians!" What an exposing commentary. I asked her about people in her neighborhood, in stores, in her clubs. Were they alive in Christ? "Of course not," she replied. "I'm so busy!" In time we helped her see she must adjust her schedule and widen her circle of friends. She made time to be with people who needed her most, and the results were amazing. She discovered that in developing caring relationships with people there were soon opportunities to share her faith.

A fisher of men is accepting. When our own character has been healed by Christ our countenance radiates acceptance. An accepted person is accepting. There are so few people whose own experience of forgiveness from God has made them accepting of the weaknesses and inadequacies of others. People need to have someone in their lives whose face and body language tell them they are O.K. even when they know they are not. We are to be the kind of people who communicate esteem, value, and worth to others. That means we must give up our costly luxury of judgmentalism. Look in the mirror! Is there a tenderness, graciousness, and openness? Are we so intent on our own thing that there is no energy left over for others?

Only Christ can produce an accepting person. His exposure of our own needs makes us considerate of others. The realization that he is at work in the people we want to take alive for him helps us to relax. We don't have to convince anyone! That's his job. While he is penetrating a life, we are to provide the accepting ambience in which that person can talk out the issues and share what he is going through. Christ is the ruminator; we are the reconcilers. Our only task is to model an alternative way to live, free of frustration and fear. We live only once and the reason Christ gave us life is to join with him in the fishing business.

For that crucial business there are three watchwords. Be prepared; be in prayer; be personal. We must allow Christ to do a
fresh work of grace in us so that what we have to share with
others is contemporary and real. Christ will guide us to the people
who need him. A good guide on a fishing trip knows where the
fish are. Christ is that kind of guide. People don't need more ideas
about the faith; they need to know what Christ has meant to us
in the deeply personal dimensions of life. That's the dynamic
that cuts through the layers of sophisticated resistance.

In the light of all this, we need to do three things. The first is
get quiet for a time with our Lord. Ask him, "Do I have anything
to share? Is there anything about my life which I want others to
have? Have I found a hope that's vibrant enough to want everyone
to have?" The second thing to do is to ask our Lord to help us
make a list of people who are his priorities for us. Then we need to
pray for each one individually and ask him to create an opportunity for deep relationships with these people. The third thing is
to ask him for one of those people for today. If we are open and
ready the Lord will arrange an opportunity which is undeniable.
We will have a tangible evidence of our prayer!

My cherished brother in Christ, Dr. Robert Munger, said recently in a covenant group we share with a group of pastors, "It
is more effective to spend time talking to Christ about a person
than talking to a person about Christ, because if you are talking
to Christ about a person seriously, earnestly, trustingly, in the
course of time you cannot help talking to the person effectively
about Christ." That challenged me to consider if I had spent as
much time talking to Christ about people as I had spent talking to
people about Christ. Prayer without sharing is ineffective, but
sharing without prayer is futile.

All this boils down to our willingness. A decision is necessary
to follow Christ and allow him to make us become fishermen
who take men alive. Mark tells us that in response to Jesus' call
the disciples immediately left their nets and followed him. Some
translations read, "Forsook their nets." Either way, the idea is that
it was a once and for all action. Our challenge is to leave a privatism
and an inverted piety and follow the Lord in his central activity
of communicating love to others. If we try to follow him without
becoming fishers of men we will not follow for long. If we want
to be with him, we must join him in doing what is ultimately
crucial to him and the people he died to save.

CHAPTER 5

READ THE SCRIPT!

Mark 1:21-45

While in Scotland recently I read an article in a daily paper which cast contemporary and humorous light on this next passage in Mark's first chapter. It was about movie producer, Sir Lew Grade.

"Sir Lew Grade announced that he was bringing forth next year a six hour television series on the life of Jesus Christ. Sponsors are the Italian State Television and General Motors, which will be the American contribution to the series.

"The director will be Franco Zeffirelli, whose recent public statements about other directors, and the general collapse of values, would make him about the only director with enough moral rectitude for such an under taking.

" 'What position will the series take on the divinity of Christ?' a reporter asked. Sir Lew said he could answer that tremendous question only after he had read the script."

There is no question after reading Mark's script. Especially the fast-moving account of his early ministry in verse twenty-one to the end of chapter one. Mark's purpose is to communicate Jesus' undeniable divinity.

There is a word Mark uses forty-one times in his Gospel. It is used five times in this passage alone. The word is "immediately." His vigorous descriptive style vividly catches the drama of Jesus' ministry, and this word presses us on as if we were trying breathlessly to catch up with the Master as he moves from person to person and from one challenge to another. The Greek word for "immediately" is *euthus*. It means straightaway. Without hesitation or lingering the Lord pressed on declaring the Kingdom of God, healing the sick, loving the unlovely, liberating the bound and uptight. He knew who he was and what he had come to do. There wasn't time to coddle people who resisted his ministry while others pressed in upon him to receive his healing and hope . . . no time to play power politics for an earthly kingdom. He was the Messiah with a mission. He was the Master on the move! The divine Son was about his Father's business.

Mark uses the word *immediately* in this passage to reveal the immediacy of divine power in response to human need. It is exposed in the way Jesus taught. He went to Capernaum and *immediately* on the Sabbath entered the synagogue and taught. Determination, singleness of purpose, and forthrightness are communicated in the way he taught. Listeners could easily tell the difference between this rabbi's teaching and that of the scribes. They were astonished. This is a very strong word. In Greek it means, "to strike out, expel by a blow, drive out or away, to strike one out of self-possession." The people were blown out of self-propriety and reserve. They dropped their cautious religious reservations and got excited. All of the carefully constructed patterns of self-containment were broken, and they were expelled out of themselves in exuberant response. The scribes had never done that for them. Their message centered around the thousand and one rules which annotated the commandments. Guilt and self-incrimination resulted. That gives us the key to the power of Jesus' divinely inspired teaching. He was the love and forgiveness he taught. His divine authority was undeniable.

That's what brought an immediate response. "And immediately there was in their synagogue a man with an unclean spirit." There's the word "immediately" again. Jesus had barely finished teaching when a demoralized man arose and cried out, "What do you have to do with us, Jesus of Nazareth? Have you come to destroy us? I know who you are, the Holy One of God." He had heard Jesus and the intention of his mission as the Messiah. Now Mark shows clearly that Jesus had divine authority by the way he exorcised the demon which incarcerated the man's body and mind —a further proof that Jesus was the divine Son of God. But note the response of the people to Jesus' action: "What is this? A new teaching! With authority he commands even the unclean spirits, and they obey him." The word for "new" used here means new in quality as compared with what is old and worn-out. What Jesus was in his person made them listen to what he taught, and what he taught was validated by the healing exorcism he performed. No wonder the news spread throughout the region. The people had never seen anything like this before.

But Jesus does not bask in the warmth of their affirmation. He left immediately and went to Simon's home. Again the immediacy of God's power is manifested in the healing of Simon's mother-in-law. Peter himself probably told Mark the intimate details of this healing. But for Mark's purposes here, it was another sign he heaped up in this passage to establish Jesus' divine Sonship.

Now the news of Jesus' healing power had become so well known that the people crowded about the door of Simon's home and followed him wherever he went. Even his prayers were interrupted when the people found his "lonely place." The reference to Jesus' prayer at this point in Mark's story was to expose the source of the amazing teaching and healing that came from him.

"Everyone is searching for you!" the disciples pleaded. The Messianic age had begun. The sick, the lame, the possessed, the blind, were healed. And Jesus presses on. "Let us go on to the next town that I may preach there also; for that is why I came out."

The next usage of the word *immediately* is found in the final healing of this passage. A leper came to Jesus begging for healing. Lepers were "unclean," and anyone or thing they touched was also unclean. But this did not dissuade Jesus. He was moved with pity. What a gracious picture Mark paints of the Messiah. In response to the leper's plea, "If you will, you can make me clean," Jesus mediated the compassionate power of God. "I will; be clean." Again the word *immediately* is used. "And immediately the leprosy left him and he was made clean."

What follows in this story needs careful interpretation for it contains a profound truth and insight into our Lord. After he had healed the leper, he "sternly charged him and sent him away at once." The verb in Greek is *embrimaomai*, meaning "to be moved with anger." Jesus' admonition was stern and strong. He told him pointedly that he must say nothing to anyone but go show himself to the priest and offer the cleansing commanded by Moses. He knew that if the man told people that Jesus had healed him, the curse of uncleanness would be on him for seven days and he would be unable to enter a town or a synagogue during the cleansing

period. That's exactly what happened. The man went out and
talked freely about his healing. It is my opinion that is the reason
why Jesus could not enter a town, but had to stay out in the desert.

In this act Jesus took the leper's curse upon himself. He bore the
rejection and the quarantine from which he had liberated the
leper. It was the shadow of the Cross and the portent of what he
would do for the sins of the whole world.

But not even this interrupted Jesus' ministry. The people came
from every quarter. His ritual uncleanness did not deter them.
Even this early in his ministry he was a magnetic attraction to
suffering people.

Mark has tried to show us here a vivid picture of the divine
Messiah fraught with the power of God. And we are forced to
ask the question Mark hoped we would ask, "How would I have
responded if I had been in the synagogue? Have I been astonished
and amazed at Jesus' message and power today? In what areas of
my life am I possessed and unable to live with freedom and love?
Who in my house needs Jesus' healing touch? Would I have gone
searching for him in the mountains, willing to interrupt even his
prayers for a word with him? Do I realize that he has taken my
uncleanness and the leprosy of my hidden sins upon himself? Has
he ever healed my personality leprosy which makes me unde-
sirable in so many of life's relationships? Am I willing to go to
him and risk ridicule and rejection and be identified with him
whatever the significant people of my life say?"

I don't know how Sir Lew Grade made out with his script, but
I know how I did with Mark's. The evidence is clear: Jesus was
who he said he was and what the early Church later declared: God
was in Christ reconciling the world!

The Messiah who moved immediately into human need whenever he found it and released the immediacy of divine power is
with us now as the resurrected, living Lord. This passage in Mark
is to quicken our faith so that we can dare to believe that what he
did then he is more than able to do now.

That presses on to the next chapter and the description of the
penetrating way Christ deals with our needs in order to release
us to live life without limits.

CHAPTER 6

WHICH IS EASIER?

Mark 2:1–12

Picture the setting. Feel yourself in it. We are in the small, sleepy fishing village of Capernaum. A main road runs through the village. Beside it and next to the seashore is a line of square, box-shaped houses built of stones. The roofs are made of saplings intertwined with sand, mud, and a tar-like substance. Tiles were overlaid to make a roof about two feet in depth.

One particular house catches our attention. There are crowds swelling about the house and inside it is jammed with people. In the center of the mass of people is Jesus of Nazareth. His fame as a healer has spread like wildfire throughout the territory. A few days before he had healed a man with an unclean spirit in the synagogue, and the news traveled all over Galilee. Now he could not move without the sick following him everywhere he went. He had left Capernaum for a few brief days, but when he returned they were waiting for him. The people would not be put off. They wanted to be near him, touch him, and have him touch their sickness.

Once inside the house we can understand why. He is preaching. As we look around over the crowd, we are amazed by the mixture of different kinds of people who were listening. Several scribes with critical, unbelieving looks upon their faces stand close to him. Then there are the newly called disciples, fishermen with a strangely different look about them. Around the inner circle are people who hang on his every word with intensity. The rest of the crowd spills through the door and out in the road. Others cluster around the windows straining for a look, a word.

Suddenly Jesus' message is punctuated by loud pounding on

the roof. Then the ceiling begins to crack open. First a pole is pushed through, causing the sand and splinters of the saplings to shower down on everyone below. Now we can see a hand reach through grasping the edges of the new hole, tearing them back. The people below are frightened and amazed. As the hole expands with the frantic razing activity, we can make out the faces of four men on the roof. The hole is now several feet wide and about five feet long. They seem to know what they are doing and are not about to be dissuaded by the consternation of either the owner of the house or the scribes below.

The men on the roof are positioning a carpetlike pallet over the hole. Ropes are tied to the four corners, and then they begin to lower it down into the room. When it reaches our eye-level we are aghast. There's a man on that pallet! Who is this? We look closely. The man is lying very quietly, as if trusting his friends implicitly. Now the pallet has reached the floor. Right in front of Jesus. What's wrong with him? Observation reveals that he has some movement in his one side, but look at the other side. It is as motionless as a dead rock. The man's a paralytic!

Now look at Jesus. What interruptibility! His preaching is forgotten, the officials of the synagogue disregarded, everyone else is excluded for a moment as Jesus' attention is riveted on this man. There's no one else in this room for Jesus now. He stoops to the man and his need. Then he looks up through the gaping hole in the ceiling and smiles with affirming approval at the pertinacity of the faith of the man's friends. A brief conversation with the paralytic quickly surmised the malady and the prognosis.

Jesus is quiet. He seems to be praying. And then his voice pierces the silence. "My son, your sins are forgiven."

The people marvel and exchange looks of amazement, then delight. But the faces of the scribes are red with rage. They quickly huddle together exchanging excited perturbation. "Why does this man speak thus? It is blasphemy! Who can forgive sins but God alone?"

Jesus knows what they are talking about in their esoteric huddle. The question he asks strikes to the vitals of the issue. "Why do you question thus in your hearts? Which is easier, to say to the paralytic, 'Your sins are forgiven,' or to say, 'Rise . . . and walk'? But that you may know that the Son of man has authority on earth to forgive sins—[Now he turns to the paralytic again.] 'I say to you rise, take up your pallet and go home' " (Mark 2:8–11). He claimed to be the Son of man. That has Messianic overtones!

No wonder the man on the pallet got up. Look at him; he hasn't stood on those legs for longer than he wants to remember. Look at him walk. We are amazed and so is the whole crowd. What begins as a private exclamation now becomes a chant of glorification. "We never saw anything like this!"

As the crowd filters away, we remain behind. Only Jesus is there with us now. We look at him and see the same compassion and unlimited power as before. Now we look at the empty pallet. It is a holy moment. Then the people of our lives flood our minds. What if we could lower them on that pallet for Jesus' healing? Think of the emotionally, physically, and mentally paralyzed people we would like to bring to Jesus. But look again. The face of the person on the pallet is our own! That's where we need to be, isn't it? What do you think he would say to us? Probably the same thing: "Your sins are forgiven. Rise, take up your pallet and walk in newness of life!"

That's exactly what happens when we put ourselves in this drama. We are moved from the crowd of observation to the pallet of confrontation. We are there! Whatever we need—the gift of faith or to be on the pallet ourselves, this is our story.

Mark has us just where he wants us and where he wanted his readers in the early church. He wanted to establish two things: that Jesus truly was the Messiah with the power of God to forgive and heal, and that we need both the faith of the paralytic's friends and the healing which the paralytic himself received.

Think a moment. With which character in the story would you identify most? The onlookers, the disciples, the scribes, the owner of the house, the friends of the paralytic, the paralytic himself? We can play all parts, can't we? There is a mixture of glorification, amazement, awe and consternation in all of us. Can that still happen? Does Jesus still forgive sins? Is he the power of healing for our minds and bodies?

Well, what would you say? If you had to answer Jesus' question, how would you answer? Which *is* easier, to say to the paralytic, "My son, your sins are forgiven" or "Rise, take up your bed and walk"?

Elsewhere in the Gospels, Jesus confounded the leaders of Israel with his arguments. But never more effectively than here.

Jesus knew that they believed in the interrelation of sin and sickness. Only God could forgive sin. If a man's sin had been forgiven by him, then the proof would be that he was healed. To show that he was truly the Son of God, he healed the man—his sins must have been forgiven because he was made well. They had one choice: either believe in him or reject him for what he claimed to be! The die was cast; his death warrant sealed.

Jesus should never have had to ask that question. The scribes should have known. But Jesus was perceptive. He caught their cankerous criticism when he pronounced an assuring absolution to the paralytic lowered down before him.

They would not have been surprised if he had immediately healed him. He had healed before; and there had been other healers. But Jesus had not come to be just another healer. His power to heal men's bodies was only a manifestation of a deeper healing he was about in the world. Jesus could see that this man before him had far more desperate needs than a paralyzed side. He could see deep beneath the surface. And in the moments of exchange, the man could see himself as he was in his greater need. He was paralyzed in spirit as well as body. He could not walk on his feet until he was ready to walk in the Lord as a forgiven man.

Jesus understood what the negative scribes should have known from their rabbis. They were among the millions who abhorred sickness but were reluctant to go deeply enough with people to get at the cause. They would have accepted the healing if only he had not forgiven the man. "Only God can forgive! He claimed to be the Son of man. We stone men to death for a blasphemous claim like that!"

Then came the question. Really Jesus was saying, "All right, you would have accepted a healing of this man's body, but it's much more difficult to say to him, 'Your sins are forgiven.' This is a greater miracle! So that you may know that I am the Son of man, with God's own power to forgive sins, I will heal this man." Jesus' action was based on three very important assumptions.

First of all, Jesus saw sin as man's basic problem. He could see what man's rebellion and separation from God had done to himself and the world. He could sense everywhere the unfulfilled purpose of creation: the distorted potentiality, the undiscovered joy, the unexpressed love. He could see how men hurt themselves and others because they would not learn to love. Everywhere he went he saw the sins of attitude, neglect, and pride.

Strange isn't it . . . Jesus seldom had anything to say about overt acts of sin. But he was uncompromising in his exposure of the subtler manifestations of man's separation. He had no tolerance for sin. He did not excuse it, accept it, compromise it or trifle with it. And yet for sinners he had all the love and tolerance in the world. The acid test for him was love. "By this shall men know that you are my disciples . . . that you love one another." Anything which debilitated love was to be exposed and confessed and forgiven!

Jesus could see the anger, hostility, impatience, and competition beneath the surface of people. He knew what these were doing to their physical and psychological health. He knew the sickening spleen this pumped into the bodies of people.

He could also see the sins of neglect. People did not care. He could see that if those who had so much would share with those who had so little, there could be a solution for suffering and poverty. He saw how carelessly people treated those around them. How little sympathy, tenderness, and warmth there was!

It is no different today. At the end of every day we realize how little we have said and done to express our concern. Needs have knocked at the door of our lives and have been turned away unheeded and unacknowledged.

Think of what could happen to transform the life of our community if we really cared for others enough to speak personally with another person about Jesus Christ. But we don't . . . and that's sin! The sin of neglect.

And Jesus took the sins of pride seriously. That's the root of it . . . he could see that some people actually believed they could run their own lives. He could see what they missed of God's love and power because they wanted to go it alone.

For most of us, dependence is a difficult thing. We have learned independence, and it is ingrained in our being. The end result is that we say with our lips that we believe but in our hearts we are still in control. Jesus' great concern was that out of pride a person could say "no" to God so long that eventually he could no longer say "yes." Not only would he miss God's power now but he would eventually live on in eternal separation in judgment for a life of proud independence.

The second reason Jesus forgave the man's sin was because he knew the result of sin on his total health and well-being. There is a tremendous relationship between our memory of past failures and our present experience of freedom. Many people are ill emotionally and physically because they have never had the experience of forgiveness. The many factors of our own failures and those of others which we have failed to forgive are part of the subliminal memory monsters stirring up trouble for our conscious health. We are now learning the close interrelationship between arthritis and the sensitive, hurt emotion in the past. Often people who pout instead of shout have churning stomachs or ulcers brought on by the hostility they feel to others and life's circumstances. Frequently, fatigue is related to conscious hiding of bad memories or tendencies. God does not will sickness. It is part of a free, fallen creation which God allows to exist because he wills our freedom to choose to love him and serve him.

It is dangerous to disguise the interrelationship between unforgiven sin and healing. We must give God full opportunity to heal our bodies. Let nothing stand in the way! His spirit of healing is at war with disease and sickness. But we hold the key! We can hinder healing by unforgiven sin within us. It would be simplistic to say that all sickness is caused by sin. There are deeply committed people who get sick. But if we look at sin as separation from God and salvation as wholeness, healing, and health, then forgiveness, love, and reconciliation with God make possible the utilization of all his healing resources. When a person accepts the healing of God's grace, he taps into the reservoir of God's Spirit who is the healing for the physical body as well. We need to care for sick people much more profoundly. If we helped them clean out any impedimenta of memories, unresolved guilt, and broken relationships, we would enable them to be all the more receptive to God's healing in their bodies.

The same is true for us. If memories of past failure still crowd in on our minds, if a sick ache groans as we remember certain people or places, if we nurse a feeling of having wasted our lives and failed to accomplish our purpose, if we know that we have allowed the pride of self-will to keep us from the joy of knowing God's guidance, because we wanted to run the show ourselves, then we need to be forgiven. We need to give God's physical healing every opportunity by having a cleansed memory and a clear conscience.

Lastly, Jesus took sin seriously because he knew what it meant to God and what it would cost him. As the author of life, Jesus knew what man was meant to be. He could see what people had done with the precious gift of life, and what they had done to frustrate others. But he came and said: I am life . . . as it was intended to be, as it can be for you!

Sin cost God the Cross. Jesus died to forgive men's sins. What does that mean? How could the death of that man . . . any man . . . the Son of man, forgive sins?

That's difficult to believe, unless we accept, as Paul said . . . that God was in Christ reconciling the world to himself . . . breaking down the dividing wall of hostility. When we consider the fact that God actually came and became one of us in order to communicate his forgiveness, what's the best way he could have done it? Words were not enough. He had to do something! He consciously took those steps demanded by love which sealed his death warrant. He loved, served, cared, exposed, and deposed until the guilt in Israel's leadership was so seared that they did away with him. He died because he loved. Men will forever look at the Cross and remember a love like that and know that they are forgiven.

That's the reason Jesus knew it was more difficult to forgive sin than to heal bodies. He knew that man's sin would cost God Calvary.

It has always been this way. If you really love people you take their sin to heart. You know what it does to them, how it twists their personalities and distorts their potential.

George Eliot has Adam Bede saying to Donnithorne when he learned the sin he had committed with Hetty Sorrel, "There's a sort o' damage sir, that can't be made up for. It's like a bit o' bad workmanship—you never see the end o' th' mischief it'll do."

That's true . . . apart from the Cross. And that kind of love is the costly love to which we have been called.

Arthur's word to Guinevere in *The Idylls of the King* portrays the kind of anguish of true love and finally is able to say, "And all is past, the sin is sinned, and I, lo, I forgive thee, as Eternal God, forgives."

But that's not easy! It never has been on Calvary or now. Which is easier? How will you answer Jesus' question? Forgiveness or healing? In the last analysis, that's not the issue—both are difficult. But one must come first. And God has done all that's necessary in Jesus Christ to assure us that we are forgiven and to enable us to be forgiving people.

With that in mind, let's return to the scene at Capernaum. Place yourself on that pallet and accept what Christ is ready and able to give. Then let's take the people for whom we have desperate concern and place them there. What Jesus did for the paralytic he longs to do for us and the people we love or need to learn to love.

CHAPTER 7

NEW WINE IN OLD BAGS

Mark 2:13–3:6

A few years ago, when I was in Beirut, Lebanon, as a leader of a Holy Land tour, some of our group attended a Lebanese Presbyterian church. After the service we participated in an informal fellowship meeting in which members of our group shared with the Lebanese what Christ had done in their lives. A translator had to make the words of each witness clear, and this wasn't always easy because of our American colloquialisms and slang.

One woman in our group gave the translator a particularly difficult time. In explaining her life prior to being liberated by Christ from religion, she used a very uncomplimentary term that her fellow workers at the office called her. Her lack of joy was obvious to them. She had been a rather grim person trying to be adequate and good enough for God. Rules and regulations dominated her pious religiosity, and she was closed and unaffirming to people who did not meet her standards and preconceptions.

When she used the name she had earned by her inflexible, unattractive behavior, the translator's face became clouded with uncertainty. At first, he could not find a word in Lebanese to translate adequately what she meant. Then, suddenly his expression brightened, and when he gave the translation, everyone laughed and nodded in comprehension. Now they knew what she meant.

The term she used to describe herself before she received the releasing, renewing experience of grace was an "old bag." Once the word was translated, we all realized that there were "old bags" in Lebanon as well as America. In fact, we surmised that there is probably a corollary term in most every language.

Let me quickly explain that I believe that being an "old bag" is not just a description of a person's age, sex, physical condition, or appearance. I have met "old bags" of both sexes among some very proper people. It can be a spiritual condition. I have met teenage "old bags" who suffer from more rigidity and inflexibility than their elders. The other day I had a conversation with a young married "old bag" who, though cultured and the model of propriety, was settled in a very highly polished rut with the traditional signs of security, including her husband, gathered neatly about her. I met one in his office several months ago who was at the prime of his career, but lovelessly religious in his legalism, and I know a retired couple whose motto is "we've never done it that way before." All these "old bags" have one thing in common: They are too rigid, dry, inflexible, and unbending to contain the tumult of the fermentative new wine of Jesus Christ. They are far too cautious, prejudiced, and judgmental to hold the dynamic of the lordship of Christ and his kingdom.

Jesus had his greatest difficulties with the religious "old bags" of his time. The scribes and Pharisees could not handle his nonconforming ministry and message. In fact, with rich humor, with tongue in cheek, he exposed them with one of his most humorous parables. How often we miss the humor of Jesus!

In the parable of the wineskins he took the familiar image of an old wineskin or bag to show what happens when the new wine of the kingdom of God is poured into the unbending framework of intellectual, spiritual and personality rigidity.

The people who listened to Jesus knew what happened to new wine in an old bag. The new wine fermented and stretched the bag, which was made from the skin of a goat. A good wineskin was soft and flexible, able to take the expanding, tumultuous fermentation of the new wine. The new wine bag stretched easily.

An old wine bag was one that had been used and was stretched —dry, cracked, inflexible. It was no longer safe to be a container of the new wine because the fermentation process would burst the skin, losing the wine and destroying the bag as well.

Jesus' parable on new wine in old bags was prompted by several aspects of the resistance and inflexibility among the scribes and Pharisees focused in this second chapter of Mark. These religious leaders were unable to contain the new wine Jesus offered because they were prejudiced about people, they erected barriers, they had lost the joy of knowing God personally and they had made their rules and regulations an end in themselves.

Religion has always been an old bag. It represents man's effort to domesticate the dynamic of faith into humanly accomplishable standards. Man's religion is his self-generated activity to do and be something to win, placate, and earn the acceptance and approval of a power or deity greater than himself. William James was right, "Religion is a monumental chapter in the history of human egotism." Jesus did not come to establish a new religion, but to be God's love incarnate. He offered men the gift of faith to respond to his love freely given. It could not be deserved by man's goodness or impeccable observance of standards.

Roy Gustafson put it with undeniable clarity. "Religion is man's quest for God; the Gospel is the Savior God seeking lost men. Religion originates on earth; the Gospel originated in heaven. Religion is man-made; the Gospel is the gift of God. Religion is the story of what a sinful man tries to do for a holy God; the Gospel is the story of what a holy God has done for sinful men. Religion is good views; the Gospel is good news."[1]

As a quality of life religion has been the greatest enemy of Christianity down through the ages. It's virulent poison has infected the Body of Christ, the Church. In each age, there have been those who tried to conceptualize an objective creedal statement of faith and elevate it to a higher position than the Lord of the creed. Fastidious religionists have drawn up long lists of requirements for discipleship and church membership. The formulations have become a "god below God" and kept people from the living Lord. The result has been always the same: The new thing the Spirit of God seeks to do in each period is resisted and condemned. Jonathan Swift said correctly, "We have just enough religion to make us hate, but not enough to make us love one another."

That makes Jesus' parable disturbingly fresh and contemporary for us. Our previous experiences, our present level of growth, our intellectual formulations, our cherished customs of church life, our prejudices based on what is familiar, all become old wineskins which cannot contain the power of the new wine of the living Christ and his innovative invasion of our lives.

---

[1] Roy Gustafson, "Contrasts," *Decision* magazine, December 1960, p. 2.

The context of this parable is crucial for our understanding. The religious leaders of Israel were alarmed when Jesus called Levi, a tax collector, to be a disciple. They were astonished when he sat down at a banquet with tax collectors in Capernaum, and they were aghast that Jesus' disciples did not fast. But they were overwhelmed with rage that he did not keep the Sabbath and actually healed a man on the sacred day. When we look at what came before Jesus spoke this parable and what comes after it in Mark's account we can see it in perspective. Each of Jesus' actions were enacted parables themselves. They proclaim five powerful aspects of the new wine the old bags could not contain.

The first is that God loves us right now, not after we become righteous. This was vividly proclaimed by Jesus' relationship with tax collectors. In his day, tax collectors were condemned conspirators. Levi and his friends were hated by the good, religious Jews because they collected import and export taxes along the main road which passed through Capernaum. The dishonest practices of some tax collectors categorized them all in the Jew's mind. They bid for the right to collect taxes for Herod Antipas. Whatever a tax collector could get above the amount he had to pay Antipas, was his own. That was the rub! Many of them gouged the people. No wonder they were hated.

Of all the people in Capernaum to be one of Jesus' disciples, Levi was the most unacceptable. But Jesus saw a man, not a category. That was the revolutionary thing about what he did. He gave an acquisitive tax collector a new name which would designate what he was to become. He called him Matthew which means "gift of God." How very different! He knew that in fellowship with him he would become the name by which he was called. He didn't have to become righteous first. Later he would learn that God's love had made him righteous.

Jesus punctuated his actions with an exclamation mark. He had a banquet with Levi's fellow tax collectors! Mark says that "he sat at table in his house, many tax collectors and sinners were sitting with Jesus and his disciples." Whose house? It either means Jesus' house, the place he made his home away from home in Capernaum, or it meant Levi's house. Either one was radical. The point is that Jesus did not require religious standards before he gave himself to people who needed him and heard him gladly. That stretched the "old bags" of the scribes and Pharisees! Pascal said, "Men never do evil so completely and cheerfully as when they do it from religious conviction."

How easily we fall into measured love and judgmental categorizing of people as acceptable or unacceptable, useful or unuseful, "our kind of people" or those who do not share our prejudices. Our categorizing computer is constantly at work sorting out people into their proper places. Jesus' spirit in us stretches our old bags to the breaking point. The issue is: What must people do or be to receive our acceptance and affirmation? Do we love them before they are lovable or have fulfilled our expectations? What if Christ had loved us that way? Paul's words tattoo the truth on the tissues of our psyches. "Even while we were still sinners, Christ died for us."

The second dynamic which fermented in the old bags was prompted by the Pharisees' consternation over Jesus' feast with the tax collectors. They said to the disciples, "Why does he eat with tax collectors and sinners?" A "sinner" here means one who did not observe perfectly the scribal law which was the protracted regulations and rules which applied the Ten Commandments to the most minute details of every situation imaginable. The term was also used for half-breeds whose Hebrew blood was mixed with other nations.

And Jesus ate with them. He loved life and enjoyed people. He usually gravitated to unpretentious, natural people rather than the self-righteous, nit-picking "old bags." Jesus did not choose to spend time with people who thought they needed nothing more. A sense of need, a desire to grow, an openness to God's flesh gift, was what Jesus looked for. That's why his response was so stretching to the old bags who were satisfied and unwilling to flex with God's new power. "Those who are well have no need of a physician, but those who are sick; I came not to call the righteous, but sinners." No wonder the scribes and Pharisees were outraged! He specifically told them that he had come for the outcasts, the nonreligious, and the people who were unacceptable according to scribal standards. That not only challenged their judgmentalism, but it clarified what should be their own agenda.

The new life in Christ is available only if we can admit our need and express our desire to grow. Religion does just the opposite. It gets God into a humanly controllable set of beliefs, moral requirements, and customs which we can fulfill and no longer feel a need. There is no need greater than no longer feeling a need.

The next dynamic which stretched the old bags was his teaching that the evidence of the new life was joy. The messianic age is to be like the joy of a banquet feast after a wedding. Jesus clearly identified himself as the Messiah here in the way he explains the reason his disciples did not fast.

The old wine bag cracked when the scribes realized that Jesus did not teach his disciples to fast. He explained that life with him was like life with a bridegroom at a marriage banquet. In that day a honeymoon was not a time away for a newly married couple but a time at home celebrating with friends. A full week was spent in celebration. A rabbinical rule of the time made it all the more enjoyable: "All in attendance of the bridegroom are relieved of all religious observances which would lessen their joy!" That was very important for the difficult, arduous life of people then.

Jesus was not opposed to fasting. In fact, he stressed its importance, as we shall see in a subsequent chapter. What he was opposed to was their sanctimoniousness which did not express the joy of fellowship with God. The reason for the fast was to think more about God and less about distracting physical appetites. A good Jew of this time fasted on Mondays and Thursdays. What had been lost was its purpose: to open a person to God. Fasting had become an end in itself.

Joy was to be the identifiable mark of Jesus' disciples and a wedding banquet was to be the quality of that joy which they shared together. The absence or presence of joy is the sure test of our relationship with the Savior. If we do not have a warm, vital expression of joy then there is something wrong with our Christian experience. It is a deep inner awareness and experience of God's grace which is manifest on our faces, expressed in our words and shared in our relationships. It is more than circumstantial happiness. True joy is the outward expression of our overwhelming thankfulness for his goodness and love in spite of what we have done or what's happened to us.

What about the church? Is yours like a joyous banquet? The worship services of a church I know are described as the place God goes when he wants to have a good time! How many churches do you know like that?

The fourth dimension of the dynamic was focused around the observance of the Sabbath. For the Jew of this time the Sabbath was a foretaste of the messianic age. It was to be celebrated in a way that encompassed all dimension of time—past, present, and future. A good Jew was to look back at what God had done for his people and then look forward to the Lord's ultimate triumph. That gave courage and strength for the present. Remember the Sabbath and keep it holy was the commandment. But the scribes multiplied that with hundreds of little rules of what could or could not be done on the Sabbath. In effect, the Sabbath became part of the religious security of the self-righteous.

That's why Jesus' disciples caused such a stir when they picked grain on the Sabbath and Jesus healed the man with a withered hand in the synagogue on the Sabbath. Mark places Jesus' teaching about the Sabbath between these two accounts. What he said broke open the old bags. If calling Levi stretched them, eating with sinners cracked them, and refusal to fast pulled them, and Jesus' attitude and teaching about the Sabbath blasted them wide open. The Sabbath had become self-centered. It was now symbolic of the Jews' outer holiness. But the Sabbath had failed in its purpose: to remind men of God and his triumphant adequacy. Jesus put it clearly, "The Sabbath was made for man, not man for the Sabbath." Then he daringly declares himself the Lord of the Sabbath. "So the Son of man is the lord of the Sabbath"—a clear, unambiguous declaration of his messiahship. There should be no question now.

As the Son of man he was more concerned about people and their needs than the complex labyrinth of religious duties. The Sabbath was created for man to enable him to remember God and make all days holy. It was God's gift to his people to help them, not hinder them. All the commandments were expressions of his profound concern to encourage people to live life according to his intended purpose. That's why Jesus did not stop his disciples from picking grain on the Sabbath. Did not David eat the bread of the Presence in the Temple and give it to those who were with him? Jesus' authority was rooted in who he was as the Davidian Messiah.

While the leaders of Israel pondered the implications of that claim, Jesus immediately enacted another life situation parable to erase any lingering doubt about who he claimed to be. He entered the synagogue on the Sabbath, and was confronted by a man with a withered hand. The scribes and Pharisees followed, watching carefully to see if he would heal the man. That would be considered labor on the sacred day, strictly forbidden by the codes. He was angered because of the hardness of the hearts of the leaders which no amount of human misery seemed to melt. Again a person was

more important than a precept. "Stretch out your hand!" he said
boldly to the man. His hand was restored by Jesus' healing power.
We are left to wonder what it is in us which keeps us from
caring about people that way. What disciplines have we established
to maintain the life of faith which blind us to the aching need of
people all around us?

What shall we do with this Jesus with his call and recall to put
people first as an expression of our love for God? The old bags
could not contain Jesus. He constantly broke out of their merciless
patterns, their walls of exclusion erected to keep people at a distance and their carefully regulated relationship with God calculated
by their own goodness and not his will.

But the last dimension of the dynamic which broke open the old
bags is found in the parable of the wineskin itself. New wine is for
fresh skins. Only a new life can contain the new wine. Jesus declares flatly that there must be a new beginning. We cannot patch
up the old life with new sayings, ideas, and religious goodness. He
said it plainly to Nicodemus, "Except you are born anew you shall
not inherit the kingdom of heaven." The old wine bag of our
previous experience, knowledge, and learning will be stretched to
the breaking point.

It is difficult for a person who thinks he's arrived to admit he
must begin all over again. Jesus had brought the scribes and
Pharisees to the razor's edge of a decision about him. Either he was
the Messiah and was worthy of their complete acceptance or he was
an imposter and worthy of death. But to accept him as lord of their
lives would mean the reorientation of their total minds and hearts
around obedience to him. He demanded surrender and unreserved
allegiance. That alone would be a new wineskin to contain the
power of his lordship.

We look back at this passage with the knowledge of the crucifixion, resurrection, and the Lord's living presence. What he hinted
at is now clear. He is the new wine! His post-resurrection dwelling
place is in the heart of the believer. If we invite him to come live in
us while we are still in control of our lives and still guided by our
own values and patterns, we will not be able to contain the new
dynamic.

There is seldom a week in my ministry that goes by without
talking to many people whose basic problem is that they have tried
to integrate the lordship of Christ into an old life. They are miser-
able as he penetrates every area of their experience and relation-

ships. Most of them are very religious but hope to hold Christ within the confines of their control. The result is usually disastrous.

I talked to a man recently who is a leader in his church. He could not be more religious as a churchman. But he is filled with anxiety and frustration. His rigid, negative personality has been poured into the regulations and taboos of his legalistic church. He has asked Christ to be his Lord and talks glibly about his reverence for Scripture. He constantly refers to his experience of the Lord ten years ago. But the old wineskin of the past cannot contain the new thing the same Lord is seeking to do in his life today.

I am amazed at how this parable of Jesus has been worked out in my own life. When I first committed my life to Christ, I tried to keep all my old attitudes and personality traits. The wineskin broke. Then I had to surrender all that I had and was. But that has to be repeated daily. What worked yesterday may not be the Lord's strategy for today. What was effective in a previous church cannot be a false security for my present church. Constant renewal and repeated relinquishment are the only things which keep my wineskin soft, supple, and flexible.

Jesus drove the point home in the twin parable. The point is the same, "No one sews a piece of unshrunk cloth on an old garment: if he does, the patch tears away from it, the new from the old, and a worse tear is made." We can't patch up an old self with the gospel.

The same is true for the church. We can be thankful for the past, but it can never be our security. Each day demands new dependence on the Lord for fresh direction. Memories of "the way we were" must always be superseded by visions of the way he is leading.

Conferences among clergy and church officers throughout the country have convinced me that spiritual leaders are among the most desperately in need of new wineskins to contain the exciting, unique power our Lord is unleashing in our time.

I have found that the greatest problem is not really the "old bags" in the church, but the empty bags. The dynamic of Christ burst the bags long ago and we are drained out. The challenge is not to trade in a mediocre bag but to acknowledge that our power has seeped out of the bags long ago. There is now no choice left but a new beginning. Christ has never been more ready. How you respond to that is crucial for what we will consider next. The strategy of Jesus is for new bags!

CHAPTER 8

THE STRATEGY OF JESUS

Mark 3:7-19

Recently, I was being interviewed on television about the power of God in contemporary life. The news analyst wanted to know if I believed in miracles today. I told him that I did and that the same power we see displayed vividly on the pages of the New Testament is available today. Then he asked this question, "What is the greatest miracle you have ever witnessed?"

I'm sure he expected me to give an account of a dramatic healing or some exception of the laws of the natural world. Though I have experienced both, that is not what I had in mind. Without hesitation, I responded, "The greatest miracle is 'the calling, conditioning, and commissioning of a disciple!'" That drew a puzzled look from my interviewer. I went on to explain that the transformation of observation into participation is one of the greatest gifts Christ can give to a casual follower. Then I marched before his mind's eye men and women whose relationship with Christ had liberated them to be contagious lovers of people and remedial reformers of sick structures in society.

"Why do you call that a miracle?" was his next question. I responded that the pressures of conformity, safety, and uninvolvement are so great that for a person to become a disciple was humanly impossible. Most people come to church for what they need and want. It is a special gift from Christ when a person sees that the same power revealed in Christ is available to us. The miracle has happened when a person urgently feels that his purpose and passion are to be to others what Christ has been to him. The strain of convincing is over; an exciting joy is evident. So much time and energy are spent in churches pressing people into doing what should be the desire of their hearts. When a person becomes a disciple, his time is the Lord's and the only question is what He wants him to do. Money and resources are put at the Master's disposal. People become the agenda. Society and its needs become the disciple's parish.

The interviewer would not allow the matter to be dropped. His last question had a cutting edge. "If Christ is still calling disciples out of the mass of followers, why are there so few disciples in most churches?" We had a fascinating conversation about why churches do so much for the uncommitted church members to inspire and entertain and so little to call and train disciples.

That question was very much on my mind when I considered this next passage in our exposition of Mark. The same motive, method, and mission of discipleship dealt with in Mark 3:7–19 is true today. The miracle of the transformation of the twelve into disciples is what our Lord wants to do with all of us.

If necessity is the mother of invention, I believe that opportunity is the father of strategy. The response of the crowds and the pressing needs of people everywhere prompted Jesus to develop a strategy for his future ministry. The urgent demands of the crowd became so persistent that Mark tells us in verse nine that he had to have a boat ready lest the crowds should crush him. The Greek word the Revised Standard Version translates as "crush" is *thlibō*, which actually means "to press hard upon." It is the same word used for pressing grapes to extract the juices. Mark uses this term several times to describe the pressure of human need, as we shall see in other passages. In verse ten, the image is stronger. Here the verb is *epipiptō*, to fall upon. The people were falling against Jesus in an effort to get him to touch them. They knocked against him in the hope that even that contact would extract his power for their needs. But Jesus saw the crowd as a potential, not a problem. That's what sent him into the hills to pray. He knew he could not touch all of the need alone. He had to reproduce himself through people who could extend to others what had happened to them. The motive of the calling of the disciples was the opportunity afforded by the gigantic response to his ministry.

In similar fashion, there is a hunger for hope today which is startling. Our hopeless period of history has created an openness to Christ which is exciting. People long for something authentic and for communicators who are personal and vital. We cannot ordain enough clergy to meet the need. And we should never try. Christ's strategy is to call disciples to extend his ministry. Out of the masses of church members, inquirers, and observers he calls disciples to multiply his ministry. We are to be among them.

Note that Mark says Jesus called those whom he desired (v. 13). That's sheer grace. It was not the adequacy, performance, or purity of those fallible fishermen, tax collectors, and political zealots that qualified them. They were teachable, open, flexible, and adventuresome. Their only qualification was that they loved him and wanted to be with him. Life with the Master was exciting, thrilling, and demanding.

Next Mark says that those Jesus called came to him. There's a note of response. They were expectant. During the course of a conversation with a fellow pastor, he asked me to pray for his congregation because they had become so bland and bored with religion. He said, "Pray that God will give them a gift of expectancy. I would love to have them come to worship as if they expected to meet the living Lord and be given his power to change the world!"

Verses fourteen and fifteen describe the miracle of discipleship: "And he appointed twelve, to be with him, and to be sent out to preach and have authority to cast out demons." Note the progression: appointment, companionship, commission, and authority. It is by the Master's appointment that we are disciples, and it is the gift of his present Spirit that we can claim what is ours. A disciple is a learner. That's what the word means. Jesus teaches by companionship. He wants to make us like himself in character and concern. Prayer, study of his Word, fellowship with fellow adventurers in which we are to each other what he has been to us, is the contemporary experience of being with him. The wonder of it all is that he is utterly available if we will be quiet, listen, learn, and live under orders. But the purpose of our relationship with him is what he wants to do through us with others. That's why he called us: so that we could be sent out. The verb in Mark is apostellō, meaning a commission to act as his representative with his credentials to accomplish his mission. The basic responsibility of the one sent forth was to preach. We dare not get hung up on our concept of formal preaching. The Greek word Mark uses is kērussō, which means public proclamation with authority. That's to be done by us in all of life's relationships. Conversation is a neglected gift for sharing the faith with others. Deep trusting relationships with others give us the right to share what Christ means to us and what he is doing in our lives. When Jesus called his disciples to preach he gave them the gift of communication which is offered every Christian who will be a disciple.

Everyone who accepts his discipleship is given authority. The word is *exousia*, meaning delegated authority. The disciples were to have God's delegated authority to speak, heal, and cast out demons, but it would be his power which would do the work. Their authority was to declare the availability of God's power. They were not to be healers containing the power to heal but mediators of the power. It was not their task to store up healing power and dole it out to whomever they desired. Rather, the need in people would be met by God's healing through them.

The listing of the disciples' names is often skipped over with unimaginative familiarity because we have repeated them so often. But look again. Some of them are given a new name as a promise of what they were to become. Continuing the Old Testament tradition of a new name to symbolize a new relationship and the potential of a new character, Jesus calls Simon, Peter—a rock. The masculine and feminine renderings of *petros* and *petra* are illuminating. The masculine *petros* means a fragment of a stone, rock, or cliff. Here it is used metaphorically for a strong, unyielding, resolute personality. The feminine *petra* metaphorically means firmness and stability like a great, massive living rock. In Matthew 16:18 Jesus said to Simon, "And I tell you, you are Petros, and upon this petra I will build my church." In other words, "You are a large, strong man but upon the living, immovable, sure foundation of my love and power I will build my church."[1] Jesus gave Simon a new image of himself, of what he was and would become through discipleship with Jesus.

In similar fashion James and John would become "sons of thunder." The lightning of Christ's life and message would be followed by the thundering response of their discipleship. How true it was to be. They became what they were named. And James was among the first to be martyred for his love of Jesus, while John became the thundering voice of love and hope in the early Church.

---

[1] I am indebted to Kenneth S. Wuest for this insight in his helpful book *Word Studies: Mark in the Greek New Testament* (Grand Rapids, Mich.: Eerdmans, 1950), pp. 71–72.

The point of this is that Christ gives us a new name as we accept the call to be disciples. What is the name which would describe you if you were completely yielded to Christ's control? What is the opposite of whatever problem or block which keeps you from being effective for him? Claim that name!

The list of disciples' names is more than a record; it's a promise. If you could focus on one word that would portray what you want to become, what would it be? If you could ask our Lord for one thing that would exemplify your character, what would you ask? Focus on that in your mind. Use it in your prayers. "Lord, this is Patience. Thank you for making the humanly impossible possible." Or, "Good morning Lord, this is Forgiveness." Or, "This is Gracious, checking in for orders!" Or, "Humble here, Lord; thanks for healing my pride!"

The new name is the manifestation of what our Lord is more ready to give than we are to receive. Dare to call yourself by the new name. Use it as an exchange for an old life. Inadvertently, we will become the name by which our Lord calls us!

This passage in Mark leaves us with a question. Are we a part of the crowd which is crushing our Lord for the extraction of power for our needs or have we been called up into the hills to be one of his disciples to communicate his power to others?

The other day I talked to a man who is training new Christians for membership in his church. He was once a part of the crowd; now his life is spent caring for others.

A woman wrote me about the excitement she feels in sharing her hope in Christ with other women in her social clubs: "Now that I have people on my heart, the worship and equipping program of the church makes sense. I need all the help I can get to be an effective transmitter of the power of Christ!"

An elderly man sees his mission as sharing Christ with the lonely, single, senior people in his neighborhood. "Sure beats being an uninvolved observer in a church committee!" he said.

A mother whose children were grown and leaving home spends her days telephoning lonely people to talk about Christ's love and to listen to people's needs.

The examples are limitless. These people are the miracles I was writing about earlier. All of life is now focused on Christ. He is their daily companion as they pray their prayers and study and become involved with people. They are not religious; they are fun-loving, affirming, "all things are possible" people. As disciples, they are living a life without limits. In their prayer and sharing groups they weekly sort out the next steps in Christ's strategy. These people are the hope for a new kind of church. No pastor can meet the needs of everyone who is ready to do business with God. He will deplete himself or have a nervous breakdown if he tries. The central task of a pastor is to reproduce himself by training disciples. Any church which is built on the pastor alone will fall on him and crush him or fall apart when he leaves. Jesus' strategy cannot be denied. It's the only way. I invite any pastor who's reading this to take an inventory with me. Who's your Timothy? What group of people in your church are you discipling to multiply your ministry? And are you laymen and laywomen ready to be discipled? Is discipleship the passion of your life? Have you ever offered your pastor your time and energy to learn all he knows about how to help people? Ask God to give you a band of disciples with whom you can meet regularly to study and discuss how to be effective in our suffering world. If you do, you will never be bored, ineffective, or insignificant again. You will be our Lord's greatest miracle!

CHAPTER 9

THE ONLY UNFORGIVABLE SIN

Mark 3:20-30

It's unsettling. Disturbing. Alarming!

What did Jesus mean ". . . whoever blasphemes against the Holy Spirit never has forgiveness, but is guilty of an eternal sin"? An unforgivable sin? Doesn't that contradict everything we believe about grace? Is there anything we can do which will make it impossible to experience God's love?

But the statement is there. We can't wish it away, nor tear it out of our Bible. It is one of the most difficult teachings of Jesus.

We read the words with awe and wonder, realizing that we are about to be ushered into the holy heart of God and then back to the nature of man, with new wisdom and insight. This is a burning bush passage. We are on holy ground.

No passage in Mark so demands that we keep text and context together as this one. The context tells us what prompted Jesus' statement, and the text tells us more about our human nature than we may want to know.

Jesus had gone to the house where he often stayed in Capernaum. He had many friends there. But some of these were alarmed at his behavior. His casting out of demons particularly concerned them. They had heard gladly his message of love and forgiveness. Many of them had been healed at his hand. Now they were disturbed by his strange behavior. He was in conflict with the scribes and Pharisees, associated with tax collectors and seemed to give little regard to the regulations of their religion. But it was his power over demons that confounded them. He was either mad or badly disturbed. So they tried to seize him, crying, "He is beside himself."

The scribes were not as compassionate as his friends. Word of Jesus' miraculous powers had reached Jerusalem. A delegation of highly trained scribes was sent to investigate and level a charge. They did not entertain the thought that Jesus might have power over demons because he was God's Messiah. Their diagnosis was set before they reached him. It was boldly and harshly spoken out of hate mingled with simplistic analysis. "He is possessed by Beelzebub, and by the prince of demons he casts out demons." Notice they did not ask him any question or try to understand his powers.

Jesus' response was remarkable in its intellectual depth and spiritual perception. His logic was impelling. "And he called them to him, and said to them in parables, 'How can Satan cast out Satan? If a kingdom is divided against itself, that kingdom cannot stand. And if a house is divided against itself, that house will not be able to stand. And if Satan has risen up against himself and is divided, he cannot stand, but is coming to an end'" (Mark 3:23–27).

The reasoning is so clear. How could anyone have missed it? Why would the prince of demons cast out demons? The implication was that only a greater power could divide the kingdom of Satan. And that's just the point they had overlooked or refused to recognize. That clears the way for an understanding of our text about the unforgivable sin.

The power of Jesus' Messianic ministry was the Spirit of God himself. The scribes had resisted that same Spirit and declared that Jesus was possessed by the prince of demons. They had rejected God himself!

The ministry of the Holy Spirit is to enable us to say Jesus is Lord. Paul put it clearly, "Therefore I want you to understand that no one speaking by the Spirit of God ever says, 'Jesus be cursed!' and no one can say 'Jesus is Lord' except by the Holy Spirit" (1 Cor. 12:3).

Resistance to the Holy Spirit is the unforgivable sin. That is not a statement of God's refusal to forgive but of man's refusal to accept.

Think of it this way. The scribes did not accept Jesus as Messiah and Lord. They sealed their own eternal doom. The same is true today. The Holy Spirit is active seeking to bring all men to an acceptance of Jesus as Lord. To refuse his influence is to close the door on any chance of eternal life. Remember that sin is separation.

To sin against the Holy Spirit is to say "no" to his gracious appeal and pleading.

For us, the sin against the Holy Spirit can take many forms. We can try to live by the message of Christ on our own power and resist the living presence of the Holy Spirit from whom we can receive the energizing power to live the Christian life. Or we can accept Jesus as Savior and resist his Lordship in our relationships and problems. Further, we can accept the truths of the Christian faith and fail to accept Christ's indwelling presence in the Holy Spirit. Arrogance and pride, fired by self-will and self-determination, can convince us that we can control our own lives, without the help of the Spirit.

But let's go deeper. When we face difficulties and problems, we are tempted to relegate the cause to some mysterious evil power rather than urgently seek the Lord's power in our need. We fall into the scribes' distorted thinking, saying the misfortune is evil, and we give up in hopeless despair. That can be true for anything from sickness to world problems. Satan cannot cast out Satan. Only Christ can do that. But to give up is to give Satan the victory.

Jesus' statement about the unforgivable sin says much more about us than it does about God. There is no sin which God is not willing to forgive. But there is a level of resistance which makes it impossible for us to ask for forgiveness. If we say "no" to the Holy Spirit too long and in too many areas of life, our capacity to say "yes" is stunted and withered.

The freedom given to us by God is a blessing which can become a curse if we misuse it in aggressive self-determination. This whole concept is frightening and leaves us with some thinking and praying to do.

For ourselves the question is, "Am I resisting the Holy Spirit? Is there any area where I am refusing to accept Jesus as Lord?" The Spirit's persistent ministry is to enable us to love Christ, serve Christ, and open our lives to him.

For others, our responsibility is to pray for the Holy Spirit to break the bind of self-will. Influence by Satan has many frightening but subtle manifestations. Many good church members are consistently refusing to say Jesus is Lord over the various dimensions of life, including their own hearts! Jesus warned that the vacuum will be filled, either by him or by evil influence.

The alarm with which we began this chapter now turns to adoration. The Lord's love has prompted a warning for us and the people of our lives. He cares about us. He called us to know and love him. But he also wants us to live with him forever. That's why he clarified the only unforgivable sin. Jesus never wants us to drift so far from the influence of his Spirit that we would no longer see our need for grace. That's what he meant: the unforgivable sin is to no longer need to be forgiven!

CHAPTER 10

BLEST BE THE TIE THAT UNBINDS

Mark 3:31–35

It was a beautiful Sunday morning. Members and friends of the church were scurrying hurriedly to their places for 9:30 worship, church school, choir practice, and prayer sessions in preparation for the morning activities. Because I was a bit late, and because I wanted to assure myself that a man my age still has athletic agility, I bounded up the stairs to my office three steps at a time. On the way up I passed a member of the choir, making her way to the choir robing room. "How's my sister?" I asked as I leaped past her. She looked a bit puzzled. "Well, I don't know your sister. Has she not been well?" I stopped at the top of the stairs and looked back with a twinkle in my eye. "I mean you! I'm your brother in Christ!" We both laughed and she admitted that her thoughts were not on her brothers or sisters in faith but getting to choir on time.

At the top of the next flight of stairs I met a church officer, a beloved friend who was waiting outside my study to have prayers with me for God's power to be released in the morning message. He greeted me with words that were intoned with manly affection and affirmation. "My brother, Lloyd!" he said; "God bless you!" I was assured, uplifted, and loved.

After the 9:30 service, a woman came out of the service and grasped my hand warmly. Then in a moment of concerned confidence she told me of a strange experience she had had in the middle of the night. She had been awakened with me on her mind and felt prompted to pray for me. The Lord said to her, "I want you to pray for your brother Lloyd." She went on to say, "I had never thought of you as my brother, but it then seemed right to talk to my Heavenly Father about you as a brother."

Later, as I reflected on these three experiences, I realized again God's intention for his people. They are to share a mutual love and encouragement which is exemplified by, but immensely superseded by, the love of brothers and sisters of a family. That's what happens to people who dare to share his love . . . they begin to share a mutual loyalty and concern.

But this realization led me into a time of frustration. What I have found with many of my people, I long to know with everyone I meet. But schedules will not stretch far enough, the hours are not long enough, the week has a weakness . . . there's not enough time to be a brother to every person. I asked the Lord about this frustration. His answer was decisive and clear. "Don't try. Be a brother to all I put on your schedule and then help your people to become a family with each other."

That was the preparation the Lord put me through long before I turned my attention to this passage in Mark. In that context, a passage which I had read often now had new meaning and power. I suddenly realized that the hope, the picture, the Lord had given me was an extension of his eternal purpose—a part of the reason he came, lived, died, was raised up, and is with us now.

From the beginning of creation, God intended that his people should be a family. Man's rebellion and fall from his intended purpose to love God and be the beloved community of his people resulted in estrangement from his creator and from his fellow creatures. The Old Testament is the bloody record of man's misuse of himself and his fellow humans.

Then God himself interceded. He came to set things right . . . to reconcile man to God and to others. Any interpretation of the life of Jesus which leaves out one or the other or both is a heresy, a distortion, a fragmentation of the truth. What we feel in the moving events of the Gospel of Mark is the tabulation of the beginning of a new creation—God in our midst recreating his original intention. Christ was God with us and for us . . . God loving and healing . . . God forgiving and reconciling . . . God creating a new people—the new Israel, his own holy people, uniquely related to him by grace and to one another as brothers and sisters in a new kind of family, the Church.

That's what makes the calling of the disciples so significant. And

as we noted earlier, he gave many of them a new name, a portent
of promise of what they would become in fellowship with him.
But groups also become the name by which they are called. That's
the thrust of the amazing message of this passage. In a strategic
moment when the followers, disciples, and opponents of Jesus were
least together in any kind of mutual concern for each other; at the
time when they were most conscious of their differences politically,
socially, and in personality, Jesus called them brothers and sisters
and designated them as his essential family!

Picture the scene. Jesus is back in the home that provided him
hospitality in Capernaum. The crowds which had witnessed his
healing miracles and heard his message of love and hope pressed
in upon him, overflowing the house and out into the streets. In
the circle around him there is an amazing mixture of humanity.
The scribes from Jerusalem are prominent. They had just accused
him of blasphemy and then had committed the ultimate blasphemy
themselves of declaring that he was possessed with Beelzebub.
Intermingled in the crowd and pressing protectively about him
were the disciples he had just called. With them were the people
who had been healed and exorcised by his power. What a panorama
of personalities! Written on those faces was the contrast of love,
admiration, thanksgiving, challenge, hatred and zealous competitiveness. Note the absurd audacity of the assumption that these
people could ever be bound together in mutual trust and loyalty.
Here was a tax collector who had been in league with Rome, next
to him was a Zealot whose passion was Israel's independence from
foreign domination. There were fishermen with little education
and sophisticated teachers of the law.

And on the edge of the crowd clustered the family of Jesus.
Rumor had reached Nazareth that Jesus was acting very strangely.
He had healed the sick, commanded demons to cower in submission, but most of all he was making claims that sounded like he believed he was the Messiah. As good Hebrews, they had reverence
for the establishment represented in the scribes and Pharisees.
Now that the leaders were attacking him openly, his family too
reached the conclusion that Jesus must be mad. What could they
do but come and take him home and tenderly nurse him back to
sanity.

They sent a message through the crowd: "Your mother and your
brothers and sister are outside asking for you." The message is

quickly passed through to Jesus. Surely he would want to drop everything, leave the crowd, and go with them.

Not so! Shock, amazement, and uncomprehending surprise greeted Jesus' response: "Who are my mother and brothers?" A murmur rumbled through the crowd. Then like a clarion call he said, pointing to the people about him, "Here are my mother and my brothers! Whoever does the will of God is my brother, and sister, and mother."

How amazed and crushed Mary must have felt! No special privilege, no unique relationship? "I gave him birth, nursed him into life, watched over him as a boy, watched him grow into manhood. I gave my life for him! Do I get nothing in return?" she must have said to herself. Or feel with his brothers and sister. "Well, that proves it. He is mad! Worse than we expected! Anyway, if that's how he feels, let him go his way!"

Yes, they had a hard time that day. But so do we as we grapple with the implications of Jesus' words. The perspective of history helps us, for we know what happened in subsequent days and months of Jesus' ministry. The family of Jesus became a part of a new family of faith. The filial ties were unloosed and replaced by the sure bonds of the family of faith. Mary became a sister in the fellowship of our Lord; James, the brother of our Lord, became a leader in the church after the resurrection.

But on that day in Capernaum they did not understand, and neither did the disciples. But as the ministry of our Lord progressed, they began to realize that their relationship to him as his new family was to be the beginning of the new family of man—the new creation, the Church. No designation could have challenged them more and given them a more vivid image of what they were to become as a fellowship of people.

When we look ahead to the post-resurrection, post-Pentecost emergence of the Church, we see the fulfillment of the promise. It is recorded that the Church met together in their homes; they had all things in common, and they sold what they had and shared the proceeds with each other.

I believe that Mark included this story in his Gospel to give specific help to the early Church at Rome. Many of those early Christians had followed Christ at great cost. Some had been rejected by family and friends because of their faith. Mark could picture the house churches meeting in Rome—groups of disciples gathering together for mutual encouragement and hope. They, too, had sought to do the will of God, regardless of opposition. Jesus had promised to every follower a new family, and their churches were a fulfillment of that promise. Coupled closely with this promise was the record of Jesus' words,

> "Truly, I say to you, there is no one who has left house or brothers or sisters or mother or father or lands, for my sake and for the gospel, who will not receive a hundredfold now in this time, houses and brothers and sisters and mothers and children and lands, with persecutions, and in the age to come eternal life. But many that are first will be last, and the last first" (Mark 10:29-31).

Two basic truths demand recognition and acceptance. The Church is to be like a family; the family is to be like the Church. The two are interlinked, one dependent on the other. But both express the two greatest needs in our contemporary society. We have lost the family feeling in the Church in America and family has lost the sense of being the Church in miniature. I want to deal with these separately and then put them together as inseparable parts of a whole truth.

First of all, the recovery of the Church as a family. The family of faith is made up of those who seek and do the will of God. Jesus modeled life as God intended it to be. He was completely surrendered to his Father. His life is punctuated by his repeated prayer, "Thy will be done!" There can be no satisfying life apart from the will of God. To know God's will means prayer and seeking his direction. It means spreading all our affairs out before him, willing to will his will. The will is the key to life abundant. With the gift of our wills we yield to God's direction and seek his insight in all our decisions and reactions.

Tennyson was right, "Our wills are ours, we know not how; our wills are ours, to make them Thine." When we make our wills his will, we know the beloved communion for which we were born. But also, we come to know a new relationship with others who are also seeking his will. A great Church is born when with one voice we cry, "In our life together, thy will be done!" The family of faith results.

James Jauncey said, "God never burglarizes the human will. He may long to come in and help, but he will never cross the picket line

of our unwillingness."[1] That's true for the Christian fellowship as
well. And George Herbert put it this way, "When the will is
ready the feet are light."[2]

There is no Christian growth without the surrender of the will.
That's the battlefield for our souls. Augustine said in his prayers
to God, "When I vacillated about my decision to serve the Lord
my God, it was I who willed and I who willed not, and nobody
else. I was fighting against myself. All you asked was that I cease
to want what I willed and want what you willed."

That's the liberating secret! The family of God is the fellowship
of people who are open to the will of God and therefore open to
each other. His will is that we love him and each other. We cannot love each other while resisting his will nor can we resist loving
each other if we do his will.

If the Lord calls us his brothers and sisters, then this expresses
the quality of life we are to have as congregations within the
Church. Jesus takes a familiar image to teach an unfamiliar hope.
We all have a sense of the mutual loyalty, concern, and commitment people in a family are to have for each other. But this familiar
image is stretched by the nature of the family of faith he lived and
died to make possible. Jesus said, "By this shall men know that you
are my disciples . . . that you love one another" and, "As you
have done it to the least of these, you have done it to me." What
we do to each other, we do to him. If he is our brother, we meet
him as elder, eternal brother in our brothers and sisters of the
Church. "This is my commandment that you love one another."
Jesus was crucified so that our individualistic and separatistic aloof-
ness might die and be crucified and be resurrected to unity and
oneness.

Here is his last will and testament . . . and the charter of the
Church.

> "I am praying for them; I am not praying for the world but for
> those whom thou hast given me, for they are thine; all mine are
> thine, and thine are mine, and I am glorified in them. And now
> I am no more in the world, but they are in the world, and I

---

[1] James Jauncey, *Lights from the Chapel Window*, comp. by Mary Jess
(Chicago: Moody Press, 1972) p. 11.

[2] George Herbert, *Evangelism Now* (Minneapolis: Worldwide Publica-
tions, 1969, 1970).

am coming to Thee. Holy Father, keep them in thy name, which
thou hast given me, that they may be one, even as we are one. While
I was with them, I kept them in thy name, which thou hast given
me; I have guarded them, and none of them is lost but the son of
perdition, that the scripture might be fulfilled" (John 17:9–12).

"I do not pray for these only, but also for those who believe in me
through their word, that they may all be one; even as thou, Father,
art in me, and I in thee, that they also may be in us, so that the
world may believe that thou hast sent me. The glory which thou
hast given me I have given to them, that they may be one even
as we are one, I in them and thou in me, that they may become
perfectly one, so that the world may know that thou hast sent me
and hast loved them even as thou hast loved me. Father, I desire
that they also, whom thou hast given me, may be with me where
I am, to behold my glory which thou hast given me in thy love for
me before the foundation of the world" (John 17:20–24).

The Church is not a channel of inspiration for uninvolved observers but a communion of involved participants. Our language
betrays us. We say we go to church, give to the church, support
the cause of the church, attend the church. Not so! We are the
Church. But a strange thing has happened over the years of history.
The church is now a programmatical presentation which can be
attended. Today we become sermon tasters, music appreciators,
Bible students, devotees of spiritual leaders, without commitment
to a family. It's possible, actually, to assume that we can have Christ
without the family of faith. But that's realizing only half of the
reason for which Christ came.

Look at it this way. You and I are struggling to live a full and
significant life. The people who come to the church have acknowledged that they need God's love and power. The church ought to
provide that. So we go, get what we need, and leave. That makes
the church a spiritual supermarket, rather than a fellowship. Our
cautious involvement is basically self-centered. We are wanting
salvation; we desire to live forever; we long for spiritual insight and
power. But the other half of Christ's resources are reserved for those
who bother to be a brother, who sustain a sister. We cannot forever
neglect the other half of the message of Jesus and expect to keep
the half we have realized.

Commitment to Christ must be spelled out in commitment to a

church. The spiritualistic heresy which has been around for nearly two thousand years is that distortion called docetism. It believes that Jesus reconciled the world without ever living in the flesh. The contemporary expression of this is in people who believe they can have Christ without accountability in a church—relationship with Christ without caring for the brothers and sisters he gives us.

From the experience of the Church as a family, we can now learn that our families should become more like the Church Christ intended. There is a dynamic interrelation between the way families live and the way the Church realizes its destiny.

I'm sure you recall the familiar words from the old hymn, "Blest be the tie that binds our hearts in Christian love." The idea is admirable. There is a quality of Christ's love that binds us in mutual concern and caring. But there is also a lesser love which binds us with the ties of guilt, compulsion, and obligation. Many of the psychological problems of our society can be traced to parents whose affection binds and ties rather than releases and liberates. We can all look back and see the influence of our families for good and ill. That forces us to think about how our present families could be more like what Jesus intended about the church being a place of liberation, a center of unbinding, a fellowship of loosening the false ties and enabling the bond of love as the ultimate basis of relationship. I am discovering this in my own family. Mary Jane and I are growing in the realization that we are fellow adventurers in Christ. Increasingly, he is the center of the relationship. The more we love him more than we love each other, the more we can love and enjoy each other. Our marriage began, really, when we shifted our ultimate loyalty, security, and need to him. Then we could begin to be to each other what he increasingly becomes to us. Neither one of us can love each other as much as we need to be loved. Only Christ can do that! When we allow him to love us, we can free each other to be Christ's persons. Then we have limitless resources of love in him for each other. The same is true with my children. As they have accepted Christ's love and lordship, I have found a fellowship with them that exceeds the father-child syndrome of dependence, rejection, rebellion, and independence. We have become friends in Christ. The Church is coming alive in our love. Thank God! That's why I think the words of that old hymn are all wrong. It should be, "Blest be the tie that *unbinds* our hearts in Christian love."

Recently I heard Dr. Richard Halverson of Washington, D.C., talk about this same discovery. He told about how each of his children has come to be in Christ and how the family is a church in miniature. I will never forget the description of a monthly dinner meeting he has with his family. His sons have ministries of their own and return to be discipled by Dick and to learn from him what he has discovered about life in Christ. But he said that he also learns immeasurably from them. The relationship is one of mutual discipleship. The Church in the home!

The commandment to honor our parents is expanded in this light. Honor now becomes the key word of the church in the family for all its members—children to parents, parents to children, husband and wife to each other. Rote responsibility, blind obedience, teeth-gritting compulsion, or guilt-oriented solicitude are replaced by enabling honor. That means consideration, commendation of worth, respectful regard, and liberating esteem. That is what the family is for! It allows uniqueness, difference, quality.

When Paul sent greetings to the Corinthian church, he included greetings from Aquila and Priscilla, together with the church in their house. That gives us the image of the family as an inclusive fellowship, open to others for informal discussion, celebration, and caring. I remember the families which included me in their fellowship in Christ when I was just beginning the Christian life. What I observed in them gave me an image of the church as a family and the family as a church which has been indelible and lasting. It set the bench mark for what I want my home to be.

There are seven steps toward becoming the church in the home which have helped me.

1. Begin with yourself as parent or child, husband or wife. We dare not expect our homes to be any more Christian than we are willing to be ourselves in attitude and action.

2. Ask for the disposition of Christ (a translation of the "mind of Christ") for your relationship to every member of the family. The only creative relationship is through Christ: to see with his eyes; to love with his love; to give with his selflessness. We can be participants in the church in our homes only when Christ has fulfilled his promise in John 14:23, "If a man loves me, he will keep my word, and my Father will love him, and we will come to him and make our home with him."

3. Be to each other what Christ has been to you. That means accepting love, forgiving, accepting, and enabling expectation.

4. Pray for and with each other. There is unlimited power available for the encouragement and direction of our lives. Power is always a prayer away.

5. Be honest about your feelings; allow an honest expression of feelings from those who live with you. Hidden feelings can hurt the family. Exposed feelings can be forgiven, used to correct wrong or injustice, and accepted as the basis of new, mutual esteem.

6. Let go of any right to each other. A marriage contract does not mean we own our spouse! It simply means God has entrusted a person to us. Our children are not our possessions or an extension of our ego. The family has no "rights" over a person. We do not belong to each other until we belong to God. We are a gift to each other by grace alone, and the gift is to be handled gently and with honor.

7. Open the doors of your home and heart for others to share what you are experiencing. Meals, family worship, and times of recreation can be the church alive in your home with other people. Think what that would do to help the loneliness in your city!

Thus the family exists as God's ordained center of psychological and spiritual nurture. It is there that the filial should become faithful. Family ties should be unbinding so that increasingly the basic loyalties to human love are released to love Christ and others. A successful family is one where Christ is center, where children and parents become friends in Christ. We are called to release our children to love others as an extension of our love for them. The test is always—have our families been the matrix in which we are liberated to love Christ more than each other?

Our need for the family feeling is never satisfied. But it can be multiplied if it is liberated. That happens when our love for one another frees us to love deeply and richly in the world. The family has done its job if we are all released to make the whole world our family.

The interdependence of the family and the church follows naturally. In the church we should learn what it means to be truly a family so the family can learn how to be like a church. The result is obvious. We will be freed to love the world.

CHAPTER 11

THE THIRD EAR

Mark 4

We all know fear. Something or someone makes all of us afraid. What is it for you? Quite apart from physical danger, what has the capacity of making you fearful? The unknown, the unexpected, the uncontrollable? Fear has many costumes for the drama of our lives. For some of us it is fear of failure. We are catatonically immobilized for fear of repeating past mistakes. Consequently, we attempt very little because we are afraid of failing again. The flip side of that is equally troublesome. We are afraid of maintaining our success. As one man said to me in an unguarded moment of honesty on a transatlantic flight, "I'm at the pinnacle of my success. I am afraid I can't keep it up. Sometimes I think it would be great if one of these flights crashed and I could go down in a blaze of glory before I fail miserably at something and that's all people remember!" Too extreme? Perhaps, but have you ever worried about keeping up the pace you've set for yourself?

Fear of change gets at all of us. Even the most innovative. There comes a time for everyone when he likes things the way he's developed them. Then someone comes along and messes up our carefully ordered values, presuppositions, habits, and life-style.

Closely related to that is a fear of loss—especially loss of people. The constellation of significant people around us is crucial for us. We don't like the loss of people through life's changes or death.

We all fear rejection. Our ideas, plans, or proposals become an extension of our egos. If they are not met with messianic wonder and delight, we feel we have failed. Often lack of affection on our time schedule in marriage is interpreted as rejection. We all need affirmation and constant encouragement. Previous rejection collects in our memories, and we soon expect to be rejected in almost every relationship. As one woman said, "I keep doing things to be sure people love me. I've had some bad blows to my ego. Seems like I keep expecting it from everyone. Guess that explains the protective shell I've built around me."

Then, too, I find that lots of us fear growth, intellectually and emotionally. We don't like ideas that force an intellectual reorientation, and we avoid penetrating conversation or analysis concerning who we are, really, and what makes us do the things we do. Many of us have tried to shut the door tightly on ruminating around in our feelings to find out what hurts. Remember the growing pains we had as kids? Do you still feel that when it comes to continuing to grow up as a person? I do!

Also, many of us fear commitments. We don't want to get too deeply involved with people or causes. We want to keep a safe distance, always sure of our retreat route. We are afraid of entangling alliances.

Another fear we all share is of the future. It's not hopeful to many people. We wonder what life will bring or do to us out ahead. A young man just out of graduate school said, "I spent all these years getting ready for my profession and now I'm not at all sure about what's going to happen. There are so few jobs open, the economy's down, and it's a sick world in which to get married and raise a family. Sure, I'm worried about the future."

But all of these fears are related to one great fear. The fear of death and dying . . . nonexistence . . . endless nothingness. How would you feel if you were to die today or before you finish this chapter? Can you greet death as a friend without anguish or despair?

Do any of these things make you afraid? Are there others? Think about that and help me answer a perplexing question: "How is it that knowing what we do about Christ's power, realizing that he is with us right now, assured of his ultimate victory in all things, we are still afraid?" Amazing, isn't it? Now we can understand and appreciate what the disciples experienced in this section of Mark.

This is one of those Mark passages which must be understood from the end forward. We must take what happened at the end of the day with the storm at night to be the context of what Jesus taught throughout the day about the awesome power of the third ear. The disciples had not heard what Jesus had been saying throughout the day. He had given them parables about how to hear, but they had not heard! Jesus always actualizes in experience what we have intellectualized. Hearing is more than having an eardrum activated by sound. That's the reason for Jesus' often repeated words in this chapter: "He who has ears to hear, let him hear." He seems to be saying, "Let your ears catch the sounds, but keep the third ear of your heart open to receive the fear-liberating truth!"

At the end of this particular day the disciples were out at sea in a terrible storm. Jesus was in the bow of the boat peacefully asleep, afraid of nothing that might happen. But when the storm reached its tumultuous height, the disciples could contain their fear no longer.

"Teacher, do you not care if we perish?" Their third ears had not registered and assimilated what he had been saying to them about the power of God. They had listened but had not heard! Earlier in the day they had been so judgmental of others about the way they received the Word of God. Now they realized they were no better; even worse. Then Jesus rebuked the wind and said to the sea, "Peace, be still!" The same admonition was desperately needed by the disciples. To them he said, "Why are you afraid? Have you no faith?" Faith is the only antidote to fear in all its grotesque shapes and forms. Now it began to dawn on the disciples what Jesus had been trying to communicate during that day. The penetration of the Lord God is not just acoustic. The nature of the response is dictated by the receptivity of the heart that receives it. In that truth is the hope for conquering our fears.

The fourth chapter of Mark uses several parables to bring together the impact of a central truth. It proclaims the way the Word of God is received, the test which indicates it has been received, how it grows in one who has received it, and what it means to the world around those in whom its seed has been planted.

The parable of the sower is really the parable of the hearers. The quality of the soil represents the receptivity of the third ear. Each of the four different kinds of soil presented to the seed, the Word of God, was familiar to the disciples and followers of Jesus. These categories of soil were also evident in the church at Rome for which Mark was so deeply concerned. He was profoundly disturbed that many who were in Christ were also in fear. Why? Our answer dare not be glib. The same kind of hearers are with us still today. What kind of soil are we?

The seed sown on the path represents the closed third ear, the hard hearts. It is unable to receive and nurture the seed. The birds in Jesus' explanation of his own parable represent Satan stealing away the seed that has been planted in the believer. The well-worn path is all too obvious: the busy life; the disappointed, hardened life. We can actually receive such contradictory data from our jaded experience that the third ear of our heart is closed. It's like the captain of the ship calling for full speed ahead and the men in the engine room putting the vessel in reverse. The engine gang in our subconscious does just that, and some of the semiconscious crew in between affirm the counterproductive order. That's why we can hear the words of Jesus, "Do not be afraid!" and our memory factors say, "You had better be afraid. Look at what's happened to you!" We listen to Jesus' words, but we do not hear.

The rocky ground in the story is the shallow listener. The third ear registers the thought of Jesus being the conqueror of our fears, but it is soon drowned out by the din of another voice demanding fear as the only safe response to life's challenges and eventualities.

There are three stages to the response given by the rocky ground to the seed. One is the quick response of joy because of the exhilarating sense of surface peace and freedom. The second stage is momentary endurance in frightening possibilities with deceptive signs of strength and growth. The third is defeat in persecution and prolonged difficulty. Acceptance of the gospel is given by rocky soil, but external pressures, combined with inner weakness, result in apostasy. There are many listeners whose soil is rocky; therefore, they have little more than a flash growth of the Lordship of Christ in their lives.

We all have some rocks in our soil. That's why it takes so long for us to grow in the Christian life, to experience the power of Christ in our personalities, and to radiate the joy of Christ in our living. Our third ear is open, but our hearing is hampered. We are afraid of what Christ might do with dimensions of our hidden, rocky, inner selves.

Note that the first category, the well-trodden path, cannot receive the seed because of the hardening caused by others. The second category, the rocky ground, cannot nurture the seed in any lasting way because of the boulders of resistance.

The thorny ground is the overcrowded life. This is the kind of listener who has a division within his heart and therefore cannot nurture the seed of the Kingdom—the rule of God in all of life. The energy of the soil is used to sustain and replenish the thorns. Jesus later explains that the thorns are the cares of the world— delight in riches . . . desire for things other than the Word. What Jesus is describing here are the contrary ambitions which choke out completely the implanted seed. The end result in this kind of hearer is that he proves to be unfruitful.

The purpose of the sowing of the seed is to make us fruitful disciples. We have never heard the gospel, really, if we cannot reproduce what we have heard and experienced of Jesus' life in other people. The same point is all too clear in his message to the disciples in the last week of his ministry. "Abide in me, and I in you. As the branch cannot bear fruit by itself, unless it abides in the vine, neither can you, unless you abide in me. . . . By this my Father is glorified, that you bear much fruit, and so prove to be my disciples" (John 15:4, 8).

When it comes to the communication of what we have heard as the test of our hearing, many of us would have to admit that we have not heard very well. We hear the gospel; it takes root in us; and yet our other loyalties, schedules, and commitments keep us from being reproductive of our faith. The seed has little energy to grow on. It's all spent on other pressures, people, and problems.

This exposes a truth I have grappled with for a long time. My reading of Jesus' messages leads me to the conviction that his power is given to us to do his work. Many of us miss what he offers because we want his power to do our work but on our schedule and according to our priorities. That's why so many of us are still gripped with fears. I meet people everywhere who are praying for power over their fears. That's the wrong prayer. We are to ask for power to do what Jesus did with people in his day and what he wants us to do today. Fears are liberated and replaced by the creative fear of missing the reason for which we were born.

But the question lingers. What thorns are draining our resources? The distracting thorns will wear us out; eventually they kill us. I know that to be true over years of futile attempts to run my own life. Just recently I had to do some very thorough weeding out of the thorns which were choking out aspects of the Lordship of Christ. And they all looked like such beautiful flowers. Some friends had to help me with my life the way a gardener often does. When I mistake weeds to be flowers in my garden, he says, "Why are you letting these weeds grow in here? They are nothing but weeds! They will kill the flowers!"

The good soil in the parable represents those who hear, accept what they hear, and bear fruit. The good seed grows, blooms, reproduces its seed, and grows again. That's what being Christ's person is all about. Good soil is ploughed deeply; it is receptive to the seed, open to its germination and growth, cultivated by the loosening experiences of life, and gives itself to no other purpose but the seed. That's the kind of third ear listeners Jesus wanted in his disciples and in us.

All of the ground which Jesus talked about in the story is to be found in any group of hearers. He has given us powers of receptivity in our third ear to hear what he has to say about his love, forgiveness and strategy for us and to have it become integrated in our lives so that it can be actualized in our experiences of fear.

Later when Jesus had his disciples alone, they asked him about the parables. He told them that parables were used because there were some who would not receive the gospel. He gave his explanation of them to those who responded and were open to him. The difficult truth in Mark 4:11, 12 about those who refuse to hear, is a hard saying, "To you has been given the secret of the kingdom of God, but for those outside everything is in parables; so they may indeed see but not perceive, and may indeed hear but not understand; lest they should turn again, and be forgiven." The secret of the kingdom was in him as Messiah. This the Pharisees refused to accept. Therefore, they could see truth but were unwilling to reorder their lives around it. They heard words but could not understand them in their hearts. He taught in parables so that they would not trifle with the ideas without commitment to him as the Son of God. The parables were given for self-evaluation, not to judge others. Judgmentalism was the Pharisee's stock and trade; truth was used to incriminate others. Jesus did not want a flash of insight which would bring surface repentance and cheap forgiveness without costly commitment to him and his Messianic mission. That's the reason the parables were a condemnation on the wilfully blind and the hostilely deaf, while at the same time they were a guide and enlightenment to those who accepted him as Lord of their lives.

Now Jesus goes on in his explanation to show what happens

when we hear and the seed takes root in us. The undeniable evidence that we have received the good seed is that people around us know it. Next, the metaphor is shifted to the symbol of light: "Is a lamp brought in to be put under a bushel, or under a bed, and not on a stand? For there is nothing hid, except to be made manifest; nor is anything secret, except to come to light" (Mark 4:21–22). Now note the emphasis again on hearing: "If any man has ears to hear, let him hear."

The point is that if we have received the good seed, we will want to give it away. Then comes the unsettling and incisive insight into our lives in Mark 4:25, "For to him who has will more be given; and from him who has not, even what he has will be taken away." What we do not use, we lose. What is not given away cannot be replenished and multiplied. Jesus is trying to help his disciples, and us, to realize that the final test of having heard and accepted the truth is that we will want to give it away.

I have always resisted haranguing people into sharing their faith. If people are reluctant to communicate their faith, it is because they have too little of it and it has not sufficiently grasped their lives. In this account Jesus is correcting a terrible distortion of God's love which was rampant at that time and is still around in subtle ways in the Church today. God's people are blessed to be a blessing, given light to light the dark world, and when a person is ablaze with God's love, he cannot hide it. But when he tries to hide it, like the light under a bushel, it will go out!

There's a further truth inherent here. When related to him our lights will shine with an undiminishable source of fuel. He is the oil of our lamps. The more we let our lights shine, the more we will be refueled. He said, "I am the light of the world . . . you are the light of the world." The two cannot be separated. But the bold truth remains: use it or lose it!

My friend Fred Grayston has learned that. For years he tried to conserve his light. He attended worship faithfully and took in the truth he heard to edify his own life. Fred was a part of several Bible study classes and prayer groups. These helped him personally and were reflected in his private experience of the faith. He was a dutiful elder in the church and a creative leader in church work. But he had never helped a person to know Christ nor had he discovered the joy of a life poured out for people and their needs. Then he discovered two liberating secrets: that all Christians are called into ministry and that the limitless resources of the Holy Spirit were given as gifts to them for that ministry. The results have been amazing. He has become a winsome, contagious communicator of Christ to others. I feel the warmth of the Holy Spirit in him, see the glow of the inextinguishable light of Christ's truth in his life, and hear the undeniable evidence in his inclusive affirmation of people. Released from private piety, he is a reproducer of his faith in others. He has spearheaded our Youth Deputation program, guided our healing ministry, and is now engaged in an extensive Televisitation Program, enabling dozens of our people to use the telephone to extend Christ's love to hundreds of lonely or uninvolved people. The more Fred gives of what Christ has given him the more he receives.

We cannot give what we do not have. But Fred has learned an even deeper truth. We cannot keep what we refuse to give away. Think of the exciting life we could all have if we gave away however little of Christ we have. The result would be a multiplication of our joy beyond imagination.

That's the truth Jesus communicates in the next section of this powerful chapter in Mark. He now describes how the seed grows. The metaphor has shifted back to seeds and hearing again. This time he wants to impress his followers about how the seed of his Word grows within us once it is heard and received. The growth is inadvertent, not obvious to the eye, but silent and secret. He anticipates the ministry of the Holy Spirit working in us. The living seed planted in good soil will grow to full fruition. That's Christian character. The Spirit is at work in us shaping us in the image of Christ. His task is to make us like him. But we are not to become impatient and pull up the roots to see whether there is growth. Our only task is to yield more and more of our lives to his control. What he has begun he will complete. Our part is to provide fertile, cultivated soil. Once he takes up residence in us he will work pervasively, persistently.

Jesus said, "The earth produces of itself, first the blade, then the ear, then the full grain in the ear." The words "of itself" unlock the profound truth. The Greek word used is *automatē*, meaning "self" (*autos*) and "desire eagerly" (*memaa*). The seed grows automatically and eagerly from the resources within itself. So it is with life in the Spirit. He grows within us, eagerly moving out the roots of power into every facet of our lives. ". . . You do not know whence it comes or whither it goes; so it is with every one who is born of the spirit" (John 3:8). The Spirit works the same way within us as he does around us. Every relationship which is sur-rendered to him knows the same persistent growth. All of life's problems when given over to his control and left there, are given the unexpected and unexplainable influence of the Spirit's inter-ventions. Life by the Spirit is therefore freer and serendipitous. We are constantly surprised by what the Lord has been doing all along. And it is only at harvest time that we know what has been developing under God's grace and for our ultimate good.

The relinquishing commitment of our lives and our particular problems may be small and meager. But for Jesus small beginnings have a triumphant fulfillment. Our cry of, "Lord, I give up! I have tried and failed. Here's my life . . . my concerns . . . the people . . . the problems . . . the perplexities." That for Jesus is like a mustard seed. To that crucial truth he now turns in the parable of the bigness of small beginnings. A mustard seed will grow into a plant twelve feet tall. The seed from which it grows can hardly be seen with the naked eye. What Jesus wanted his disciples to know was that however small this willingness to receive was, God would enable it to grow into greatness.

But that's difficult to hear. We think bigness is best. We wait for the spectacular. But all God wants is a beginning, however small. That's about all some of us have right now. Life looms with its fears, and we wonder if we can take it. We can't. But our admission and submission are beginning enough for Christ.

The disciples hadn't done that. They had not listened, heard, or understood. They were spiritually hard-of-hearing. That's why the storm at sea at the end of the day matched the storms inside them. The whole day had been spent telling about the fact that the good seed could be planted in them and that they had been elected to be God's good soil. God was in charge, and he would bring to fruition in his own time what he had begun. But there was still a thought raging in them that made the storm at sea a source of fear.

Jesus was with them, and they were still afraid. We dare not press our incredulity too far; we're not very different. Note that they called him Teacher when they cried out, "Do you not care that we perish?" They had not *heard* either that he was more than their rabbi nor that he was more than capable of handling their fright, even though he had told them that he was Messiah and that God's full power was available to him.

The story of the disciples at sea in the storm is an incident that is itself a type of parable. Mark used it to help the early Church face the storms in which it found itself tossed about. There is much symbolism here. The boat was symbolic of the Church in early art; the sea represented the uncertain movements of evil; and the winds and storm suggested the unpredictability of life's conflicts, persecutions, and difficulties. Mark is trying to tell his readers at Rome that just as they were frightened at what was happening to them under Nero's rule, the apostles had been frightened and unable to trust that Jesus would bring them to shore safely on that stormy night.

What does all this mean to us? Has the seed of the Word of God and his kingdom taken root sufficiently in us to give us the assurance that there is no one or no thing which can separate us from his care? . . . that nothing can hurt or destroy us ultimately? If so, we can live in a world like ours confidently and unafraid.

But the question which faces us is this: Have we used the third ear of our inner heart to receive the Lordship of Jesus Christ and allowed him to conquer our fear of people, life's eventualities, and of death itself?

Now how do you feel about the fears that we enumerated at the beginning of this chapter? Can you accept that Jesus is with you on that sea? Can you hear him say, "Please, be still!"

CHAPTER 12

THE STRANGER INSIDE

Mark 5:1–20

Are you ever haunted by the memory of previous failures or mistakes? When you are quiet or alone, does your mind ever drift back to memories which hurt or cause remorse? When you meet people who remind you of previous inadequacies, do you feel bad? Can a familiar place, situation, or circumstance open the gates of memory and inundate you with what you felt were forgotten feelings?

Do you ever have feelings of self-incrimination? Do you ever feel that you should punish yourself for not having done something or for having done something you knew was uncreative or wrong?

Do you ever ruminate over what you have said or done, rehearsing why you acted the way you did? Have you ever felt absolutely brilliant twenty-four hours after a conversation or situation and wonder why you did what you did?

Do people's attitude or reaction to you ever throw you into an anxiety reaction about your capabilities or adequacy? Do the rejections of people often confirm your own feelings of doubt about yourself?

Have you ever felt like resigning from the human race, that people and groups would probably make it better without you?

Do you ever feel alienated from yourself? What I mean is, do you ever feel that you are bordered on the north, south, east, and west by yourself and you do not like what you discover? Do you find that you don't like the company when you have a visit with yourself?

Do you ever feel all wrapped up in yourself and realize that it's a pretty small package to offer others or our society?

Do you ever feel alienated from people when there seems to be no obvious reason for such a reaction?

Do you ever experience longings, desires, appetites, ambitions, conflicting loyalties, fantasies, illusions of grandeur—the desire to be someone else?

Does life seem to pull you in a multiplicity of directions so that you lose touch with yourself?

We all could answer yes to many of these questions and could respond affirmatively to them for others we love. Our answers to this personal inventory prepare us to consider the story of the healing of Legion in Mark 5:1–20.

We are likely to wonder what an account like that has to do with us. Are there such people still around? If we stretch our perception, we can probably name a few, but what does that have to say to us? Who is like Legion? Hardly anyone, we say!

But wait . . . how did he get that way? What caused that extreme condition? On a scale of one to ten in a test of how healed are our memories, how alienated we may be from ourselves and others, how frustrated we may be with life's demands, how fragmented we may feel by pressures, Legion would probably register a 10 of extremity. But could it be that there are some of us who would register 1 or 2 or possibly 5?

The reason for taking this passage seriously is that we are all troubled by Legion's symptoms to some degree. We may not be ready for the tombs of self-inflicted punishment, but we're often troubled, hoping no one knows how bad we feel at times.

Note that both ends of the alienation scale are registered in this passage. That keeps us from thinking it has little to say to us. How clever of Mark! He shows the extremity of human need in Legion and a much subtler sickness in the herdsmen and townspeople. But both groups were possessed. Neither wanted Jesus to bother them. The demons in Legion cried out to be left alone; the people begged Jesus to leave their country and trouble them no more. We all get to that state of misery where the familiarity of the feelings of unfulfillment are at least more secure than the possibility of change in ourselves or our institutions.

There's a word from the Lord in this passage for all of us. When I began my studies of this passage, I asked the Lord what we could possibly say to our contemporary society through it. His answer came after long and patient listening. "Lloyd, plumb the depths of what made Legion the kind of person he became, and you will write for multitudes of people who have the same seeds of distortion in them. Look at what the passage says about human need, and all of the little Legions will be blest.

"But be careful about being simplistic about demon possession. That's dangerous territory. If you simply say that Legion's problem was that he was possessed by demons, you will cooperate with Satan in making people feel that perhaps they too are possessed. If that is communicated, they will become vulnerable to demonic influence. Whenever people suspect that may be true, the door is wide open for Satan to sow his deeds of destruction.

"Legion got to the state he was in by a series of contradictions to his created nature. The compulsive repetition of this got him to the place where Satan could take control. Show people what prepared the way for Satan to take control of Legion. Warn them of subtle patterns which can become equally dangerous if persisted in too long without help."

With that, I turned my attention to Mark 5:1–20 with a new perspective. Using a bit of sanctified imagination, this is how I picture what happened to Legion.

There was great excitement in the otherwise sleepy, peaceful village of Gadara. The herdsmen had returned from the grazing fields near the foreboding tombs beside the Sea of Galilee with unbelievable news. They were so frightened and awestruck that they could barely talk. Their faces were alive with wonder. People came together in the village square to listen to their erratic recounting of an incomprehensible tale. Could it be true? Some scoffed, while others listened, hardly daring to believe what they heard.

Finally, the leading shepherd spoke for the others: "You all know about the demoniac . . . you have heard him rave in madness late at night. And you have all warned your children never to go near the tombs for fear that he would harm them. You have locked your homes at night for fear that he would come back to the village. We have never known that he is harmful, but we have been afraid and our fears have been aided by rumors. We who have lived here a long time have watched him as he became possessed by an unclean spirit. We saw him change from being a useful, kind person, a loving father and husband. Remember when he began to act strangely and said things we didn't understand? And you remember, too, when he finally left his family and went to the tombs to live alone. Well, listen to me . . . with our very own eyes today we saw him healed. Believe me, he's out there in the tombs and is just as normal as we are. A healer from Nazareth came ashore after the terrible storm and actually talked to the demoniac as if he were not mad! After they had talked, the healer cast the evil spirits out of him, and he became quiet and calm. But we must do something! When the healer cast the demons out of the demoniac, he made them enter a herd of our swine. If he does any more of this, we will lose our herds."

The people in the crowd joined the speaker in jeering protest. The loss of the herd of swine had enraged them. They exchanged the hateful glances and words of people who are gripped by a mob frenzy.

That is, all except one. On the edge of the crowd stood a frail, worried woman with eyes wide with wonder.

"Can it be that my husband is really healed?" For years she had hoped against hope that something would happen. She had known her dreams to be dashed again and again by each new sign of his growing depression, restlessness, self-hate and bitterness. Were they taunting her with an idle tale, or could it be true?

She turned on her heel and ran toward the tombs, whispering her hopes and dreams and forcing back the tears. The others followed close behind, ready to jeer in judgment as they had through the years.

When she reached the tombs, she saw the splendid spectacle for herself. There he was, seated quietly, fully clothed, talking to Jesus. She paused a short distance away, wondering what his response to her would be, still fearful in her heart that it could not be true.

Then he saw her and looked her full in the face in a way he had not done in years. She knew it was true. His face was calm and tranquil, and his eyes danced with a joyous happiness.

The truth came tumbling out. He told her about Jesus and the secrets of love and forgiveness he had learned. And he shared with her the marvelous story of how Jesus had freed him from the awful bonds that had crippled him emotionally and mentally for so long. Now he wanted to tell everyone about Jesus. He had asked to be one of his followers, but Jesus told him that in order to stay well and free from the evil forces which had made him ill, he should tell others about his healing and show them how they too could be well.

Together, they watched Jesus and his disciples get into their boat to cross back over the sea, and arm in arm they lingered until he was out of sight. Then they returned home to a new life of mutual love and the excitement of sharing the good news.

What Jesus Christ did for the demoniac of Gadara is what we need him to do for us. As we read the story carefully, we see a penetrating presentation of the drastic results of the same seeds of sickness that are growing in us and in our society.

This story can be easily by-passed as irrelevant to us because of the ancient language used to describe the man's sickness. Yet, Mark has given us a dramatic demonstration of what happens to a human being who is separated from God and tries to live on his own resources. To a lesser degree this man is a picture of what we can all become. The language of demons and exorcism may seem a bit bizarre and extreme, but the more closely we look at the account, the more it reads like a case history of the kind of emotional disorder we see all around us in more subtle degree. And with emotional problems and illness so prevalent in today's world, we may get some help and insight by asking what happened to this man in the first place. What was it that had wrenched this otherwise calm and creative human from his moorings and turned him into the restless, resentful recluse he had become?

And this is precisely what Jesus had wanted to know when he first met him.

"What have you to do with me? Leave me alone!" the man had cried.

Jesus didn't react to his raving rejection. With love and empathetic tenderness he asked, "What is your name?"

The question carried greater implications than a casual inquiry about a surface surname. Jesus wanted to know him as he really was and he was hoping to discover how the man felt about his illness. It was like saying, "My friend, what's the matter? I can see that you are deeply troubled. How did this happen to you?"

The man's answer revealed tremendous insight into his problem: "My name is Legion."

How often he had seen the Roman legions billeted in the great cities of the Decapolis. What the troubled man was trying to say was: "Who am I? I am many. There are driving forces within me that nobody knows and I dare not tell. They are like the countless soldiers of a Roman legion. There are numberless appetites, desires, frustrations, fears, angers, hatreds, loyalties, dreams, and aspirations in me that I cannot understand. I have no centurion to make them march in order. They go off in all directions."

Sounds familiar, doesn't it? We too are legion. We don't know who we are, for we are many. We want to be loving, but so often we are hateful and envious. We want to care, but we are careless. We yearn to think of others, but even our most magnanimous acts camouflage self-concern. We want to serve Christ, but we are ambitious for security and position, for things we can taste and touch.

When the psychologist William James lectured at the University of Edinburgh on pragmatism, a little old cleaning lady listened from a far corner. "What did he say?" she was asked by a friend later.

"Ach, the like of me canna ken what he said, but he gave a grand speech on fragmation, or something like that."

Fragmation . . . ah, a good word, that. It describes Legion's sickness. He was fragmented indeed—not whole, divided against himself.

And Jesus was his Savior. He brought salvation—"wholeness" —oneness with God and oneself and, eventually, with others. The Savior's name was Jesus for he came to save from sin, the great fragmenter.

Let me suggest what I think had happened to the Demoniac. First, look at Legion's legacy. Like all of God's people, he had been endowed with a conscience. Huckleberry Finn was right, "Conscience takes up more room than all the rest of a person's insides." That was true for Legion. Over the years all the things he had learned to be right and wrong had blended within him. Then, like every human, he went against what he knew was right—probably in some little thing at first. Then he heard the alarm signal within, and he felt guilt. But he told no one. Soon he began to dislike himself for what he had done. But because he believed that he was the only one who ever thought or did these things, he hid his acts and feelings. Then he disliked himself all the more. Soon he was deeply depressed and became obsessed by the thoughts and actions which were causing him to feel guilty. And it wasn't long before his self-hate manifested itself in hurting those he loved. He began to say and do the things he didn't want to do and say. He cried out for help, but always in ways no one could understand. He was "just confused and sick," they would say. There was no one he could talk with who would listen and understand. The syndrome became an established pattern: conscience, condemnation, and finally compulsion.

Mark fills us in on the hopeless prognosis. In a few descriptive sentences he tells us the result of this deceptive behavior: The man had an unclean spirit. This was an ancient way of saying that he was possessed with a demonic force which compelled him to do strange and evil things he did. Actually, the term "unclean spirit" was a way of describing a disturbed person much as we categorize people with our terms of psychoanalysis today. It tells us little about Legion, other than that he acted in an irrational, unacceptable way.

But Mark goes on to explain further. The man lived among the tombs. He separated himself from society. The tombs above the steep slope on the bank of the Sea of Galilee provided a grim theater not unfit for the tragedy of isolation which was staged. This was the final expression of the Demoniac's withdrawal from people. Perhaps he had lived in the dishonesty of duality all along and now it had its fatal result. Before, he did not *want* to be with people; now he could not be with them. The patterns of hiding from reality had begun long before this. He did those things which caused him guilt and which he could not confess; then he felt depressed.

The result of hiding what we are and have been always produces sickness like that. It's interesting that "alienated" was the word used in antiquity for an insane person. The alienated person is out of touch with himself, others and reality. And Legion was alienated.

As we have seen, Jesus knew the relationship between sin and sickness. He could see how hidden failures festered in human nature. When he dealt with the woman by the well in Samaria, he helped her recall all that she ever did as a first step to help her toward emotional and spiritual health.

Another look at the story reveals that the Demoniac could not be restrained. This was but the final stage of the rebelliousness which probably had plagued him all his life. Rules were to be broken, laws to be manipulated, authority to be resisted. We all have a battle with the confines of conscience. But we cannot deny the core of conscience in all of us, rebel as we may. The source of this man's guilt was that he could not be responsible for his own actions within the confines of community. He had to break out.

Think of the many ways we break out! Those of us who are impeccable in moral behavior are rebellious in so many subtle ways.

We are constantly breaking the chains of any restrictions. We want to run our own lives we say, by attitude, if not in word. This man's self-control was out of control. He wanted to run his own life and ended by running away from life. He could not be responsible for his own actions in relationships to others. A deeper bondage than ever resulted.

Then we are told of his uncontrollable restlessness. He wandered to and fro in the mountains crying out. An inner turmoil brewed within him. But again this was but the final outcome of years of restlessness which he had never learned to express creatively. He was a man in desperate search for inner peace. He hadn't found it in people or things. Nothing he could do or be would suffice. His hungers drove him until he became the unacceptable sociopath that he was, unfit for self or anyone else.

The final manifestation of this kind of pattern was that the Demoniac became self-destructive. He hated himself.

Our patterns of self-hate are manifested in little ways. We overeat, overindulge, overwork. We depreciate ourselves in word and deed. Jesus' nostrum of healing was to encourage and help the man to see himself, to accept and love himself.

Now, let's look at Legion's liberation. Once Jesus had helped him gain insight into his problem, Jesus was incisive in prayer. He didn't by-pass the need for self-understanding, but he did not stop there. Jesus helped him to pray, and he prayed for him. With a decisive prayer of exorcism, Jesus commanded the evil possession to come out of the man. To assure him that the miracle of release had occurred, Jesus commanded the evil spirits to enter a flock of swine. And they proceeded to march off the cliff right into the sea. The man need never harbor these feelings again. The swine were symbolic confirmation of Legion's release—the evil spirits were gone forever. If the swine had been raised for the feeding of people for profit, should they not be used for the assurance of the healing of a person?

Finally, let's examine Legion's love. Now he was clothed and in a right mind. The Greek word used in our text means a healthy mind, one that exercises self-control and is able to curb one's passions. Here, a wild man was transformed into a strong, integrated person capable of love. Martin Buber described a healthy person as one who steps forth as a single man and talks directly to men. That's the miracle we see at the end of this Scripture passage.

Jesus gave Legion, who could now be called Wholeness, a practical prescription for continued health. Immediately the man wanted to stay with Jesus in order to maintain the state of peace he now felt. But Jesus knew that honesty coupled with restitution would be the only way the man could stay healthy. So he sent him back to the very people with whom he had lived to tell what had happened.

I suspect that during the conversation Jesus had talked with the man about sharing honestly with the significant people in his life. No longer would he have to turn the guilty feelings of his life back in upon himself. Now he could frankly admit what he was and tell others what God had done for him. The secrecy which made him "sick of himself" no longer would upset the physical and mental balance of his life. Each day before the sun set he would balance the short accounts of life with honest confession.

In Legion's healing we see what our healing can mean. Jesus Christ has promised to meet us in our need. He comes and asks, "Who are you?"; yet he knows us as we are! He sees the Legion of compulsions, concerns, desires, and dreams. And we are free to tell him all about ourselves. We need no hiding place among the tombs. The variant forces within can come tumbling out and be banished. There is no need to live on with guilt or remorse. We can turn all of that over to Jesus, and he will give us a new name.

CHAPTER 13

DARING TO BELIEVE

Mark 5:21-43

There are eight different responses to Jesus in this passage. Each one represents some one of us in our experience of the gift of faith. But before going on I want to define faith. It is God's enabled, engendered response to his love in his Son. We never possess true faith; true faith possesses us! It is that gift which is given with an authentic encounter with Jesus Christ. It originates in the soul when we see Jesus and respond to the love we feel from him. Luther said, "Faith is a living, daring confidence in God's grace. It is so sure and certain that a man could stake his life on it a thousand times."

Faith, then, as it is exposed in the New Testament, is not an effort, a striving, a restless seeking, but a response to love, the love of God in Jesus Christ. The faith, or lack of it, in the eight categories I find in this passage determined the response to the immeasurable riches of healing, help, and hope which were freely offered by the Savior.

In Jairus we find faith born out of the womb of difficulties. Here was a man of prominence, wealth, power, and social prominence. He was a ruler of the synagogue. This meant that he was the leading elder in the local fellowship of Jews. His only daughter, twelve years old, was lying at the point of death. All other resources of her healing had been exhausted.

In desperation Jairus fell at the feet of Jesus and pleaded, "Come and lay your hands on her, so that she may be made well, and live." The invitation is insistent. The Greek word used is *parakaleō*, "I beg of you, please!" And how did Jesus respond? The passage goes on to say that Jesus went with him. That is always the response to authentic, God-given faith.

This is the first example of faith. It is that which comes out of disturbing concern for the people we love. It grows through the realization that there is nothing left for us to do. All other avenues have become culs-de-sac of despair. The need coupled with Jesus' display of power equaled the gift of faith.

There are some of us right now who face life's impossible situations and needs in people we love. We do not have to produce faith to get God's attention. He has our attention and wants to give us the gift of daring faith. He places in our expectant hearts the hope that he can do something. And we can pray boldly knowing that the hope came from him.

D. L. Moody once said, "I prayed for faith and thought that someday faith would come down and strike me like lightning. But faith did not seem to come. One day I read the tenth chapter of Romans, 'Faith cometh by hearing, and hearing by the Word of God.' I had up to this time closed my Bible and prayed for faith. I now opened my Bible and began to study, and faith has been growing ever since."

So it was with Jairus. His relationship with Jesus produced confident faith; it was not faith that produced the relationship. Later Jesus gave him the secret, "Do not fear, only believe!"

At our church we have what we call Prayer and Healing Services. After we've prayed and meditated on God's Word, the opportunity is given to the people to come to the chancel for the laying on of hands for specific needs. The fact that healing begins with a relationship with the Savior and this permeates out into the physical, emotional, spiritual, and interpersonal needs of people is always stressed. We also emphasize the power of intercession for other people. I am continually amazed to witness the interrelationship between our lifting up the Savior with his forgiveness and love focused in the Cross and the expectancy of the people who come forward. But, really, this should not surprise us, for he said, "When I am lifted up . . . I will draw all men to myself" (John 12:32). What he promised about his resurrection happens each time we uplift him in teaching and preaching, coupled by the honest sharing of what he has done in our lives. When the gospel of his winsome love and dynamic power is made clear, the gift of faith is given to people to dare to believe. Astounding miracles have happened in the lives of people as a result of the intercessory prayer of others.

One night a young couple were in our congregation who were scheduled to meet with a lawyer the next day for the final plans of divorce proceedings. They had been brought to the service by one of our members. After the power of Christ was proclaimed and witnessed to by others, the gift of faith was explained. By faith, the people were told, they could grasp the forgiveness and new beginnings offered by Christ. When the elders took their places in the chancel in keeping with James 5:14, "Is any among you sick? . . . call for the elders of the church," the man who had brought the couple was given the gift of faith to believe that Christ could heal their sick marriage. He went forward for prayers of intercession for them. When he returned to his pew, the husband and wife asked, "What did you pray for?" "You two!" he answered. "I prayed that you might give Christ a chance with your individual lives and that you might seek help for your marriage." They were stunned. Then the husband felt an undeniable urge to go forward. When he could not subdue it any longer, he moved forward and knelt before one of the elders in the chancel. This elder helped the man to ask for the gift of faith to believe that a change in his marriage could take place. This enabled the young husband to commit his own life and the future of his marriage to Christ.

When he returned to the pew, his wife asked, "What did you pray for?" The man was obviously moved. With tears he said, "You! I simply thanked Christ for you and, whatever happens, to take care of you." It wasn't long before she was on her way to the chancel!

But the amazing thing was that at the end of the service, just before we closed the time of prayer and the laying on of hands, they both had returned to the chancel. The sight of the two of them kneeling together was moving.

The next day they went not to the lawyer but to a marriage counselor. The marriage was saved and now is being deepened by consistent, remedial help.

It was the gospel of hope that attracted them in the service, but it was the gift of faith which impelled a response to claim what was offered.

The next category of faith in Mark's account is exemplified by the woman who touched Jesus in the crowd. In her we see the kind of faith which arises out of personal need within ourselves.

The crowds pressed in upon Jesus as he went with Jairus to meet his daughter's need. Imagine thousands of people, a river of humanity, the currents moving swiftly, irreversibly. And in that crowd was a woman who had suffered from a hemorrhage of blood for twelve years. She had tried physicians; none had helped her. Luke, a physician himself, simply said, "The woman could not be healed by anyone."

She had tried all the known prescriptions for her illness—eleven were listed in the Talmud: ashes of an ostrich egg in a linen rag in summer and a cotton rag in winter, barley corn from the dung of a white she ass, tonics, astringents, etc. But nothing worked. In the meantime she had been suspect, could not live in her own house, was ostracized from society. The words of Leviticus 12:19–25 help us understand that her sickness made her ceremonially unclean. She was treated like a leper. Her clothing, anything she touched, her home, bed and belongings were unclean. This was why she was able to get through the crowd so readily—people would draw back whenever she came close.

Mark tells us that the woman had heard reports about Jesus. In the Greek there is a definite article before the name of Jesus. The English name Jesus is a transliteration of the Hebrew name of Jehoshua, very common in Palestine then. The definite article implies "the Jesus." There is the motivating power for her faith; she had heard about *the* Jesus. Could he do for her what he had done for others?

As she moved through the crowd, she said to herself repeatedly, "If I touch even his garments, I shall be made well."

Her faith is imperfect, to be sure. She seems to think that the power of Jesus is magical or mechanical, that there is no need for him to know who or what she is.

Then it happened! As she touched him, she suddenly felt in her body a deep physical sensation which gave her health and hope. And Jesus stopped with a question which exposed his sensitivity and individualized caring. "Who touched me?"

An impersonal touch brought personal attention. The incarnate reservoir of divine resources felt that power had gone from him. He knew that his power had become personally applicable to someone in need. Who was it?

The Greek word used to express that the woman knew she was healed is *ginōsko*, to know by experience. She knew that her scourge which had brought her calamity and punishment was gone. But Jesus also knew that something had happened. Here *ginōsko* has a prefixed preposition, *epi*, giving the force of intense knowledge. He was intensely aware that he had been a channel of God's healing. That's the reason he looked about with avid interest for who it was. He knew that the gift of faith could not be used for a magic deliverance without knowledge of him as the healer. No surface solution would suffice. Superstition and magic would not do. Whoever it was could not have his power without knowing him personally. He was always concerned that people know the dynamics of deliverance and the continued cure for lasting health in the soul as well as the body. Whenever he healed, he made it clear that faith had made the sick whole again. This faith alone could keep a person from a worse fate.

Finally, with fear and trembling, the woman came forward to identify herself. She was self-conscious at being the center of attention. What would the Lord's attitude be to one who sought to draw upon his miraculous power without his knowledge? Would he reverse the blessing? She felt like a criminal confessing a crime. Though she was healed, her image of herself, impressed by years of rejection, was of one still unclean and therefore unworthy of the undeniable healing she felt within herself. She fell trembling at his feet and, as Mark says, she told Jesus "the whole truth."

What a phrase! The whole truth. Faith's response to Jesus does that for all of us. The whole truth of her sickness, rejection, loneliness, and despair. Personal liberation comes from that!

Jesus' eye caught the woman's. Now a deeper kind of healing was in progress. Love, forgiveness, and hope flowed from his eyes into her soul.

Then, in effect, he said, "Go into peace." That's the meaning of the Greek: Progress into your new life of peace, which is healing, integration, oneness, wholeness. Then the secret which we most need to learn was given: "Your faith has made you well." The priest in the temple would have required something quite different: two young pigeons, one for a sin offering, the other as a burnt sacrifice. But Jesus by-passed the Levitican requirement and offered her the results of both offerings, and yet so much more.

Jesus wanted the woman to know what God had done for her

and now offered her for continuing health. But he also wanted her
to know what she had offered God. That she needed to understand
for staying well spiritually as well as physically.

Her touch was expectant. She must never lose that. Her hope
that she could be healed, implanted by the very God who had
healed her, should now be used for all of life's challenges and problems. Unfortunately, too many of us are not expectant. We are not
open to the implantation of God's dream and so we limp along on
broken legs of human impotence.

The woman's touch was also one of persistence. She kept pressing
into Jesus. Her words, "If I can only touch him!" were not discouraged by the crowd. The immensity of the crowd, the difficulty of
reaching him, the unlikely chance that he would notice or care, did
not dissuade her. She would not give up until she was healed.

But, most important of all, her touch was one of faith in Jesus.
That's where the miracle began. The actual healing was only a
result. Jesus wanted her never to forget that. She was now plugged
into a power which would unlock his potential in the future. The
same Lord, the same healing, the same joy would be available for
all things.

Complete openness resulted. Because she told him the whole
truth, the whole gospel was available to her. He could show her
what the cause of sickness had been and how to live now in health.
In similar fashion, when we tell him the whole truth and spread all
of our hidden secrets before him, he can then give us the whole
truth about himself and his power. Peace of body and soul will be
an evolving realization.

This category of faith is found in many of us who want results
without relationship in our prayers. When we shoot "quickie"
prayers out to Jesus, hoping for help but not for him, he says, "Who
touched me?" Then he looks with penetrating eyes, searching for
us who want his benefits without his personal blessings. He, himself, is the best answer to any prayer.

Jesus says, "Are you the one who wanted *something* from me? I
offer you *someone*. Myself. I have been at work in you motivating
that prayer. It was the gift of faith which gave you the daring. I
will work with you to make the answer the best possible one for
your ultimate good. Grow in peace. Your faith has made you
whole!"

The disciples' reaction to Jesus' question "Who touched me?"

provides us the third type of faith. They caught the impossibility of it all and expressed what we have thought about in more reflective moments. The truth penetrates our minds and permeates our emotions. Can it be possible that our Lord cares about one person on our tiny earth spinning in a universe which is but a small part of the great galaxies of universes?

"You see the crowds pressing around you, and yet you say, 'Who touched me?'" The disciples could not imagine that in a crowd like that with everyone touching and pushing each other that Jesus would feel the individual touch of one person in need.

Behind the disciples' question was this deeper question: How can you know about the needs of individuals in a crowd like this? Strange, isn't it? After all the disciples had witnessed and experienced of Jesus' personalized caring for them, why should this individualized awareness be so impossible and astounding?

Mark's account stands for itself. It balances off the scale. The answer to the disciples' question is not vain intellectualizing, but experience. Before we answer the theoretical question we must answer the personal one. Have we ever tried to press through the crowd? Has the Lord ever failed to respond? The answer is not always on our agenda or according to our preconceptions. But there's always an answer. As a living, hoping, asking, daring man I know he cares! That sends me back in love to the masses I used to muse about with irresponsible intellectualism.

Could it be that the disciples never had that kind of personal touch with the Master? Perhaps they didn't have the woman's immutable faith. Maybe that's what troubled them. They didn't have the courage, the audacity to reach out in faith. And they had access to him without the crowds! Jesus was right about them, "You receive not because you ask not."

The messengers from Jairus' house who arrived on the scene at that moment give us a further example of a type of inadequate faith. They represent those of us whose faith is always limited on the basis of what we can see. The possibility of an intervention of God is not part of the equation of their faith. Observable facts always equal potential reality. In this category we see the negative influence of distorted faith in others.

"Why trouble the Master any further?" they ask. "Why go on with this quest for the healer?" Note the effect on Jairus. The news of his daughter's death crushed him. Now he must carry the burden of the messengers' negativism also. He might have responded to the sad news with a new and difficult request that Jesus help her back to life. But this is snuffed out by the unbelief of his employees. Jesus had to bolster his faith in the defeated context of the limited vision of others.

Into this category march many of us. We do not have a clear vision of what Christ can do. We call it realism, but usually it is lack of faith because the data is always calculated around observable human resources. We give up too soon! We have no windows in our souls to look out to Jesus' immense possibilities. Calculatable facts are not the last word. When we take our readings from them alone we not only get bogged down, but we drag others down with us. The messengers almost did that to Jairus. But Jesus was not dissuaded.

I am fascinated by the next category of faith in this passage. Jesus had an inner circle of affirmative, faithful disciples he could trust to take with him into the despair-infected home of Jairus. He allowed no one to follow except Peter and John. Why? Because the miracles of the Lord could not be done in the presence of doubting, unbelieving observers. The ambience must be positive for God to work.

I have known this all through my own ministry. The congregation in which the gospel is preached has a great influence on what happens in peoples' lives. When there is expectancy and surprisability among the people, the power of God can work freely. Billy Graham said to me recently in the Hollywood Bowl when we celebrated the twenty-fifth anniversary of his Crusades, "I could not preach with power nor lead anyone to Christ if it were not for the positive prayers for the blessing of God by thousands of believing people." And just before he got up to preach, I said, "I'm praying for you, Billy!" His clear blue eyes flashed when he said, "I need that more than anything in all the world!"

So often when I am called into a difficult situation to pray for some sickness or need, I have seen the power of God limited by unbelieving, resistant people when it came time to pray. I never pray for the gift of God's healing or deliverance when someone who is closed to the possibility is present.

This is also true for the Church and its programs. We are an institutional anachronism in society because of the limitations we put on God. We aim at little and hit it. We attempt things we could do without the Holy Spirit and are proud that we accomplish them. We even thank God for things we did on our own strength. When we dare to pray for his vision and attempt it by his power, that's when the adventure begins.

The questions which come to me when I contemplate this category of faith are disturbing. Would I have been among the inner circle of faith-filled disciples Jesus would want with him when he attempted what others deemed impossible? How about you? Would the people who are on your church boards be included? Would the people who determine our destiny in positions of authority be there?

Some of us would be in the next example of faith: The professional mourners at the home of Jairus. Jesus *saw* the wailers, Mark tells us (5:38). The word used for "see" in Greek is *theōreō*, which means to examine with a critical, careful, practical eye. Jesus could see the level of their faith. God's people had always been swelled by the numbers of wailers and mourners in Israel's history. Moses had his fill of them in the wilderness on the way to the promised land.

The mourners at Jairus' home were professionals. They were paid to wail for the dead. It had become a tradition and custom to have them at a time of death. We, too, can become professional, by developing a habitual pattern of grief or negative reaction. After a while it comes naturally. We slip into saccharine shibboleths at a time of tragedy which require little empathy or passion; we cannot grasp the situation and enter into it with sensitivity; our trite truisms don't fit!

I was introduced one time to an official in a company who was described as "our professional 'no' man." Equally disturbing to me was a pastor friend's reference to the officers in his church whose stock reply to any suggestion was, "Great idea, but it won't work here!"

The professional mourners in this story were so intent on grief that they could not make way for grace. When Jesus said the child was not dead but sleeping, their weeping turned into frenzied laughter of embarrassed unbelief. The scornful laughter exposed the tragedy of inflexible, superior knowledge.

Jesus implied two things: death is not tragic, it's like sleep; and when God wills, even death can be reversed in resurrection. Our

Lord's prognosis of Jairus' daughter, if taken literally, meant that she was in a state of suspended animation. There are two words for sleep. *Katheudo* means natural sleep; *koimaomai* is the sleep of death. Jesus used the first of these words. The perspective makes all the difference. Jesus saw her supposed death as a sleep from which God's power would awaken her.

The little girl herself gives us a further type of faith. She is the recipient of the influence of the others' faith. Jesus took her by the hand and said, "Little child, get up." The words imply a tenderness, almost as if Jesus had used the little girl's nickname.

In the little girl we find a category of faith not often explained. She received healing at the mercy of God through the prayers of others based on the gift of faith. We are all recipients of power, insight, wisdom, safety, guidance, and love because of the prayers of others' faith. No one can live without it; no one who has come along at all has arrived without the investment of the faith of others.

I could not live, study, preach, counsel, lead people to Christ or do even life's slightest task without the prayers of others. Nor can you without the prayers of the people who care about you.

Have you ever wondered what might have happened if you had not prayed for people? Or what might be happening to you if others were not praying right now?

I am grateful for the greatest prayer warrior I know, my mother. She never gave up on praying that I would meet the Savior. Then my college buddies, Bruce Larson and Ralph Osborne, prayed me into the new life and have never stopped praying since. Since that time I have never been without a band of faithful interceders who ask for God's best for me. I would be lost without them and miserably ineffective without the power God releases in me because of their prayers.

In Jesus we find the supreme example of authentic faith. Here is faith as it was meant to be lived: never in a hurry; time for people; wide open to God's power; a flow of healing miracles; a limitless source of wisdom and vision. He meant that to be our quality of faith when he promised, "These things I have done, you shall do also!"

There it is! That's the kind of faith we are to have. The more we are with Jesus, study what he said, dare what he did, are influenced by his life, the more of his faith we will have in us. If

Jesus has promised to live his life in us, could it be that his faith can be reproduced in us?

Notice the commanding presence of the Lord throughout this whole passage. Look at him when he first assures Jairus, when he gives peace to the woman, when he confronts the doubt of the messengers. But most of all, observe him at Jairus' house. He is the Master of the situation as he banishes the wailers, selects the confident prayer circle to go to the little girl's room, and commands that she get up from her sleep. There's the picture of the kind of faith available to you and me. When people fall apart we are put together by grace; when life collapses around us we are the indwelt people of strength and hope.

Faith is God's greatest gift. Through it we are able to appropriate all that he has made available to us in Christ. The new life, power over death, the dynamics of prayer, and the capacity to love others are all unlocked through the gift of faith. The Lord is available to motivate and mediate this gift to us. The result will be confidence and trust; new possibilities, not just problems; hope and help for the hurts of life.

CHAPTER 14

"THE SACRAMENT FOR FAILURE"

Mark 6:1–13

There's a great difference between taping and doing a live television program. The great advantage to taping is that you can do a retake, or, through the clever skill of an editor, mistakes and goofs can be edited out. Retakes, though costly, give the performer a chance to more closely approach perfection, while live television takes raw courage and at times the acceptance of less than the best.

But in life there are no retakes and there are far too many reruns on our inadequate performance. Wouldn't it be great if life were more like a taping in which we could rehearse and do things over, deleting our bumbling failures?

We all have one thing in common! We have all known failure. We feel the anguish that comes with the realization of some ineptness, inadequacy or ineffectiveness. If a retake was only possible on whatever we did or said or wished that we hadn't! We can ruminate and recount the events with 20/20 hindsight of what we would do if we had another chance. Others feel something more than that: we have had second chances but have repeated the same mistakes. For some of us our failures are like pockmarks on our psyches. We can't forget, try as we will. This is one subject about which we are all experts.

Our failures are focused in different ways. We have high expectations of ourselves. It's difficult to accept when we miss the mark of those expectations so badly. We all want to be effective people and yet must end most days with ineffectiveness staring us in the face. Our performance in life's opportunities is so far from what we want it to be. But it's in our relationships that most of us feel life's most excruciating failures. Ever wake up in the middle of the night and rehearse what you said or did with a person? I find I am very insightful at four in the morning about what I should have done. I suspect that everyone who reads this has someone, perhaps a list of people, whom he feels he has failed. Parents, friends, a spouse, our children, people who work for us or for whom we work. We've all done some regrettable things to people. Sometimes we are incarcerated with the memory when it seems too late to say we're sorry, or the failure is irreparable, or restitution is no longer possible. Our prayer is a pitiful plea, "O God, will I never be able to forget?"

Most of all, we know failure when it comes to our faith. Not just the little sins, but the sin of the failure to live life as God intended it to be, to use our amazing potential, to utilize his gifts and power.

Some years ago I met a young man who had received a large inheritance from his grandfather which he refused to use. But the will had some very particular instructions. He had to use 90 percent of the inheritance for human need. The remaining 10 percent he could use for himself in any way he wished. Yet out of rebellion and a false sense of independence, the man would not use his inheritance for either himself or other people.

How like our failure to take what is ours from God! Paul apparently found the same reluctance in the Corinthians when he challenged, "Do you not know that you are God's temple and that his Spirit dwells in you?" We do not take what is ours because we don't know what we have been given and we will not accept it when it's made clear to us.

But there's no failure which eats at us more than the failure to communicate to others what we have been given. Why is it that it's so difficult for us to share the joy and delight of being in Christ? We hold the secret of death and life. People can live forever if we introduce them to Christ. They can experience abundant living in him now if we will only communicate what we have. Yet many of us refuse because we are either too busy or we hope desperately someone will do it for us. But what about our failure when we do try? We all know what it's like to have love refused and our hope in Christ rejected or ridiculed. Who hasn't felt that if he had more skill or knowledge, he might be able to break the resistance barrier and unstop the deaf ears? Yes, that's the most anguishing failure. But what can we do about our failures?

It's comforting and reassuring to know we're in good company at this point—Jesus failed. In this sixth chapter of Mark we have a tabulation of one of his deepest failures. When he came home to Nazareth he wanted his loved ones, neighbors, and friends to experience what others elsewhere were discovering. The same power to heal, forgive, and restore hope which had been displayed so spectacularly in other places is what he longed to give his own family and townspeople. Yet, Jesus failed. I am thankful that it happened! Because out of his failure, he gave his disciples and us a sacrament for failure.

A sacrament is an outward sign of a deep, inward experience. In baptism we have the Sacrament of the Covenant. The visible sign of the forgiveness, cleansing, regeneration, and new life in a person who has experienced Christ. A believer's baptism is affirmation outwardly of what Christ has done inwardly.

The same is true of Holy Communion. The bread is an outward sign of Christ's broken body, the wine is the sign of his blood shed for our forgiveness. When we take the elements we accept what Christ did for us on Calvary.

In this passage from Mark, Christ gives us a third sacrament. A sacrament for failure—an outward action to expose an inward condition. Jesus said, "And if any place will not receive you and they refuse to hear you, when you leave, shake off the dust that is on your feet for a testimony against them." What that means is that we are to shake the dust off our feet as a sacramental sign that in our hearts we have accepted forgiveness for failure.

Some background will be helpful here. The rabbinic law provided that when a Jew returned from visiting a Gentile nation, he was required to shake all the pagan, non-Hebrew dust off his feet. This was done as a testimony against the nonbeliever. Jesus used this practice as a basis of interpreting his own failure and in order to give the disciples a therapeutic way of handling their failures then and in the future. He knew that learning to fail successfully was an important part of discipleship.

It was said of Napoleon that he had a great facility for victory but no strategy for failure. That's the reason he diminished so miserably. Charles Kettering once said, "It's not a disgrace to fail. Failing is one of the greatest arts in the world." Jesus alone can teach us the art of failure.

The text and context of this passage blend together. Jesus' own experience in Nazareth and what that meant to him is the context. His own teaching out of that experience given to the disciples becomes our text.

Recently, I heard music played on a quadraphonic set of four speakers, and that reminded me that we need to hear the good news of what Jesus said about failure in a fourfold blend: what it meant to the disciples, what Mark wanted it to mean to the Roman Christians, what it means to us personally, and what it can mean through us to people in our lives who have failed.

Mark tells us that when Jesus arrived in his hometown, he was invited to speak in the synagogue where he read the messianic passages of the prophets. And he clearly identified himself as the long-expected and hoped-for Messiah. But the people could not accept that. After all, he was one of them! Their own lack of self-esteem precluded the possibility of accepting the idea that this carpenter from their own town could be the Messiah. It always works that way. Lack of self-esteem flows over into negation of others. Affirmation is niggardly given when our own image is negative. More than that, Jesus had been a tradesman among them. They could not imagine that one who had repaired their oxen yokes or fixed their broken things was God's appointed Messiah to heal their broken hearts. Could any good come out of Nazareth?

Rejection in his hometown marked a dramatic transition in Jesus' ministry. He now went out among the people, not just in the synagogue or among the Jews, but wherever people heard him gladly. The closed door of Nazareth made him turn to God's open door and preach the good news of the Kingdom to people everywhere. Hillsides, the seashore, a fishing boat now became his pulpit.

The failure at Nazareth also signaled the beginning of the disciples' missionary journeys. He sent them out two by two to multiply his ministry. He gave them his authority to do what he had done. But he gave them something more. With his own failure ringing in his heart, he gave them the way to face failure. Nazareth had slammed the door. So would the leaders of Israel. It is an ominous sign that the crossbar of an execution cross could also be used as a gigantic doorjamb.

There are few of Jesus' teachings which are more helpful to us. Once we discover how to handle our failures we will become gracious communicators to people everywhere who need freedom to fail and to learn how to use their failures creatively. To do that we need to know what this pronouncement about failure doesn't mean before we can discover what it does mean.

First of all it does not mean it's okay to quit when the going gets rough. Nor does it mean that we can cut off people who have cut us off. We have no business saying, in a paranoid snit, "If you don't like me, go your own way!" If people don't happen to like us, there may be some cause in us as well as our message. And we don't have the right to close the door of a second chance on people simply because they have closed the door on us.

What it does mean is that we are to go on in spite of failure. When we meet disappointment we are not to be completely stopped. We are to close that chapter and go on to God's new chapter. Henrietta Mears, that great Christian leader and educator, used to say, "Failure is not sin. Faithlessness is."

There are four things that flow out of the rich resources of Jesus' teaching in this passage from Mark.

First, don't develop a failure fixation. The self-imposed image of ourselves as failures becomes the inadvertent compulsion. When we ruminate over our failures, they become the focus of our future. In time we may get to the place where it feels better to fail than to succeed. We keep repeating the same patterns which force us to fail. I know a woman who has failed at four marriages. She is compulsively drawn to losers whom she feels impelled to redeem. And now she is thinking about a fifth. She is madly in love and can't see that the new candidate for her reformation is the same as the previous four.

That may seem a bit bizarre and extreme. But there are many people who are too proper ever to consider divorce and yet they develop patterns in marriage which become a syndrome. They cannot break free of the imprisonment of that negative, repetitive attitude or action to try what God might want for them because that old, bickering, hostile, self-negating habit has become the psycho-cybernetic cycle of their life. It results in a terrible failure bind: it feels good to feel bad. The same thing is true of students. Once failure becomes a repeated pattern, success is feared more than failure. We become the composite of our memories of inadequacy rather than the hope of what God can do.

But failure can be the source of new dependence on God for the future. It can bring us to the end of ourselves and to a desperate surrender of the mess we have made. Remember, there is a tragic arrogance in us that makes us feel we must atone for our own failures. That's one thing we cannot do. But trying sets the pattern more deeply than before.

Harry Overstreet once said, "We make our mistakes; and unless we are allowed to use our share of them without being driven into self-distrust, we lose the power to venture." That's it! Note that Overstreet advises us to use our mistakes, not have them use us. They can become the raw material of discovering how to grow. Any inventor or creative artist must learn this. And so must the adventurer in the new life in Christ.

Jesus seemed to be saying to the disciples: Go on! Don't indulge in self-incrimination, remorse; go on to the next opportunity more dependent on God than ever before. Paul learned this. He shared his discovery through what the Lord said to him. "My grace is enough for you; for where there is weakness, my power is shown the more completely" (2 Cor. 12:9, Phillips). That's why he could say to the Philippians, "Forgetting what lies behind and straining forward to what lies ahead, I press on toward the goal for the prize of the upward call of God in Christ Jesus" (Phil. 3:13–14). But Paul could do that because he replaced the failure syndrome with the confession, forgiveness, new beginning cycle. His emphasis on sharing the dynamics of Christ's death and resurrection daily meant he could surrender his failures and be resurrected to new freedom to accept the next opportunity. And the Spirit was with him. "The Spirit helps us in our weakness; for we do not know how to pray as we ought, but the Spirit himself intercedes for us with sighs too deep for words" (Rom. 8:26). The Spirit is with us to help us learn from our failures and grow as people through them. Then the Spirit prays in us what we don't know how to pray for ourselves. When we are down, he lifts us up to dare to contemplate and accept the next challenge which God will resurrect out of the burnt-out ashes of our failures. The author of Hebrews gives us the same formula: admit what we have done and are, and then get on with the business of living— keeping our eyes not on a problematic past but on a Christ-oriented future. "We are all poor sinners, thwarted and stumbling in our course again and again, but at least let us keep running the race with patience, looking to Jesus!"

Instead of focusing on failure and making that the goal of our life, we look to Jesus, the author of the future. It's out of failure, when we are broken in our own aggressive assertiveness that the Lord's power is shown to us in a way we would never be able to observe in life's smooth and easy times. Christ can break the fixation of failure!

I remember a time when I sat with friends in a hospital waiting room while their small son was having heart surgery. We had been there about an hour when we heard the surgeon's name called on the intercom. The father's face turned white. The surgery was to last five hours. Something must have happened. We rushed to the nurse on the floor. She told us the little boy was dead. Later the surgeon came to explain. He was compassionate and tender; the strain of failure was on his face. Afterward, I walked with him and talked about how he handled failure. As a Christian, his answer was profound. "I did my best. We all did. But we failed. Now the problem is that I will have dozens of operations like that one this month. If I think only about this one failure, I will soon become incapacitated as a surgeon. What would be worse than that immobilization? I must keep on working, learning, perfecting my skills. And God is at work with us. I must go on with him or the demons of despair would soon destroy me."

Tennyson put it clearly, making the same point,

> I hold it true, in him who sings,
> To one clear harp in diverse tones,
> That man may rise on stepping stones
> Of their dead selves to higher things.
>
> . . . .
>
> I hold it true, whatever befall
> I find it when I sorrow most;
> 'Tis better to have loved and lost
> Than never to have loved at all.[1]

The past, with its dead selves of default, discouragement, and defeat, need not be an impenetrable road block, but stepping stones to higher things. Don't indulge your remorse; it will make you sick. Don't ruminate over failures; they will become the goal of your life. Allow the failure to bring you to the Lord. That will enable you to shake the dust off your feet and go on!

[1] Alfred Lord Tennyson, *In Memoriam*.

The second thing we can learn from Jesus' strategy for failure is: don't play God. He created us in his own image; we return the compliment. We insist on trying to run our own and others' lives, and we view failure as anything which has not gone our way. To be able to shake the dust off our feet and go on means that we must trust God and his gracious remedial love. Many of us stay on in a situation or with a person where we have failed like a bull dog with a rag in his mouth. If we don't do it, it won't be done; if we don't say what needs to be said, it won't be said. So we stay on indefatigably trying to justify our failure when our Lord already is on to the next phase. He says, "Shake the dust off! Leave the past to me!" The disciples had a difficult time with that. They insisted on doing what they wanted to do. So do I. I want to make amends, straighten things out, atone, backfill. I insist on battering down closed doors while the Lord stands in an open door beckoning me on. "Lloyd, I'm over here!" the Lord says. But I reply insistently, "Just a moment, Lord, I'm not finished! Not yet!" And I blast away. Again he says, "Lloyd, I'm finished for now with your part in that situation; you come with me. Behold, I am the door!"

Do you ever have that problem with people, situations, unsolved problems? Don't play God. That is what I need to remember; I imagine you do also.

Many of our repeated failures are because of our aggressive reluctance to trust God to continue working where we have failed. He is still in control. Be sure of that!

Often, however, the circumstances are such that we are not able to walk away from a person or a place where we have failed. The same relinquishment is needed even then. We must stay where we are but without the tenacious grip of control. This is especially true of marriage. We are to surrender our mate, saying to the Lord, "My mate's future is in your hands. Help me to communicate your patience, love, and understanding. I abdicate my fastidious insistence on straightening out this person. My agenda is to affirm, not to recast." You see, what we have prayed is essentially the same—only by God's guidance we stay in the situation as his person with real freedom because we trust him. The same is true for a job, our friends, or a problematic community.

That leads us to the third insight I receive from this passage. Allow the fear of ultimate failure to free you from the fear of failure. Does that sound redundant or ambiguous? It's not. If the purpose of life truly is to know our Lord, be shaped in the image of Christ, to grow in him and with the power of death defeated so that we might live forever with him, then the only real failure in life is to miss that. All others are adjustments to circumstances. By comparison to our ultimate purpose, our little failures are put into perspective. We can see them for what they are. The disturbing fact is that millions of people who seem to know little of daily failure are failing in the real reason for which they were born. Equally startling is the fact that many of us are upset with daily failures and focus on them because we have not been liberated by the expulsive power of the fear of the failure which could determine where we spend our eternity. But if that anxiety is dealt with by Christ, all other little failures can be exhorted and exorcised. We can face the truth about ourselves and learn from it because we cannot do anything which will make God stop loving us! The monster of fear of failure is gone. We do not have to live with the frustration Edwin Arlington Robinson described in his poem "Nicodemus,"

> "What has truth done to us
>   That we must always be afraid of it,
> As a monster with a shape unknown." [2]

Shake the dust off your feet. The future is a friend, not a monster!

The final thing I see in this passage is crucial to the people around us. Believe in what God has done with our failures and we will be able to accept the failures of others and help them with them. When we shake the dust off our feet, we have realized God's forgiveness. We are now possessed with a power that the world needs most. There is a winsome freedom in a person whose feet are dust-free. This is not arrogant self-assurance. It is Christ-confidence. That's what the people around us need more than food or financial security. The world is longing to find some way to handle failure, and we have it. It's happened to us!

There is a tenderness, an inclusive acceptance of others from a person who has faced failure and found Christ's forgiveness and freedom in a life of second chances. There is a receptiveness about

---

[2] Edward Arlington Robinson, *Collected Poems* (New York: Macmillan, 1937), p. 1186.

people who have been through it. The "I understand!" is written on their faces. That's what Christ in a person looks like. Failure has softened judgmentalism and severe criticalness. The result is that we are ready to help those who are failing around us. We can share how light the feet are to run into the future when the burdensome memory of past failure is shaken off. Because our failures have led us to Christ, we can use what he is teaching another person to be the doorway to the new life. People are more than ready to receive Christ's forgiveness and new beginning. But they think they are the only people in the world who ever failed like they have. If we perpetuate the lie by refusing to be vulnerable about the failures which shaped our character, we will have shut them up in their incarceration of self-incrimination—perhaps forever!

I have a friend who is a very effective witness. There are dozens of people in Christ and in our church because of him. I asked him to tell me his secret. "No secret at all. I just tell people about what Christ did and is doing right now with my failures. There is always communication. That's the one thing everyone knows about. There is immediate identification. Then I share what the Savior can do!"

Look at your feet! Any dust on them? The dust of past failures, the incomplete, the inept, the insecure? Shake it off! Let's get on with the forgiven life!

CHAPTER 15

PEOPLE PRESSURE

Mark 6:14–29

Perhaps it was because the subject was on my mind that I heard the comments with particular sensitivity. I often hear the same complaint, but this week it was unusually persistent.

A woman said, "I'm under tremendous pressure from my son these days. I can't seem to satisfy him, however hard I work. He really puts me under pressure."

A young man said, "My parents have fantastic goals for me to take over the family business. It's not what I want to do, but their pressure is unbearable."

A college woman said, "I'm being pressured by my boyfriend to live with him before we are married. You know . . . sort of try it out . . . to see if we are right for each other."

A husband said, "My wife is never satisfied. Whatever I do, however much I make, it's never enough. Life with her is like living in a pressure cooker with the lid fastened down and the heat on high!"

A secretary said, pointing to her phone, "That little black thing is driving me silly! At the other end of the line are people who make impossible demands and think they are the only people alive!"

A middle-aged wife said, "My husband thinks my faith is silly. When I feel his resistance to Christ I wonder if I'm wrong and confused. As a result, I've developed two lives, one with him and one when I'm with my Christian friends."

An elderly woman said, "My sister thinks she has all the answers about the faith and tries to convince me of her point of view. I feel pressure to become her brand of Christian. But I keep thinking, 'If it means being like her, I don't want it at all!' When she calls, I just hook the phone on my shoulder and let her rant on while I do other things. A half-hour later, she's still on the line blasting away, but I still feel pressure."

A young pastor at a clergy conference said, "I hardly know who I am any more. There are so many points of view in my congregation; I can't please them all. Everyone wants to capture me for his camp and get me to shape the church around his convictions. The pressure makes me want to leave the ministry!"

All of these folk are suffering from people pressure. Most of us can deal with the pressures of schedules, responsibilities, and needs which place a demand on us. But people . . . we all know their pressures! They expose any area of ambivalence or uncertainty within us. By them, we are pushed into doing and saying things we are not sure we want to do or say. And we end up disliking ourselves for being so malleable in the strong molding binds of pressurized people.

I remember visiting the office of a man who is in charge of efficiency and productiveness for a large corporation. It is his responsibility to reorganize the company, increase production, clear the deadwood out of the staff and boost sales. When he was hired, he demanded and received absolute authority from the board of directors of the company. With this power, he has become famous for getting things done, but his methods are highly questionable. His nod of approval can make a man succeed, and his thumbs down signal can diminish an aspiring career.

On the wall of his office is an artist's black line drawing of him. It isn't an especially complimentary caricature, but apparently it expresses his feelings about himself. The drawing pictures a grim character with a hard-set jaw and protruding determined eyes peering out beneath furrowed John L. Lewis type eyebrows. Underneath the picture is the caption, "I don't live under pressure, I create it!"

We all know people like that. And we all know pressure from people. Perhaps we are among those who create it.

People pressure is the exertion of force from an individual to do, perform, react, develop, or achieve according to their demands, images, and values. Through the use of personality strength, persistence, and willful influence a person tries to mold the direction of our thinking and response, if not our personalities and beliefs.

There are many methods that are used: words, approval, withdrawal of affiliation, the shout or the pout. The result is frustration and the denial of our selfhood and freedom. We want to please, gain approval, and be popular. But often the price is high.

Herod Antipas lived under pressure from people. The Scripture we read from Mark is a sad analysis of the web of human pressure in which we can all become entwined. Our text is pathetic: "The king was exceedingly sorry; but because of his oaths and his guests he did not want to break his word." Poor Herod. He was not able to resist pressures from people and do what he knew was right. The circumstances of the scriptural situation may seem a bit unreal for application to our life, but the underlying problems of pressure are the same for you and me, and about as indefatigable. Our exposition is focused on that pressing problem.

Mark's vivid account of Herod's helplessness under people pressure is actually a parenthesis in his sweeping chronology of Jesus' ministry and the mission of the disciples through the villages of Galilee. Herod's conscience was stirred by word of what Jesus was doing. "It is John the Baptist whom I beheaded, risen from the dead," whispered the despot when he heard of Christ. He was stung by the sharp sting of remembered sin. Exposed was the puppet prince of Galilee with all his deceptions and disguise torn from him, a frightened man in anguish with a tormented memory.

A bit of background here will be helpful. There are several references in the New Testament to the various Herods. We need to sort out the one referred to in this passage.

When Jesus was born, Herod the Great was king. He was the frightened king who was visited by the Wise Men from the East. It was this Herod who was responsible for the massacre of the children in Bethlehem in his fanatical effort to destroy the child who could threaten his rule.

Herod had married many times. But three of his marriages have significance here. Herod Antipas, the Herod of this passage in Mark, was born to Herod the Great and Malthake. By another wife, Mariamne, he had Herod Philip. In marriage with still another Mariamne, a Hasmonean, he fathered Aristobulus. Thus far in our study of this twisted family tree we see that Herod Antipas and Herod Philip and Aristobulus were half brothers. Herod Antipas married the fiery daughter of the king of the Nabataeans and Herod Philip married Herodias, the daughter of Aristobulus, thus actually she was his niece. Philip and Herodias had a daughter whose name was Salome.

Now the plot thickens. Tennessee Williams could not have written a more sordid plot. Seldom in history has there been such a series of matrimonial entanglements and incestuous involvements. It was sometime before A.D. 23 that Herod Antipas went to Rome for a visit and met his brother Philip's wife Herodias. She was a willful woman who knew what she wanted and usually got it. Antipas was her ticket to power and influence. He bought into a cheap, stolen relationship for which he would later have to pay with the high price of his own soul.

Together the two set off for Palestine. It is said that there is no wrath like a rejected woman's spite. Not so! There is a greater wrath. It is the indignation of the rejected woman's father. And Antipas' rightful wife's father was waiting for him when he returned to Palestine. News of Antipas' marriage to Herodias had gone before him. The queen's father was king of the Nabataeans, an Arab tribe whose capitol was Petra. He raised an army from the desert and marched upon Palestine. This is the reason Antipas had gathered his forces at Machaerus, situated on the barren heights of Moab above the Dead Sea. This was the stage of the drama which is played out in our Scripture.

But not all of Antipas' difficulties came from his former wife's kinsmen. The Jews were greatly enraged by the marriage to Herodias, his brother's wife and his own niece. He had broken the Jewish law and had raised the indignation of the people.

It is in this context that the last act of the drama of the life of John the Baptist was played out. John was under pressure from nothing except the moral demands of the ancient covenant. The king was as unrighteous as the people to whom John prophesied. John was afraid of nothing and no one. In the tradition of the prophets of old, he declared the truth as he saw it. He exposed evil wherever he found it, and he didn't need to look beneath the surface to find it in Herod Antipas' court.

John's ministry attracted and interested Antipas. He admired his God-empowered courage. He was just enough a king to see greatness and respond to it in John. But he was not strong enough to take the personal implications of John's message. Antipas listened to him gladly, the Scripture says. There was a creative pressure on Antipas through John's message; it was the pressure to change and repent. But there was another pressure from Herodias which was greater. She had come to hate John because of the prophecy he had leveled on their marriage: "It is not lawful for you to have your brother's wife!"

In time Antipas gave in to the unrelenting pressure from his wife to have John thrown into prison. But his personal loyalty to John prompted him to have him imprisoned in his own castle at Machaerus. Antipas visited him often in the dungeon, but with each visit Herodias' anger increased. Her grudge was focused in pressure on Antipas to have John killed. We are told that the king was perplexed. He was at his wit's end to find a way to ponder John's truth and placate his wife's anger. The perplexity of pressure: he was under the pressure of the truth he heard from John, and at the same time he was pressured by Herodias' vindictive venom. Antipas couldn't execute John because of one pressure, and didn't dare to release him because of the other. He was stalemated on the razor's edge of indecision and indecisiveness. What a condition in which to find one's self!

But Herodias was not to be outwitted by a roving prophet, however righteous her husband thought he was. The time came for her to make her move. It was on the night of his birthday celebration that she intensified her pressure to inhuman proportions.

Her people props were carefully deployed. The courtiers and officers of Galilee had gathered for the sumptuous reveling of the birthday celebration. These were people Herod wanted to please and impress. At the height of the debauchery, Herodias had her daughter Salome dance the voluptuous ritual dance usually done by prostitutes—a striptease.

When Salome began her dance, the loud laughter of the drunken throng died down. All eyes were on her whirling, writhing movements. The intensity of the music quickened as she cast aside one veil after another, leading to the climax of naked sensuality.

Herod was half-maddened by the spectacle. His own lust was heightened by the response of his guests. And then, at the conclusion of the dance, Antipas made his fatal mistake when he blurted out to Salome, "Ask me for whatever you wish, and I will grant it. Whatever you ask me I will give you, even half of my kingdom."

Half his kingdom indeed! It was to cost him his soul and the whole of the Kingdom of God.

Herodias was ready in the wings to prompt her daughter with pressure.

"Mother, what shall I ask?"

The pretentious queen didn't have to think long. She quickly whispered her heart's desire: "The head of John the Baptist."

Now the king *was* under pressure! He had made a boisterous promise that he would do anything. He was trapped. Under the pressure, he gave the order. The awful act was accomplished: John was beheaded.

Now the pressure was off . . . for a time at least. He had pleased his wife and had postured power before his guests. But later there developed a different pressure, far more excruciating than any human pressure. Now the pressure of guilt and fear haunted him. When news of Jesus' ministry reached him, he was under pressure again—the pressure of God. Was this John risen from the dead? The king couldn't rest. His father had murdered all the male children of Bethlehem when Jesus was born. Now loyalty to Jesus had been born in the hearts of thousands. God had the final word; he always does!

The story we have retold from our Scripture text may seem extreme in its circumstances and bizarre in its results, but the implications are known by every one of us.

There are five groups of pressure-producing types in this account. We can find ourselves in one or perhaps several of them.

Willful Herodias was a *pressure person*. She is reincarnated in people we face in our own lives. These are the people who have never learned how to employ love-motivated influence on others to help them do what is creative and constructive. Personality power is used to get what they want. Little or no thought is ever given to the ultimate welfare of the person on whom they put pressure. Argument, persistent demands, sly conniving, relentless bombardment, and bartered affection are some of the weapons used by the pressure person. They want what they want when they want it. They will shout, flout, and use clout!

We resist being considered in this category. But think about the ways you get your will accomplished. How do you go about it? We all face the dilemma of how to impress people with our desires and get them to do what we want. Some questions in a "pressure-person inventory" will help:

1. In accomplishing your desires, do you ever withhold affection,

approval, or affirmation until a person has done what you want?

2. Do you ever use power to get a person motivated to move on your carefully outlined plan?

3. Do you ever use fear of retaliation or rejection to keep people in line?

4. Do you ever harangue a person by repetition of your desires long after a person has heard and understood your desire? That is, until you are sure your plan will be followed, do you keep nailing it to the wall tenaciously?

5. Do you really believe that the people of your life are capable of discerning what is right and doing it? Do you trust that once acquainted with the facts, they will be able to act intelligently and responsibly?

6. Do you feel a responsibility to straighten people out to get them to do what you want?

7. Can you state the truth as you see it and leave it there?

The pressure person is exposed by these questions. At center, he is an insecure, arrogant person. The pressure production is motivated by self-idolatry. It is rooted in a terrible insecurity and nurtured by unexpressed anger. It wants to rule because it has never been ruled by truth. It corners people because it believes it has a corner on the truth.

How about you? Are you living under the pressure of a person like that? Are you a pressure producer like that? The opposite of manipulation is motivation. Which have you been using lately?

What about our marriages? How do you get your mate to do what you believe is best?

What about our children? When we want what is best for our children, how do we encourage them to do it, especially when they don't agree? What do they do with their freedom after the heavy hand of our discipline or threats has exhausted their effectiveness? Think of the inner-retarded adults who are still living under the pressure of parents long dead! Have we communicated, modeled, and enforced the values and convictions which will produce inner-motivated people after our pressure is off?

What about our parents? All of the young people reading this have probably found some strategy of getting what they want from their parents. Is the pressure creative?

What about the Church? How do we move a great institution toward the goals and priorities of the Kingdom of God? How do we get a pastor to do what we want, preach the way we think he should, or perform the way cultural and historic presupposition demands? Or, on the other hand, how do we keep him off certain subjects or force him to develop the church that fits our mold? How do we domesticate a prophet? And equally frustrating, how does a pastor motivate his people? What are the potent, father-image weapons of a parish pastor who cannot trust the truth he proclaims or the people's capacity to be guided by the Spirit in their response?

One of my friends who is a vestryman in a Church of England parish once said of his bishop, "He was a high ranking officer in the Royal Navy Chaplaincy. He still thinks he's an admiral and this diocese is a ship. He always acts as if he would make us walk the plank if we don't do what he wants."

Every leader must learn how to implement his vision without threats of force, authoritarianism, or loss of livelihood. Until people share the development of a vision they can do little to support it.

The second category of pressure producers is represented by Salome: the *ploy of pressure*. There was no hatred in Salome's heart for John the Baptist. She was a lovely young woman of sixteen or seventeen when she was forced to leave her childhood home in Rome for the wild regions of Galilee. But unlike most teenage young women who are asked by their fathers what in all the world they want, she could not answer for herself. She was a ploy, a pawn on the chessboard of her mother's tragic maneuvering for power.

Whatever the facts of the case, Salome became a conduit of pressure on her stepfather, and she participated in the murder of a man of God.

Could it be that Herodias anticipated the outcome of her daughter's sensuous dance and had coached her carefully in what to do if she were asked? We have all been used as a ploy of pressure and we have used others in that kind of gamesmanship. When affection is shown to one to stir jealousy in another, when loyalty is shown to one person to pit him against another, when admiration is shown for one person to create productivity in another, when time is spent with one group to bring another into line; we use people as things to produce a desired result. Have you ever done that? Be sure of this: If you ever use another for that purpose, you will someday be used yourself.

I recall a man who was not having his needs met in his wife. To get her attention he developed a relationship with another woman. He left clear tracks so his activities could be followed. When his wife discovered them she was angry at first and then began an inventory of what she was withholding from her husband. They were reconciled at a deeper level in their marriage and the other woman was forgotten. Forgotten? Yes . . . by the man to whom she was a ploy, not a person. "There seemed to be no other way," he said "and wow, am I being loved now!" "And what is going to happen to this other woman?" I asked. He had no answer.

There are ploys of jealousy, competition, and comparison. We all use people as teaching devices to try to pressure others into being or doing what we want. The same thing is lacking as in category one: the respect of the inner motivation within people to do what is right because it's best for them.

The third category of pressure is found in Herod's friends. These are the *pressure perpetuators*. They said nothing. No one jumped to Herod's aid to make him question what he was promising and proposing to do. They just watched him stew in his own juices of arrogance. No one spoke out against the terrible act of cruelty.

Obviously, they too were under pressure and simply passed theirs on to Herod. They needed Herod as much as he needed them. How often our pressure is transferred to other people. We subtly suggest to people what they should be or do, and then hold them to it by sometimes silent but not very gentle persuasion.

The question for us here is, "How free are the people of our lives to try, perhaps fail, but always grow in their own true uniqueness?" As one man said, "My wife never says much about what I do, but she lets me know when I don't measure up. I feel her omnipresence all the time. I filter everything I say and do through the question, 'What will my wife think?' Someday I may break out and do just what I want!" The interesting thing about this man is that he in turn creates terrible pressure on his kids and the people who work for him.

Pressure perpetuators always do that. They are a wide-open pipeline for the flow of pressure on others because they themselves are under pressure. When we feel inadequate, lack self-esteem, are under pressure in our work, we pass on the sickness.

One young man commented, "Dad is going through a rough time. Sales quotas, a difficult boss, and his own sense of incompleteness are really making life unlivable at home!"

When Jesus outlined to his disciples the necessity of the Cross, Peter put him under pressure. He became a tool in Satan's hand when he tried to dissuade Jesus from what he knew he had come to do. Jesus finally had to say, in T. W. Manson's translation, "Out of my way Satan! For you are more concerned with human ambitions than with the purposes of God!" So were Herod's friends who became perpetuators of pressure. Our need for approval and acceptance, or our desire for dominance makes us vulnerable to pressure—group and personal.

But there's another category of pressure. It came from Herod himself: "Because of his oaths . . . he did not want to break his word to her."

Promises, promises! The ones we make to people and to ourselves come home to roost. They create pressure on us. In this category are all the things we swear we will never do as well as the things we become committed to with far too little reevaluation.

How often we create our own pressure. One person I know finally came to the conclusion that the reason he overworks is so that he will have a built-in explanation of his inadequacy. He can always say, "Well, who could have done any better with all I have to do?" The promises he made himself were always unrealistic, but he seldom could admit it. We should always keep our promises open to renegotiation with others as well as with ourselves. If we don't, we will constantly try to live up to the standards we have set. We will pressure ourselves to save face, or maintain our image. The motivation is not from within, but from an external picture of what we think we ought to be and do. Life becomes excruciating when we assume the task of pressuring ourselves to accomplish our idea of perfection.

Herod kept his word . . . but what a word!

All right now, what can we do with pressure? The answer is found in still another category: the *pressure purifier*—God himself. He is the only one who can be trusted with the unique person within us. He is the only one who knows and wills our ultimate good. Often people, ourselves included, can neither exert creative pressure nor use it for redemptive purposes. There are two worlds for all of us, the world from within and the world without. And of the two, the first is always the harder to conquer. Only God can do that!

He provides the equalizing pressure of purifying love. Day by day, as we respond to his gentle, persuasive pressure to renew, reform, redirect, we grow in courage. We become inner-motivated people. We know who we are in the light of who God has destined us to be. Herod's demise began when he closed out the voice of God and listened to others. The overtures of love were resisted because it meant a change of his life, relationships, and values. No wonder Herod was under pressure. But he gave in to the wrong pressure! There are those times when God speaks, when the issues are sharp and clear. Then there are other times when we must persist in our prayers while God gets us ready for the answer he has made ready. He's reliable; trust him! The habitual prayer, "Lord what do you want?" is the source of creative pressure. Each impulse is a part of his holding direction.

> Have thine own way Lord,
> Have thine own way,
> Thou art the potter, I am the clay.

Our story closes with the excruciating words, "The king was exceedingly sorry." For whom? John? He should have been sorry for himself. He had said "No!" to God and "Yes!" to people pressure.

If you are tired of being sorry . . . of looking back over life's broken promises, easy compromises, and leagues with evil, then try a different kind of pressure . . . the pressure of love. It will give courage to resist human pressure and receive God's pressure.

CHAPTER 16

BEING OPEN TO THE IMPOSSIBLE

Mark 6:30–56

"Come on, let's be realistic! I believe that God can do wonderful things, but this is impossible!" a man said to me the other day. Ever hear that said? Ever say it yourself? Many of us have received answers to prayers which boosted our faith. But most of us have areas of life that we write off as too big for God or not within the realm of what he can or will intercede to help or heal. We build a neat, ordered list of things we can talk to God about, and the rest we take with what we call faithful endurance. We decide what is proper to pray for and what is impossible. As our faith slacks, our impossibility list gets longer.

I have a friend who carries what he calls his "write-off book." In it he lists the things he can write off on his income tax forms. It occurs to me that many of us have "write-off books" of a very different kind. To write off a person, situation or problem is to decide what's impossible—what can never be made to happen. A woman said, "I know it's not Christian, but I have written that group off—it's impossible!" And a student said, "My parents are impossible! They will not see things as they are. I've stopped trying to help them. I guess I've written them off."

Check your "write-off book." Who or what has made the list?

Mark 6:30–56 is a vivid account of Jesus' efforts to liberate his disciples from the limitations of the impossible. This is another one of those Markan passages that are understood better when read backwards. When we see what happened at the end, we can realize what Jesus was trying to do at the beginning.

In the light of what happened at the end of the day referred to in the Scripture, we can understand what Jesus was trying to teach the disciples all through the day. They were frightened by the storm at sea and were unable to appropriate the secret of dependent discipleship he had tried to communicate repeatedly. The territory of their faith was limited by the boundaries of the possible, fenced in by human capacities. Throughout the day he had tried to help them invade the regions of the impossible—to push back the frontier of their own possibilities.

The first thing he tried to teach them was to "come apart" or their faith in God's power to reach beyond human possibilities would fall apart. The disciples had just returned from their missionary journey throughout Galilee. They had seen God work through them in a reproduction of what they had been witnessing in the Master. They were excited, delighted, and filled with the nervous energy of success and victory. It seemed like a time to press on with the enthusiasm of their spiritual high. Instead, Jesus told them to, "Come away by yourselves to a lonely place, and rest a while." The strength of Jesus' admonition is arresting. The Greek carries the explanation of not just, "Come away by yourselves," but "Come away for yourselves." Jesus knew that the disciples needed physical and spiritual rest at times of exhilaration as much as at times of frustration. He wanted them to experience what they had seen God do in others. He was saying, "Come away, love yourselves enough to give God a chance to do his miracles in you even as you have seen him do them in others." The desert place he recommends is the place of privacy, uninhabited by needy people. Jesus himself was always cautious to take time for rest and quiet. Now he knew that his disciples, who were overwrought and exhausted, needed to "rest in the Lord."

The reason for Jesus' insistence is related to the happenings of that whole day. There would be challenges and opportunities which would require a quality of daring openness to God's potential for human need that only personal renewal could release. They could be enablers of the impossible only if the impossible was repeatedly happening to them. As Elijah, after his defeat of the priests of Baal, was most vulnerable to depression after great success, so too, the disciples were in the dangerous position of feeling that what was happening around them and through them was dependent on their own strength.

My own most perilous times are after a triumphant Sunday in which I have seen the power of God convict, liberate and heal people. Or when I have finished a conference filled with the exuberance of seeing lives changed, I find that's when I need to be quiet and alone with God. It's then that God gets to me! In solitary prayer he gently asks, "Lloyd, you have seen me work miracles and do the impossible. That is good. But now, what about you? Your body, mind, and spirit are drained. Don't mistake your excitement for spiritual power. The things you have witnessed are my gifts. Ask yourself, 'Have I realized for myself all that I preached? Have I experienced the new life I have talked about? Have I found the peace I have communicated to others?' You cannot look back on what I have done any longer. Now we must look ahead at what I am about to do. I will be able to continue to do the impossible around you if you allow me to do it in you right now. Be still and know that I am God!"

What Jesus offered his disciples, I require every day—a period of rest each week, and an extended time in rest and study each year. The word for rest in our Scripture is translated from the Greek word *anapauō*, which means to "cause or permit one to cease from labor in order to recover and collect his strength." It is a gift we give ourselves so we have something to offer back as a gift to God. The middle voice is used here meaning, "to give one's self rest, to take rest." Often we have so little to offer God because we have accepted so little of what he has offered us in quiet communion.

There's a story of a man who had a very unusual dream of heaven. When he arrived, he saw a giant Christmas tree loaded with presents. And when he inquired of God what these were, the Lord responded, "These are all the gifts I offered you during your life which you refused to accept."

Several times in this passage, Jesus' ministry was punctuated by retreats into quietness. He knew, didn't he? He understood what the disciples, and most of us, hear with such reluctance: "Come away *for* yourselves . . . if you want to work *for* people's needs."

And those needs were never far away. Wherever Jesus and his disciples went the people followed with frenzied persistence. What a pitiful picture our Scripture passage paints! The throng ran from place to place around the seashore trying to catch a glimpse of him, listen to him, touch him! As they ran, their excitement gathered a crowd of expectant followers from each village until the crowd of five thousand were waiting for Jesus when his boat landed on a

distant shore. His response was always the same: He had compassion on them because they were like sheep without a shepherd.
This is a vivid description of humanity—of the Church, of you
and me. Never forget, his response is always one of compassion.
Out of that, he taught them the good news of the Kingdom of God.

It was late in the afternoon that the disciples' inability to venture
out into the impossible was exposed. The crowd was tired and
hungry, not unlike the disciples after their missionary venture.
They must have felt that their concern was magnanimous when
they said to Jesus, "It's late, send the people away to get food in the
villages." Was this compassion on the crowd for their exhaustion
and hunger or a desire to get away from the pressing needs of
people for a while? Whatever their motives, their calculations
were within the limitations of human potential. Little more than
the calculations of a commissary official who knew that the food
for such a crowd of five thousand would have to be provided from
many sources. The disciples were not open to the impossible!

The Master's response implies more than the words convey at
first glance. "You give them something to eat." What he seems to
be saying is, "You have seen God do the impossible through me
and at your own hands . . . what do you believe he can do now?
It's your responsibility to trust God for the answer. That's why I
wanted you to come away and rest this morning . . . so that you
would be replenished to trust God anew today! Didn't you receive
enough courage from him in your prayers to believe that he could
handle a problem like this?"

Think of how often our calculations are based on what is immediately available through human resources. Even after times of
tremendous experiences of God's power, we react with the paralysis
of human analysis of what is available through our personal potential. I believe God wants us to use all of the resources put at
our disposal, but never to stop there. I am convicted by the many
times I have said, "I don't have enough strength; the needs are too
great; there's not enough money; there's too little time; I just can't
do it!" And the Lord's response is, "Silly man, I never intended
you to do it on your own power. If I had, I would never have
called you to get into a position like this. I have allowed this situation to help you to order your life on my power, not your potential!"

We can all empathize with the disciples' response, "Look here,

Master, you know we don't have more than a few denarii between us; do you want us to go and try to buy enough bread for this crowd? It would cost at least two hundred denarii. You know that! Are you trifling with us?"

Jesus' next question was to underline the inadequacy of their human resources. "How many loaves do you have? Go and see." He knew that the people had not brought food with them. They had been too excited to plan that far ahead. Except one little boy—Andrew found him—had brought five barley loaves and two fish. I'm afraid my response would have been like Andrew's, "But what are they among so many?"

There have been many explanations of what happened at this point. There are some who say that the little boy's generosity in giving up his loaves and fishes created the miracle of influence, that when the people saw his generosity, everyone brought out his own hidden snack. Lovely sentimentality, but it hits wide of the target of Mark's account or his purpose in telling the story. Others have said that Jesus broke the five loaves, and because people were satisfied with the spiritual bread he had given them in message, they were no longer in need of physical food and were filled. An evasion again! The point here is that Jesus did a miracle. He multiplied the loaves and fishes and fed all the people. Mark is careful to drive this point home because he concluded the account by saying that the disciples gathered up twelve baskets full of broken pieces of fish and bread.

Linger for a moment over the words, "He broke the loaves and gave." The Greek verbs are in different tenses. The first implies that the act was instantaneous, and the second is imperfect, implying a continuous act. The breaking was immediate; the giving continuous. The multiplication took place in the Master's hands between the breaking and giving. My mind darts to the Cross. He was broken for us, and as the Bread of Life, he keeps on giving us what we need.

Jesus had amazed the crowds, but his desire was to astonish the disciples. He wanted them to get away from this fresh manifestation of God's providing power and allow the miracle to happen to them. That's what he's up to all the time. The miracle for which he came was the transformed life, fully dependent on God, and completely open to a surprisable awareness of what God could and would do. The breaking of the loaves and fishes and the miraculous multiplication was only a portent and promise of what should be happening to them.

It was that which was to be put to the test at the end of that day. Jesus sent the disciples back out to sea while he retreated into the mountains to pray. By the time he returned to the seashore, the disciples were in the middle of the sea and in trouble again— the winds and the waves were against them. I think he purposely let them go out to sea alone to give them an opportunity to trust the God of the impossible. When it was obvious that they were gripped by a turbulence which matched the sea against which they rowed, he came to them walking on the sea. Like a gentle parent, he hovered over them, giving them full opportunity to apply what they had been learning through him.

A single phrase tells us so much. "He meant to pass them by. . . ." That is, he was not planning to intercede; he wanted them to handle it by themselves with raw trust in God. Perhaps that's where many of us are right now as we read this. We are in that kind of an impossible situation or wrestling with a complex decision. We feel all alone while we pull on the oars. Perhaps we're even a little angry because we feel we are pulling harder on our oar than the others who are with us. But he is close by. Be sure of that!

When we are in trouble, our reaction is like the disciples'. We want help right now! But they were frightened, and who of us wouldn't have been? They thought they saw a ghost, a disembodied spirit of Jesus. And they cried out with a shriek of terror which came from the depth of their throats.

Then he spoke to them. The words have been repeated millions of times to frightened, disturbed followers through the centuries of Christian history. "Take heart, it is I; have no fear." That's what we all need to hear right now, isn't it? The word for "take heart" is *tharseō*, which means "be of good courage." His personal assurance is very strong. Literally, he was saying, "It is I and not any one else." In that context he gives the imperative command, "Stop being afraid!"

The disciples, like us, were in transition. They had witnessed the power of God all day, but now needed Jesus' personal presence and power for the crisis they were facing. The concluding statement of this paragraph tells us the reason the disciples were astonished that Jesus could come to them and deal with their fears:

". . . for they did not understand about the loaves, but their hearts were hardened." A hard heart is one that is callous, dull, incapable of grasping new truth. Here the heart is a composite of the entire inner man—reason, emotion, affections, and will. That's the reason they could not understand. Mark is telling us that they could not put the two things together in their minds. The verb used here is *suniēmi*, meaning that they could not join the breaking of the loaves and Jesus' capacity to come to them in their need. The miracle of the afternoon did not last as the basis of confidence for the dark hours on the stormy sea.

Previous vision will not match present crisis. But why? Why can't we carry the inspiration of previous encounters with the Lord into present difficulties? Perhaps it's because we have so much negative data in the computer and the response to present challenge is the failures and inadequacies of the past.

My wife and I were wrestling with a problem in our work that seemed unsolvable. Then we began to realize that we had faced similar concerns in each of our parishes. We began to go back over the many times we had felt the same mood of uncertainty. And we began to laugh as we remembered the way the Lord interceded with the right guidance, the gift of just the right staff people, a breakthrough of vision and love with leaders at the strategic moment, the response of the congregation which was so obviously the Lord's inspiration. The Lord had not by-passed us at sea. He came to us and calmed the storm inside us. We both knew it when together and from the deep recesses of our souls, we heard him say "Courage, Lloyd and Mary Jane, it is I, no one else, give me your fears!"

Just before writing this chapter I experienced the most exhausted feeling I have known in a long time. A few days before I had had to take the "red eye special," an all-night flight east, to interview two candidates for our staff. After the interviews, I caught another night flight home in order to be in the office for meetings all the next day. By Wednesday I was feeling jet lag and a bit of physical frustration. And on that particular Wednesday I was scheduled to teach a series of Bible classes at 6:30 A.M., 10:00 A.M., and at 7:00 P.M. At noon that same day I was to meet with one of our officers to review a crucial responsibility which I needed him to take. When I sat down to lunch, a wave of exhaustion hit me. I didn't know how I would make it through the soup course. Then the man stopped the conversation and said, "I just want you to know that the Lord has been talking to me about this luncheon. In my prayers the last few days I have felt as if the Lord was saying, 'Carl, be open to what Lloyd has to say to you. I want you to say yes.' "

As he said that, I felt a jab of energy flow through my body. Suddenly, I wasn't tired any more. To think that the Lord had gone before me to prepare the way! Now there were three persons at that lunch, and the Third Party said, "Take heart, it is I, none other."

Matthew has an added dimension to this same account of Jesus' coming to the disciples at sea which underlines the message the Lord seems to be teaching us (Matt. 14:28-33). Peter apparently felt more confidence than the others when they saw Jesus walking on the water. He exemplified the confidence the miracle of the afternoon should have imparted in all of them—that is—almost. He says, "Lord, if it is you, bid me come to you on the water." What boldness! Jesus' response was immediate, "Come." Peter took the brash step of faith out of the boat and walked on the water. But then he saw the wind and waves from a different perspective. He took his eyes off Jesus and focused his attention on the danger. That's always fatal! He began to sink and cried out, "Lord, save me!" Jesus immediately reached out and caught him. His words to Peter are words most of us have heard all too often, "O man of little faith, why did you doubt?" The answer to that question is the basis of this study. He doubted because he suddenly realized that he was beyond human power and only the Lord of the impossible could help him.

This all becomes very personal when we picture that boat as the realm of our resources. We are all wondering what it might be like to stop measuring the possibilities of what we can produce or perform on our own skill and energy. The first step out toward the impossible is the most treacherous. But it's after we have taken it that the peril starts. We take our eyes off the One who alone can help us, we look at reality and say to ourselves, "You fool! What are you doing out here?" That's when we sink. But even then the impossible happens again: our Lord catches us by the hand and holds us secure to safety.

A man attended our Sunday evening prayer and healing service. He had a profound need in his life. After a deep time of prayer, singing, and quiet meditation, the elders took their places across the front of the chancel to be available for the laying on of hands. The power of God to heal and make us whole, beginning with our relationship with him, then with ourselves, in our memories, throughout our emotions, and then into the very tissues of our bodies—was explained. I acknowledged that we could not have the gift of healing without the Giver, so people were encouraged to turn their lives completely over to God and accept his love and forgiveness before presenting him with the impossible situations which brought them to the service for healing. Through the gift of faith this man realized he had never surrendered his life to God's complete control. When the invitation was given to come forward for the laying on of hands by the elders, the man said that the most difficult thing he ever did was to stand up and take the first step into the aisle. As he walked down, his heart pounded and he wondered how he had ever had the courage to make this move. When he knelt and the elder gently laid a loving hand on his head, he gave his life and problem to God. He's a new, radiant man. What was an impossibility by all human standards is now a reality. But it was the first step out of the boat of his reserve that made the difference—the Lord did all the rest!

There are some first steps out of the boat I need to take today. What about you? Let's review our list of the impossible things in our lives we face right now. All reason and reality seem to say that there's little hope. The need may be in ourselves, in someone we love, or in some complexity in our work or community. In our prayers we should focus right now on whatever prompts us to say, "Well, I can believe God can do great things, but this is impossible!"

Now, this takes us back to where we began: "For your own good, come away and rest." We need to be quiet to discern how to pray boldly and with relinquishment. Don't ever pray for the impossible without deep fellowship with and guidance from the Lord of the impossible. And don't forget that the disciples went away to rest together; they needed each other and so do we. Often, after we have been alone, discerning the impossibilities on our own strength, we need fellow adventurers in the new life to remind us of God's possibilities and of what he has done with their own insufficiencies. Then together we can listen to the Lord say, "With men this is impossible, but with God all things are possible" (Matt. 19:26).

CHAPTER 17

TRADITIONAL BUT NOT TRIUMPHANT

Mark 7

When I was a pastor in Bethlehem, Pennsylvania, we introduced a lovely custom to the Advent celebration. We had a florist weave pine branches into a beautiful Advent wreath which hung in the center of the chancel. On each of the Sundays of Advent we lighted one of the four candles on the wreath. It provided wonderful symbolism and heightened the anticipation of Christmas.

I remember vividly the day the wreath was being hung for the first time. One of the members happened by the sanctuary. He watched the proceedings with growing consternation and he said angrily, "We've never done this before!" When he found me in my study, he unloaded the full blast of his criticism. "What is this pagan use of candles and pine branches you have introduced into the sanctuary of God?" I tried to explain the meaning of observing the Advent Sundays in preparation for Christmas. "It's an ancient tradition," I told him. "Advent indeed!" he said with a Scroogelike snarl. "That's just more Romanism," and he turned on his heel and stomped out.

At the opening of the service on the first Sunday of Advent, I lifted the taper and lighted the first large candle and called attention to the coming of Jesus, the light of the world. When I caught this member's eye as I finished the explanation, he seemed unmoved and unconvinced.

Each Sunday of that Advent, we repeated the symbolic practice. People responded with appreciation for this visual demonstration of truth. On the last Sunday of Advent that year the man came to me and apologized for his critical, negative attitude. He said he saw the value of the practice and hoped we would do it every year.

Just before Advent a few years later, the florist was late in the preparation of the wreath. He called me to say that he would have to hang it late in the evening. On that Saturday afternoon, the man who had been critical at first bolted into my office. Before I could explain about the last minute hanging of the wreath, he sounded off again—this time with a different criticism. "I have been watching all day for the wreath to be hung. It's a great tradition. We can't do without it! Our people are used to it. They expect an Advent wreath! The children love it. How can we have a proper Advent celebration without the lighting of the Advent candles?"

Strange isn't it? A few years had made a new custom for that church a tradition. Now it was a crucial thing to have an Advent wreath!

Remember the old radio jingle competitions? All you had to do was save a number of box tops or labels and complete a statement in a few words and send it in. You could win everything from a Little Orphan Annie watch to a vacation trip. "In thirty words or less complete the following sentence, 'I like Wonder Fluff Shampoo because . . .'" the mellow tones of the announcer would articulate.

What if you had to complete this statement: "It just wouldn't be the church without . . ." How would you complete the statement? I'm sure all of us would be able to complete that statement quickly and with conviction. For some of us it would take more than thirty words to list the absolute minimum ingredients for a great church.

We've all seen the familiar sayings, "Happiness is . . . ." The humorous and sometimes ridiculous things which are written make for attractive posters or greeting cards. What would you write if you had to complete "Christianity is . . . ." For most of us we would have to say that the Christian faith is a combination of customs which familiarity has encrusted into tradition. The danger is that we may celebrate the traditions of Christianity and miss Christ!

Now, I like traditions! Acquired practices of doing things in a particular way that the years have enshrined can be very meaningful. They can give unity to life, order to our family and friendships, and a common heritage to galvanize loyalty and spiritual dedication. I am a traditionalist when it comes to the Scripture as the Word of God; the absolute adequacy of Christ for abundant living, now and in eternity; the Church as the fellowship of the beloved; and worship as the encounter with the Living God. I am a traditionalist when it comes to patriotism and loyalty to God's dream for democracy in America. I am also a traditionalist when it comes to a sprig of heather, the bagpipes, and the lovely customs of Scotland.

Last summer when I visited New College, Edinburgh, for a few weeks of study, I was alarmed by the modernization of those old hallowed halls of theological learning. On previous visits since I was a student, it was always a sentimental journey in nostalgia among the memorabilia of tender remembrance. Now things were all rearranged. But as I walked about, I realized that the important things were unchanged. The library was modernized but still filled with magnificent treasures of learning. The classrooms were outfitted with new chairs and modern equipment of teaching, but the quality of teaching was still excellent. Last of all, the chapel was rearranged, but the open Bible and the seats of the professors and students were still in place. Lots was changed, and yet, nothing was changed that was important.

So, I believe in traditions—when they do not distract us from the essentials. But what happens when traditions become more important than the truth they were meant to convey? What if our traditions of worship and customs of the faith become more important than God?

That's exactly the issue of this passage of Scripture. Jesus and his disciples did not fulfill all of the traditions of ancient Israel and were bitterly criticized by the Pharisees and scribes. The issue in this passage was that the disciples didn't perform a ritual washing of their hands before eating. It wasn't that the disciples were dirty, but they were not observing the traditional ritual cleansing before eating. The word for "defiled" in the text is koinos, meaning that which is common to everybody. It refers to the profane as contrasted to the hallowed or sacred. Their hands were ceremonially unclean.

Some background will be helpful here. The Jew was guided by the Law. This meant first and most importantly, the Ten Commandments given to Moses. Secondly, the Law included the Pentateuch, the first five books of the Old Testament. In those, the great moral principles of the commandments were spelled out for the Jew to interpret and follow for himself. Then, added to these two sources of guidance was a third, which became the focus of Jesus' conflict with Israel's leaders. It is called the tradition of the elders.

This referred to the definition of the moral principles in their most minute and explicit detail. Around the third and fourth century before Christ a group called the scribes spelled out the specific implications for every possible application. The result was thousands of rules and regulations to keep the Jew pure and distinct from the culture in which he found himself. But, unfortunately, Israel's leaders became more committed to the scribal tradition than to the commandments themselves.

Later, these scribal rules were summarized and became the Mishnah. At Jesus' time these were not written but were a part of an oral tradition handed down from one generation to the other of the scribes. However, the written form, which is available for us to study, gives an insight into the conflict of our present passage.

It was not hygienic, but ceremonial uncleanness, which bothered the scribes about Jesus' disciples. Before every meal and between each of the courses of a full meal, a Jew was supposed to wash in a very special way. The water for washing was to be kept in large stone jars, free from any impurities. This water was to be poured over the hands with the fingers pointed upward so that the water flowed over the hands and down to the wrists. Then each hand was to be rubbed by the closed fist of the other. But, because the water on the hands was no longer pure, the hands were held together with the fingers pointing downward. Now water was again poured on the hands from the wrist down, running over the fingertips. After this the hands were no longer considered defiled or unclean. And it was through this act that the Jewish scribes believed that not only the dirt, but the uncleanness of contact with unsacred things and people was washed off. To fail to do this was not just bad etiquette but was a dishonor to God.

This ritual was coupled with dozens of regulations on the cleansing of eating utensils and dishes. A cup or a vessel could be made unclean if touched on the inside but not on the outside. It made little difference who touched the outside of a cup, but if the inside was touched, the crockery pot or cup would have to be broken. The fact that our Scripture text mentions vessels of bronze is very significant. If these were touched on the inside, they must be boiled and purged of the impurity.

Now consider this in the context of Matthew's record of Jesus' sayings about cleansing. "Woe to you, scribes and Pharisees, hypocrites! for you cleanse the outside of the cup and of the plate, but inside they are full of extortion and rapacity. You blind Pharisee! first cleanse the inside of the cup and of the plate, that the outside also may be clean" (Matt. 23:25–26). Do you catch what he is saying? Jesus deliberately accuses them of breaking their own carefully delineated rules. He makes their regulation a parable to teach the disturbing truth that they are like their vessels . . . washed on the outside, which was not required even by their own rules, but inside they were unclean, unwashed, and impure. His message was clear: Your inner self needs to be purged by fire and the boiling water of a profound cleansing.

With ardent audacity, in Mark's account, Jesus goes on to spell this out. He quotes Isaiah 29:13 to show that the inside of the vessel is the heart. This was his concern for the leaders who quibbled with him.

"This people honors me with their lips [the outside of the cup], but their hearts are far from me; in vain do they worship me [external pretension of holiness], teaching as doctrines the precepts of men [the oral tradition devised by humanly contrived compulsiveness, not required by God at all!]. You leave the commandment of God [the Mount Sinai guidance of God for how his people were to live with him and each other], and hold fast the tradition of men [the rules and regulations became more important than the commandments, and often, God himself!]."

Now see our traditions in the perspective of this passage. The heart of Christianity is the heart. The essential purpose of our faith is to bring the heart of God, Christ himself, into touch with the heart of man, his deep inner self—man himself as he is in the inner springs of personality. The traditions of the Christian faith, and in a broader sense the traditions we have acquired for the practice of the Christian life, as well as the customs of the Church, are often more important to us than the Messiah who came. We participate in the same gamesmanship as the scribes. Our oral and written traditions keep us from receiving the Lord of the Church. John's words sting, "He came to his own, but his own people received him not; but to all who received him, who believed on his name, he gave power to become the children of God."

The next sections of Mark 7 portray the results of traditionalism. Jesus paints a vivid picture of what traditionalism does to our basic relationships with the people closest to us, ourselves, and the people we are to reach with the love of God.

Jesus drives home his point with the illustration of the misuse of tradition to keep a person from fulfilling the commandment about responsibility to one's parents. He touches the raw nerve inside most of us about parental concern. The acid test of any tradition is that it serves to extend the basic purpose of the commandments to love God and people. In this case, the traditions of the elders had debilitated the basic reason for our being—love.

Let's go deeper. Jesus reminded the scribes of the basic commandment to honor father and mother. Then he pointed out the tradition they required which contradicted that: "You say, 'If a man tells his father or mother, What you would have gained from me is corban (that is, given to God)' " The strict performance of this scribal regulation became a slippery evasion of the responsibility of practical love. The word *corban* means a gift, anything which was set aside and dedicated to God. It was sacred and set apart from all common uses. When a thing was declared corban it could no longer be used for ordinary purposes. What happened was that people evaded parental care by this tradition. If a man declared his property and resources corban, sacred and dedicated to God, he could then say to his parents in need, "Sorry, I can't help you. All I have is dedicated to God." This then gave room for terrible misappropriation of resources to avoid helping people. In most cases, much of what was declared corban was still used for oneself. It was gross piosity that precluded pity. Most of all, it missed the profound truth that the resources of God are to be used for people. Tragic neglect of the essential nature of the commandment was practiced in the name of God. In a fit of anger a person could swear an oath, "Corban is anything I have which may ever be needed by you!" The vow then became unbreakable and gave license for irresponsibility.

That says more to us than we may want to think about. It exposes the way we use tradition in the practice of our religion at anytime. The purpose of our life is to receive the gift of the Savior and offer all we have and are to him. All of life is corban, a gift to be dedicated to God. But Jesus' test of corban is that everything we have be used to meet human need. What is dedicated to God must be committed to his ministry to people. Do the customs, busyness, frantic activities, which we say are dedicated to observe the Savior, keep us from new love and tenderness being expressed to the people around us? As one woman said, "If I can make it

through this church bazaar and keep my sanity, I'll be O.K.!"
Or a man exclaimed, "I can't take one more church committee!" Or
two mothers during the holidays agreed wistfully, "Wouldn't it
be great if we could skip all the frenzied obligations at Christmas
time and just enjoy our families?" And consider what a church
member said about the sharing of the peace of Christ with other
members during the Communion Service: "I come to Communion
to get peace, not give it. I don't like to turn to the members around
me and say, 'The Peace of the Lord Jesus be with you.' That's
just not Presbyterian!" For this man the customs and traditions
of cultural Presbyterianism held a higher authority than the ancient, biblical giving of the peace by the priesthood of believers.
He wanted to "take Communion" but would he *have* Communion
on this individualistic basis?

Next Jesus again deals with the cause of all this: the true inner
uncleanliness, our heart trouble. His teaching on false tradition is
continued by showing that no amount of the rearrangement of the
estrangement of our outer lives with traditional rituals will touch the
real source of our trouble—the inner heart. The ultimate test of
the value of any tradition is, "Does it deal with our heart trouble?
Does it penetrate into our lives and help us see what we are in our
inner selves and allow God's love, judgment, and forgiveness to
heal our true natures?" The traditions of Christianity must be
evaluated by the test, "Does our celebration of the faith get to the
heart of the matter?" Will we be able to look back over the
activities of this year and say, "Well, this year the activities of the
church didn't get at me, they got to me"?

The point is this: Jesus came to save his people from sin. That's
the meaning of the name he was given. "You shall call his name
Jesus, for he will save his people from their sins." He was Immanuel, God with us. He came not to establish the traditions of a
new religion but to get to the inner heart of people's need. His
life, message, death and resurrection were to reconcile us with
God eternally. And that wondrous process for each of us begins in
the healing of our inner selves. Our memories are liberated with
forgiveness, our personalities are reformed around the person of
Christ himself, our turbulent drives and needs are satisfied and
reordered around his guidance and direction. The heart becomes
his home. "The Father and I will make our home in you." The
Christmas carol suddenly has meaning, "Where meek souls will

receive him still, the dear Christ enters in." Then we can sing, "O come to us, abide with us, O Christ, Immanuel."

Once again the river of Mark's thought here in the seventh chapter catches us and carries us out into the deep. The story of the healing of the Syrophoenician woman's daughter was a brash departure from tradition. Here is Jesus' enacted sermon. He attacked the citadel of the traditional religion of the scribes and Pharisees. This tradition led to separation and not inclusiveness. Now he purposely strides into Gentile territory to declare with his travel that he came to love and save all men. To go from Galilee to Tyre and Sidon and then back through the middle of the Decapolis would be like going to Glendale from Hollywood by way of Bakersfield! He purposely went into Gentile territory as an enacted parable, a living sermon, to declare that to be God's person meant inclusiveness. It was an extensive circular tour to prove a very important point.

There he met a Gentile woman who personified what he had been trying to communicate. He incarnated Isaiah's prophecies that he was to "shine as a light to lighten the Gentiles" (Isa. 42:2, 6). Mark's purpose in telling the story is to show that Jesus came not with human resources, but divine, Messianic power which was equal to any problem, and was to be shared with all people, even the Gentile nations. He emphasizes it three times. Israel would not learn that it had been blest to be a blessing. Later the Church was inverted with exclusiveness and for a time existed as a sect of Judaism. Even after the dramatic breakthrough to the Gentile world through Paul, and later Peter, the Church struggled with time-tattered prejudices.

We suffer from the same problems. The Church today is often tempted to repeat the mistake. We become the exclusive Israel and our Gentile world is the excluded people we don't like or approve or who are not our kind! Our Tyre and Sidon is any realm of life which needs the Savior; our Syrophoenician woman is any person within our sphere of influence who needs Christ's love and hope through us.

Jesus had stressed that religious exclusiveness was useless because no outward separation can remedy the inner pollution. His new life would bring inward cleansing and outward fellowship with people. Now we can see exactly what was happening in the miracle singled out in this chapter.

A Gentile woman discovers Jesus and begs him to heal her daughter. He is whimsical and tender in the way he deals with her. The dialogue is for the disciples' ears to teach them a very crucial point. Jesus says to the woman, in effect, "Salvation belongs first to the Jews. Is it right to take food meant primarily for the children (the Jews) and give it to the dogs (the Gentiles)?" The meaning is: I am a Jew. You know how Jews think about people like you. They speak of themselves as the children of God and you people as dogs. What do you say to that? The woman takes the dangling bait and rises to the occasion. "That's true," she answers. "The children should have the food first, but most children feed scraps to the little dogs beneath the table." What a brilliant answer! Jesus is delighted with her wit and persistent faith. He immediately grants her request, and when the woman returns home, she finds that her daughter is well. I can imagine that Jesus caught the disciples' wondering eyes. "And what do you make of that?" I suspect he said to them. They had much to ponder. Jesus broke tradition, he cared for a foreigner, his healing was at a distance. They could not rationalize the miracle, nor can we. It makes us fall on our knees and exclaim, "Only the Messiah could do that!" And that's just where the Lord wants us to be.

But the implications again are powerfully clear. What traditions, prejudices, and worn-out equivocation keep us from loving and helping certain people?

God broke through time and space to redeem us so that we could break out of our carefully erected compartments of reserve. Life in Christ ought to do that! Think of someone you don't like and do something out of love for him. Consider the people whose beliefs and practices are different. Make a list of the people God wants you to care for and ask him what love demands. In the name of the Christ enact your love in practical caring and friendship. If we don't, our Christianity will be traditional, and we will not be triumphant!

The last portion of chapter seven caps off the message. It focuses our attention on the One who is the source of the quality of life exposed all through this chapter. The purpose of the account of the healing of the deaf stammerer is to underline that the One who supersedes tradition, who calls us to freedom and joy, is truly the Messiah. The last verse gives meaning to the whole account. The people say, "He has done all things well; he even makes the deaf hear and the dumb speak" (Mark 7:37). I like an annotated interpretation of that. "Now we see that he has accomplished all that Isaiah said he would. Even the dumb speak and deaf hear." There is no question now. Everything the prophets said is fulfilled. Jesus is the Messiah. His word is enough. All power is vested in him. He said to the deaf mute, "Be opened," and immediately his tongue was loosed; he could hear, and he spoke plainly.

But this all becomes very personal. Jesus is not only the Messiah but he is the personal encounter of the presence of the living God. The moving aspect of this passage for me is that Jesus took the man aside, away from the crowd, and dealt with him privately. Jesus came to save the whole world, but that becomes particularized in the private way he singles each of us out and deals with us as if we were the only person he came to save, and our needs were the only important thing for him at the moment.

I like that! He deals with us one by one. Christ is for the world, but he is for me, not against me. The wonder of it all is that when we first meet him he takes us aside to heal our hearing so we can listen to his words of love, and then he loosens our tongues so we can speak and sing his praises. Our healed ears become the open door to our hearts, and we feel and know that he is *the* Lord, that he is *our* Lord, and then with loosened tongues we can declare him *everyone's* Lord.

Let Christ take you out of the crowd. Right now allow him to transfix you. Feel his loving hands grip your head, touch your ears, hold your gaze on his face. Now with unstopped ears hear him say, "I did it all for you. Bethlehem was for you, the Mount of Beatitude was for you, the message of Galilee was for you, Calvary was for you, the open tomb was for you, the Upper Room was for you, my living presence in the Holy Spirit is now my gift to you." And in response we can all shout, "He has done all things well! Now I can celebrate life! Here is my heart. Everything I have is corban to be given away in your name. Tyre and Sidon, here I come!"

CHAPTER 18

WHAT WOULD IT TAKE TO SATISFY YOU?

Mark 8:1–10 and 8:14–21

The couple's marriage was in deep trouble. They had come to see me as a last effort to find some way to stay together. The minute they entered my study, I noticed their body language indicating the separation which had grown between them.

I have a large couch in my study and each of them sat down at either end, almost pushing the armrests off in an effort to sit as far from each other as possible. I thought of the contrast with young couples who come for marriage counseling before their weddings. They sit together huddled in the center of the couch. As I talk about the joy of Christian marriage, they wink at each other, hold hands, and exchange affirmations.

Not this couple. They couldn't get further apart. The distance on the couch was symbolic of what the years of discord had done to them.

I opened the conversation with a question, "What was it that made you fall in love in the first place? What was it about each other which set you on fire, attracted you, made you want to live together? What was the dream you had for marriage then? What has happened to that dream since then? Where are you right now?"

The man answered first. He gave a few trite and pat phrases about what he had liked about his wife. And then he opened the floodgates of a vitriolic stream out of the cesspool of his hidden agenda. He began to tell me about what his marriage was not, all that his wife was not, and what he had dreamed marriage would be that had never happened. He went on for what seemed like an hour.

His wife was filled with embarrassment that another person now knew his opinion of her. She fidgeted, crossing and uncrossing her legs. Her hands were fisted and her arms were held tightly across her chest. Finally, she could take it no more. She leaped to her feet and began pacing the floor. I prayed. There was no telling what might happen. Then suddenly she marched up and got eyeball to eyeball with her complaining husband. This is what she said: "Will you never be satisfied? What would it take to satisfy you?"

Then there was silence. I continued to pray. The man reeled under the psychic blow of the penetrating question. He was shocked and couldn't answer. It was a turning point for him. From that moment we began to make progress and in subsequent sessions he allowed God to deal with his seemingly insatiable critical nature.

The question the woman asked her husband, however, has persisted in my mind. It comes back to me often as I observe the mad scramble of all of us for security, affluence, stability, and the satisfaction of our voracious appetites for what we can taste and touch. Recently I did an inventory of the truly satisfied people I have known. I couldn't think of very many. I reflected back over the churches I had served, the great Christians I had known, the personages of literature about whom I had read, and I could think of only a few deeply satisfied Christians. Many were committed to Christ but remained curiously ambitious; some surrendered to Christ's will but were still disturbed by their desire to have power and control; others were dedicated to the cause of Christ but were still acquisitive in their little "kingdom of thingdom." I wondered: Does Christ satisfy? If so, why do we spend so much time and effort to acquire the things which eventually displace our ultimate loyalty to him? Is it possible to find our satisfaction in Christ alone?

Suddenly the words of our text from the account of the feeding of the crowd of four thousand in Mark 8 leap off the page. "And they ate, and were satisfied." Jesus had compassion on the great crowd that had been with him. The disciples had forgotten what Jesus had done to multiply the loaves and fishes for another crowd a few weeks before: "How can we feed these men with bread here in the desert?" "How many loaves have you?" Jesus replied quickly. "Seven!" was their frightened answer. Then Jesus took the loaves, gave thanks and gave the multiplied pieces to the disciples to distribute among the people. The same was done with a few small fish. After they had eaten, Mark gives us this astounding word, "And they ate, and were satisfied." They were satisfied not only with the nourishment of the bread, but also with the nurture of Jesus' presence. What they heard of his message and saw in his deeds met the spiritual hunger in them. Jesus himself satisfied them at the core of their being.

But not the disciples! The very ones who had been the hosts and servers of that miraculously prepared meal were not satisfied. Look at them at the end of that day. In verse fourteen we see them. worried and troubled when they set sail on the sea because they had forgotten to bring bread! They had only one loaf and were concerned that they might be hungry at sea. Seven loaves had fed four thousand, but they could not imagine that Jesus could feed twelve of them with one loaf. "We have no bread!" they exclaimed. Jesus patiently took them back over what he had done to satisfy the crowd. "Do you not remember?" he asked. He made them retell the story, recounting the amazing facts of what had happened. Still no comprehension of Christ's sufficiency registered. We can feel the Master's pathos when he sternly demanded, "Do you not yet understand?" No, they hadn't. Nor do we.

How can we forget so easily? We forget the times he has intervened and multiplied our inadequate resources. Our memories are dull when it comes to new challenges and difficulties. We wring our hands, our hearts ache with worry, our minds are confused by dangers. What would it take to satisfy us?

But, isn't it wrong to be satisfied? Isn't that the problem of Christian history? . . . the Church? . . . self-satisfied Christians —the bastion against change and growth? What would it have been like if the prophets of Israel had been satisfied in the midst of an apostate nation? What would Jesus have been like if he had been satisfied with the world he found? Would he have given his life? What of the martyred saints of the ages? What about their consternation with things as they were? Think of what would have happened if Christians had always been satisfied with society!

That forces us into a deeper question about what it means to be truly satisfied. "Why is it that the most Christ-satisfied people of history have had the greatest dissatisfaction with the world around them? Why is it that the deeper we grow in Christ, the more dissatisfied we are with our present stage of growth? How does Christ satisfy us?"

Listen to Isaiah. He was asking the same question in the context of his times: "Ho, every one who thirsts, come to the waters; and he who has no money, come, buy and eat! Come, buy wine and milk without money and without price. Why do you spend your money for that which is not bread, and your labor for that which does not satisfy?" (Isa. 55:1–2).

Inventory any week, day, or hour. Why do we spend our time for things which don't satisfy? I found an obscure passage in Proverbs which gave me direction: "The leech has two daughters; 'Give, give,' they cry. Three things are never satisfied; four never say, 'Enough': Sheol, the barren womb, the earth ever thirsty for water and the fire which never says, 'Enough' " (Prov. 30:15–16).

That forced me to delineate the things in me which keep me uncreatively unsatisfied. What are they for you? Power, popularity, success, sex, food? What if we had all that we could get? Would it be enough? I doubt it. We become driven by these needs and not by Christ. But admitting that is the beginning. Until Christ satisfies our profound hunger spiritually we will use even his causes to satisfy our human hunger for ego satisfaction. My study of the creatively dissatisfied people of history reveals that they were fed by Christ, filled with his Spirit, nurtured in the lasting nutrition of his message. Only that could fill the Christ-shaped hunger in their hearts. Then their dissatisfaction grew around anything in them or their society which kept people from being fed by the Word of God which had satiated their own hunger.

The Cross is the feeding place for Christians. Our insecurity is fed by his love; our self-justification created by the hunger pangs of our failures is fed by his forgiveness; our aggressive competitiveness is filled by a purpose big enough to displace our distorted affection. The knowledge of Christ's presence and power is an intravenous feeding which is never unattached. He surges strength into us. But it is the indwelling of his Spirit which provides the lasting satisfaction. Not just an overpowering presence around us but an empowering presence within us. Paul knew what that meant. "Christ in you, the hope of glory!" That alone can fill the gaping hole in our natures.

Then, flowing out of that comes healthy self-satisfaction. Christ's love heals self-condemnation. We are free to take delight in ourselves, to love ourselves as loved by Christ. We can begin to enjoy being ourselves by being thankful for the gift of uniqueness God has given us. That security gives us the remedial energy to change anything about us which contradicts our Lord.

The wonderful result of that is that people suddenly feel a liberating satisfaction from us. Many of them know already what they need to do to be better people. Our delight in them gives them the courage to try to be different. I know so few people who have ever felt the unequivocal satisfaction of someone else for them. They believe they must always *do* something to be loved. Not so when a Christ-satisfied person invades their life with the overflow of his love for them.

I have found that people who have experienced the balm of Christ's Spirit deep in the hurts of their own psyches become agents of healing with others. The result is that satisfaction helps people deal with the dissatisfaction they feel about themselves and their lives. That's how Paul helped the troubled Roman Christians. "I myself am satisfied about you, my brethren" (Rom. 15:14).

Christ-satisfied people have what I call divine unrest, a discontent with anything which hurts or frustrates people in our society. From their sure love in Christ they can move out to be change agents.

My personal witness is that I have found Christ able to satisfy. At the end of each day, year, challenge, or opportunity, he forces me to look back at what he has been able to do with the hard clay of my humanity. Like the disciples, I often forget and worry about having enough bread. But when he reminds me of the ways he has invaded my meager potential with his power, I am satisfied that, as he gives each day, he will show the way. With every thought of my mind, fibre of my body, feeling of my emotion, decision of my will, I am captivated by the conviction that Christ is able. He proves it to me again and again. I have eaten; I am satisfied.

In that light, I can answer the question with which we began: "What will it take to satisfy you?" "Christ, my Lord!" And I say with the Psalmist, "Bless the Lord, O my soul, and all that is within me, bless his holy name! . . . who satisfies you with good as long as you live so that your youth is renewed like the eagle's" (Ps. 103:1,5).

If we experience that, we will become a sign to our generation. To that hope we turn our attention next.

CHAPTER 19

A SIGN FOR OUR GENERATION

Mark 8:11-13

If you had to pick out a personality or type of person from the people in Jesus' life, who most vividly characterizes your response and relationship with Christ, who would you choose? Could you say that you are most like Peter in your impetuous abandonment of all you have, or like Andrew in faithful commitment of however little you are, or like James and John in lusty desire for spiritual adventure and challenge, or like Thomas in searching intellectual integrity?

If I were to be honest, there are times when I would have to say that I am most like one of the Pharisees! Does that surprise you? The Pharisees have suffered so badly as the whipping boys of 1500 years of New Testament interpretation that it is difficult to see anything positive about them. We have learned to hate these judgmental, critical religionists. Each time they appear on the pages of the New Testament they are either getting data to be used against Jesus or pressing charges for his destruction. We picture them as a strained, snooping band of fact-finding religionists. No wonder our caricature of a Pharisee is a negative, judgmental person. How then, can I admit that I am a Pharisee?

The passage we just read gives us a picture of an aspect of Phariseeism with which I identify and empathize. The more I have studied this passage and mulled it over in my mind, the more a new image of the Pharisees has emerged. Two things become very clear as we take a deeper look into this passage. The Pharisees were responsible men who waited to be sure, and they were unable to act even when they were convinced.

The Pharisees had to be positive; it was their job. They were

the protectors of the Old Testament tradition, its rules and regulations. They had a responsibility to God and to the people to test
any new leader who emerged. There were many who claimed to
be the Messiah but were not. The tests were clearly delineated.
Israel would have victory over her enemies, there would be peace
and God's people would reign supreme. But most of all, there
would be some tangible sign from heaven, a visible, audible inter-
position from God to prove that the Messiah had come. The rabbinic commentary, the Peshitta, taught that when the Messiah
came, he would stand on the roof of the temple, and those who
doubted would see light streaming over him. Josephus tells us
about the revolutionary Theudas who professed such signs of Messiahship.

So the Pharisees had to have proof. Was Jesus the Messiah or
not? They wanted some tangible verification to convince them
beyond any doubt.

We are all like that; we want to be sure. The disciples of John
asked one crucial question, "Are you the one or shall we look for
another?" "Are you the answer to the riddle of life, the complexity
of existence, the tensions of living, the pains of dying?"

The Pharisees wanted certitude, and so do we. They were cautious, and so are we. The world needs people who will wait to be
sure. There are so many thoughtless statements, unexamined
causes, and well-intentioned but meaningless activities. How easily
we can go off in all directions.

But when does caution become constriction? When does investi-
gation become an excuse for inactivity? The Pharisees wanted a
sign for certainty. There is nothing wrong with that. So much
depended on the right sign being given. But they were so filled
with preconceptions that they tried to force Jesus to perform signs
which would satisfy them.

How many Pharisees there are of this kind in the Church today.
They are not sure; they have never had any experience of Christ
personally or any manifestation of divine power to convince them
that Christ is alive. And so they wait—off on the sidelines, critical
of what is going on in others and negative because it has never
happened to them.

The great sin of most church people is neglect. We don't think
much about God, we seldom pray, we spend little or no time
studying the Bible, we are embarrassed by people who talk about

what they believe, and we keep our feelings private. We are really unsure about Christ. What difference did he make, is he truly God's revelation, can we know him today?

What more could Jesus have done; what more could he have said to convince the Pharisees? What did they want? Mark tells us they wanted a sign from heaven. They were not satisfied with the love-motivated miracles of healing of human sufferings. Jesus never performed a miracle for the sake of convincing anyone of who he was. His miracles were all prompted by need in people. The blind, the lame, the demented, the confused, the dispossessed —all found a miraculous response from Jesus. There were no claps of thunder, no lightning, no fire from heaven, no spectacular voice from the clouds. Instead there was the miracle of love at work in human need.

But this was not enough for these Pharisees. Because they had not been recipients of Jesus' personal love, they wanted a tangible physical sign from the sky that indicated truly he was Messiah. Because they could not see the sign he was in himself and sense the miracle of his love, they had to have an outward manifestation to prove to the eye what only the heart could know. Signs were demanded by those who did not believe, but in reality signs were granted only as a manifestation of belief. Again and again Jesus said, "Go your way healed, your faith has made you well."

How like these cautious Pharisees we are! We wait for some tangible evidence that Jesus is alive and in control. We do not want him, we want only what he can do for us. We wait for some healing, reconciliation, answer to need, or direction. If we receive that, we will believe. We bring crises to Christ, but never ourselves. We want answers to prayer, but not *the* answer to our life.

Jesus' response to the Pharisees was direct, "No sign will be given to this generation." The original Aramaic is very strong. Jesus swears that there will be no sign. He sighs deeply, expressing a combination of disappointment and sorrow. Why could they not see the signs of healing already performed? "This generation" is a corporate term for the undecided and uncommitted who looked on but were not involved. He alone was God's sign. They would have to know him before they could be sure.

In Matthew's account of this same incident, Jesus says that there will be no sign except the sign of Jonah. This helps us understand. The sign of Jonah was the miracle of God's overarching, intervening, redeeming care. Even though Jonah rebelled against God and took the wrong ship to escape doing what God told him, God intervened and saved him. When finally he did proclaim the message of God's sovereign Lordship over all to the people of Ninevah, they responded and believed in spite of Jonah's reluctance. This same God was at work in Jesus. Free, unchanging love was offered in him. The sign of Jonah would be culminated in the resurrection where God would use the worst that man could do to give man the best that he could offer: his love.

Now the amazing thing is that while those who demanded a sign would never have one, those who discover that Jesus Christ is God's greatest and final sign of his love and power will themselves become living signs in their generations.

At the close of Jesus' ministry, he promises his followers that signs will follow those who believe. There will be evidences of God's power at work in them which will be a sign to others of what can happen to a life fully submitted to him.

We wonder, "What would it take to convince our modern world of cybernation and détente that Jesus is the answer to our needs?" What kind of sign would lead people to say, "Oh, now I understand!" or "Now I believe!"

There is still no more convincing sign than a human life fully committed to Jesus Christ. This reveals to people that Christ is alive, when they see what knowing him personally has done for you and me.

Throughout the Book of Acts the term "sign" is used repeatedly. Wherever the new Christians went, wonderful signs of God's power to heal, release, love, forgive, and renew were evident. Signs and wonders should be the mark of a living church.

J. B. Phillips catches the spirit of what we have been trying to say:

"Yet we cannot help feeling disturbed as well as moved, for this surely is the Church as it was meant to be. It is vigorous and flexible, for these are the days before it ever became fat and short of breath through prosperity, or muscle-bound by overorganization. These men did not make 'acts of faith,' they believed; they did not 'say their prayers,' they really prayed. They did not hold conferences on psychosomatic medicine, they simply healed the sick. But if they were uncomplicated and naïve by modern standards, we have ruefully to admit that they were open on the Godward side in a way that is almost unknown today."[1]

How have we come to Christ today? Have we come like the Pharisees, to argue and demand a sign? Have we been aware of all the signs God has given already? Elizabeth Barrett Browning was right,

> Earth's crammed with heaven,
> And every common bush afire with God;
> But only he who sees takes off his shoes;
> The rest sit round it and pluck blackberries.

What more can Jesus do to convince us? Nothing. It is done. The Cross is the sign of his love. If we take him at his word and trust him with our lives, the power of his love will transform us and make us a sign to our generation that Christ is alive, of what life was meant to be, and what can happen to a person who trusts him completely.

---

1. J. B. Phillips, *The Young Church in Action: A Translation of the Acts of the Apostles* (New York: Macmillan).

CHAPTER 20

ONCE MORE WITH HEALING

Mark 8:22–26

I have had two conversions. One was to Christ; the other was to Christ's people. The one set me free to love him and myself; the second liberated me to love people. For the first I had to accept what he had done for me, and for the second I had to receive what he wanted to do through me.

The good news of the gospel melted my resistance and self-centered adequacy. When some friends modeled the gracious, forgiving love of Christ in a deep, caring friendship, I wanted to know what made them the inclusively warm people they were. They pointed me to Christ as the answer. Then they helped me use my mind to consider the message, life, death and resurrection of Christ. My emotions responded to the love I felt for what Christ had for me. I confessed my sin of separation from him manifested in my rebellion and insistence on running my own life. Then I reviewed the sins which had come as a result of that. A moral and personal inventory dredged up the mess I had made of life, and I relentlessly exposed to Christ and my friends the failures I thought I would never tell anyone. At that point my will took over and the last-ditch battle for the control of my life was on!

After days of struggle, I made a conscious decision to surrender the control of my life and future to Christ as my Savior. The result was that I could see what I had been blind to for so long: I saw Christ as he was and myself as I was in need of him. This decision opened the floodgates of my heart, and I received love from Christ as I had never known before. I felt loved and eager to love myself as loved by him. I could actually feel what Paul meant when he said, "But if we have died with Christ, we believe that we shall also live with him. . . . So you also must consider yourselves dead to sin and alive to God in Christ Jesus" (Rom. 6:8, 11). I felt alive, full of hope, adventure, and excitement. Yes, there have been times when I have felt that reality more intensely than others, to be sure, but the assurance has never left me that I belong to Christ and that he liberated me from blindness and boredom to live for him.

But I still had problems! The Saviorhood of Christ did not free me from them. And most of my problems were people. I did not know how to love people without using or manipulating them. My subconscious was filled with experiences which had frightened me. The computer within was filled with debilitating memory factors of what people had or had not done to me. Inadvertently, I repeated the pattern in my own life with people for a long time after I met Christ as my Savior. I could not see people as they were in their need and potential. A friend shocked me with the truth. "Lloyd, I hear you talk a lot about Christ's love, but I don't feel the vibes of love from you!" Christ was closing in to show me a second dimension of his love: his Lordship. He forced me to grapple with the truth that I was still so focused on my own agenda that I had not accepted his. People were his agenda.

Again, the Lord gave me a loving fellowship of friends to mediate his power. In a group with which I met regularly, Christ forced me to see the terrible contradiction. I was frozen emotionally and people around me in my family, the church, and my friends were hearing the words of love without feeling the music. I had a rudder of rhetoric but no sail to catch the winds of the Spirit of Christ.

At the end of one particular meeting which had focused on my need, the group asked me if I wanted to receive the indwelling of Christ as Lord to give me the power to love people. In the group we practiced the laying on of hands when we prayed for each other. This was Christ's appointed hour for me. I'll never forget it! The group gathered around me, each placing his hands on my shoulders and head. As these friends prayed, I felt a warmth pervade my body, an electric vitality shoot through my brain, and a new power surge through my emotions. Then quiet and peace. We all thanked the Lord for his gift and claimed a Spirit-empowered love for the future.

That was my second conversion. I was healed of those memories and feelings which incarcerated my potential for being a loving person. The new capacity for feeling, giving and receiving love began to grow from that day and it has never stopped. I often ask for the renewal of that love in my own prayers, and the indwelling of the Spirit of Christ has continued his limitless flow of love. I see people differently now and what I have to give is more than a bartered, equivocal affection; it is the love of Christ himself. What a difference!

I have told you this personal account because it is my own experience of what I believe happened to the blind man who received a two-dimensioned healing. Christ laid hands on him twice. The first enabled him to have sight; the second enabled him to see people. Christ gave him what he needed—once more with healing.

Mark has a marvelous way of focusing the truth in a personal illustration. After passages of teaching, conflict with the establishment, and resistance from Jesus' disciples Mark tells the story of the healing of a blind man. He is the intimation of incarnation. What Jesus longed to have happen to his disciples and urgently prescribed for Israel's leaders is that they would recognize their blindness to the truth—about themselves, life, God and his plan and purpose for them. In speaking to his followers Jesus referred to Israel's leaders as blind guides: "Having eyes to see, do you not see?" Mark will have accomplished his purpose if we can see ourselves in this blind man and experience both levels of healing Jesus came and lived and died for and is alive again to perform right now.

The unique aspect of this miracle is the particular thing Jesus wants from all of us. As with no other healing of blindness recorded in Scripture, this account focuses on a second laying on of Jesus' hands. Here we meet a half-healed man who needed to be healed more thoroughly.

Let me suggest an interpretation built on an exposition of what happened to the blind man. There are three characters in this amazing drama: Jesus, the Light of the World; the man as he was after the first healing; and the man as he was after Jesus laid his hands on him a second time.

Look first on the Light himself! Light surrounds all of the nativity stories of his birth. "The people who sat in darkness have seen a great light and upon them has a great light shown" (Matt. 4:16, Isa. 42:6–7). It was the light of a star that guided the wise men to the Christ child. The angels came to the shepherds with a burst of light. The darkness of the night on which he was born is symbolic of the darkness in men and this world. There was deep darkness in the inner souls of men. Learning, religion, and governments had done little for the spiritual blindness of mankind.

As God's light in the world, Jesus illuminated the darkness of men's understanding of who God is and what he created man to be. The symbolic use of light as the nature of his mission and message punctuated his ministry. Wherever he went he healed the eyes of the body, mind, and soul; the physically and spiritually blind alike said, "Once I was blind and now I see!" He was a shaft of light, the Morning Star piercing the darkness, and his promise was "Blessed are the pure in heart, for they shall see God."

That's what he continues to do as the resurrected living Christ today. The world is still dark after two thousand years of his illuminating light. But no one who has ever experienced a personal relationship with him can live in darkness. His light dispels the darkness of our ignorance, the hidden dimness of our emotions, and shadowy paths of the future. What happened to the blind man is the greatest need of all mankind today.

Many of us will find ourselves in this second person of the drama. We have received enough sight to know that we are insufficient, that we cannot make it on our own and that he alone can give us strength and guidance and hope. But we are among the half-healed Christians.

The evidence of the first touch is that we have been able to see at all. Light has come into our hearts, and we know there is reality outside ourselves which was beyond our grasp before. The first breakthrough has enabled us to say, "Jesus is my Savior," and to see in him the answer to our problems. We are like the disciples with Jesus—convinced but not changed. We see the truth, but it is not clear enough to be a basis of life. Our response to Jesus' question, "What do you see?" is "We see trees like men walking!"

Seeing the truth is always relational. The healing of Christ is to bring him and the people of our lives into focus. But we are half-healed, and a partial healing always results in a dim view of people. He has a gift to give us: a second laying on of hands which will enable us to clearly see things, reality, truth, people. We are to become people who will to do his will, who want the loving touch of his Spirit, are able to see people clearly, and are empowered to love them.

Could there be a greater tragedy than to accept Jesus as the Light and then live with fuzzy, unfocused images of him, ourselves, and people? But often the Light is too bright for eyes which have grown accustomed to the dark prisons of our own preconceptions and prejudices. There are times I see more of Christ than I am willing to follow; more of myself than I am willing to confess and change; more of people than I am able to accept, forgive, and care for personally. The secret is that our Lord never shows us more light than we can stand. That's why the Christian life is ever evolving and developing. Each day more light; each day further responses and growth.

The final test of how much we see of him is how well we see people around us. When I contemplate the quality of vision Christ would want us to have, I think he would want us to love him by seeing, truly beholding, one another. Wouldn't you feel you had spent a fine day if the people around you truly saw your potential as well as your problems?

I called a friend after last Christmas to wish him well and ask about the kind of Christmas he had. "It was the finest Christmas we've ever had" was his response. He went on to explain that there was a deep feeling of love and mutual acceptance which pervaded all the members of the family. They seemed to be open to each other and warmly affirmative about each one's joys and struggles. "It was as if we saw each other for the first time," he said.

How would you like to be able to say that for every day?

How many of you feel like the man who said, "I don't think my the distorted focus of her image of me!" Well, that takes time and wife has ever looked at me, really, I mean, as I am—not through the distorted focus of her image of me!" Well, that takes time and about people. Relate at a distance; it's not so costly. Indeed! But what shall we do with this Christ of the second touch?

There is a frustration I feel in many Christians who have the picture of what life can be but do not have the power to live it. That frustration can be healed by an even greater gift than our salvation. He offers himself, his own Spirit, to live in us. We were never meant to produce the Christian virtues to please him. That's where so many of us have missed the gift. We have wanted to do for him what only he can do in us.

We all need a second conversion—this time with healing. His

indwelling love can heal the memories, the hurts, and the frigid-
ness which keep us from seeing and loving people.

What do you see? Trees? Things to be used? Or people to be
loved? Remember Mark tells us the blind man begged Jesus to
touch him. That's one prayer Jesus will never refuse.

CHAPTER 21

LIFE'S ULTIMATE QUESTION

Mark 8:27-30

Life's ultimate question was first asked on the road to Caesarea Philippi. Few places could have provided a more significant locale. Then, as now, alternative answers of man's longing quest for meaning and security were all around.

Jesus, walking ahead of his disciples, was silhouetted against the city in all of its Roman glory. Rising up out of its center was a translucent temple of white marble built by Herod the Great in honor of the Caesars. Around it were magnificent villas and palaces added by Herod's son Philip who had renamed the city to honor Caesar, and to impress his own name in history!

The power of Rome was in the air, but so were the hauntingly vivid memories of the pagan god, Baal—once so powerful in that region. The city had in fact been called Balinas in honor of the fertility god before Philip renamed it. Ruins of temples and shrines of Baal orgy worship punctuated the landscape.

Framing the view and overshadowing the region was Mount Hermon, metaphor of Israel's quest for God. Sharp recollections of the strategic times God had encountered great leaders of Israel undoubtedly filled the minds of the disciples. Even on the slope of Hermon a cliff with ancient inscriptions and niches containing statues of pagan gods gave stark reminder of the conflict Israel had faced affirming its resolute monotheism.

It was here, in the region ambiguous with symbols of man's religion and pride and passion, that Jesus stopped. He turned and confronted his disciples with these words, "Who do men say I am?"

It was a leading question. But a deeper and more penetrating one was to follow. This was not the question of an insecure leader seeking to know his standing in the public opinion polls. It was a probing inquiry designed to determine the extent to which men were discovering the true nature of his mission and message.

The answers were really very complimentary.

There had been one or two denigrating titles—winebibber, friend of publicans and sinners, blasphemer—but the disciples by-passed these. They rehearsed instead the more serious speculations as to whom the Son of man was.

They told him that the fears of Herod Antipas had promoted the theory that he was John the Baptist raised from the dead. Others believed he most actively fulfilled the prophecy of Malachi and that he was Elijah come to prepare the way for the Messiah. Still others believed that the vision given to Judas Maccabaeus had come true: He was Jeremiah who had come with a golden sword to wage war for the deliverance of the chosen people. Others simply said that Jesus was one of the prophets.

It was in this significant moment that Jesus pressed home life's most important question. Surrounded by geographical and topographical evidences of man's answer to the riddle of life and in the emotional context of the varied opinions, Jesus asked, "But who do you say that I am?"

Only one could answer. It was not a levered response, and it didn't come quickly. Simon's answer was seasoned by deep thought. His face was radiant and his voice alive with the excitement of discovery and insight as he answered: "Thou art the Christ."

Matthew records the full statement: "Thou art the Christ, the son of the living God."

Clearly Simon acknowledged Jesus not as a prophetic forerunner of the Messianic age, but as Messiah himself. It is true this had been hinted at before when Andrew and John announced hopefully to Simon that they had found the Messiah. Philip had told Nathaniel that they had found the one about whom Moses, the Law, and the prophets had written.

Now, as a fact of revelation from God's Spirit in this moment of high spiritual drama, Simon knew it was true. He now knew for himself that Jesus was the expected Messiah. And he knew, too, that this beloved and winsome person with the dust of Palestine on his sandals and the world in his heart was the Son of God. In a strange, mysterious way he was God with them.

We too are surrounded by the ways men have tried to answer

life's deepest questions. We live in a world of military might. Defensive barriers are drawn. Stockpiles of sophisticated weapons are more important than food, as young nations struggle for recognition and survival. A fourth world emerges with a new kind of black power. And now, with the pushing of a button single nations can unleash enough nuclear power to destroy the world.

Men sit in seats of electronic power creating needs and shaping thought. The gods of science and technology are about to be tried in the marketplace. Symbols of the occult are ubiquitous. What is right continues to be judged by what is expedient and pragmatic.

In a world like this Jesus Christ still puts the question: "Who do men say that I am?"

We must be frank to admit that he doesn't fare as well in our century as in the first. Our generation would be quick to answer: He is a historical character . . . a poetic idealist . . . a beautiful, sensitive but misguided person who is obsolete in our cybernetic, technopolitical world . . . a myth of men's creation . . . a good example . . . a fine moral leader of a new social order . . . a picture on a church wall. But is this enough?

In the midst of these clamoring answers Christ still demands silence. As we approach prayerfully, he stops each of us and puts the penetratingly personal question: "But who do you, for yourself, say that I am?"

Who is Jesus Christ now? What he was and did is not in question, but who and where is he now? Is he a separate God? If so, don't we end up with two separate Gods—even three, a tritheism, when you affirm your belief in the Holy Spirit?

You ask what God is like? Look at Jesus! Jesus Christ is God in his approach to man. He is the full, final, never-to-be-repeated unveiling of God to man.

The Spirit who created the world and sustained it through the generations, the Spirit who called and cared for his people, who gave the Law and raised up prophet, priest, king, and soldier was the same Spirit who came to reveal his essential nature in Jesus of Nazareth. He focused his face for men to behold in Jesus. When we talk of the Holy Spirit, we do not speak of another separate deity, but the same Spirit continuing his activity with man.

The question stands. Who do you say Jesus Christ is? He is God's historical revelation of himself. He is God's invitation to man. He is God's Spirit reaching out to your spirit in forgiving love and power. He longs to be the living Lord of our lives.

Who do you say that he is? Your answer is tremendously important.

Your answer determines your relationship with God.

If we believe that Jesus Christ was God incarnate, and that God continues to approach us in Christ, then we can know God only as he comes to be known. Jesus said, "I am the way, the truth and the life. No man comes to the Father but by me." This is true because the Father comes to his creation only through his Son. Therefore, the more we know of Christ, the more we know of God—for God is Christ coming to us.

We cannot by-pass Christ to get to God, for God has willed it otherwise. We must come to grips with his message, see his death for our sins, know he is alive and dare to live under his lordship.

Your answer determines your capacity for daily life.

Christ is God's abiding presence with us. Jesus said, "Lo, I am with you always . . . even to the end of the world." He sustains us in loneliness and gives power in weakness. He gives direction in indecision and wisdom in times of confusion.

If he is only a myth or a poetic idealist who lived 2000 years ago, then we are alone—dreadfully alone—to face life and its ambiguities and complexities.

How you answer determines your character and conduct.

Does it make any difference what you believe? Try to follow the Sermon on the Mount without the help of the living Christ and you'll end in despair. Jesus never meant us to try to live that way without him.

The more we read about what he said and the more we listen to him in prayer, the more we become like him in our character. Conduct follows in a selfless, other-person orientation that gives and forgives.

How we answer determines our capacity to love.

Our relationships are radically altered as we live in fellowship with Christ and allow the depth of his love to heal us. Christ's love is unmotivated by us and unchanging in spite of what we do. When he lives in us, we find we soon have the capacity to love others in the same way with a love that cares and dares.

How we answer determines our courage to die.
Underneath all our insecurities and fears is the ultimate fear of nonexistence. We are afraid to die. Not so for the man who belongs to Christ! Long before physical death he has passed from death to life. Death has been swallowed up in victory—Christ's victory.

No pleasant moral teacher or gentle guru could do that. Only God in Christ can defeat death. If he is the Christ to you, death has lost its sting.

How you answer determines where you will spend eternity.
We will all live forever. But where? With whom? The Scriptures are very clear: "He who has the Son has life; he who has not the Son has not life. This is eternal life . . . that [we] should know thee the only true God and Jesus Christ whom thou hast sent" (1 John 5:12; John 17:3).

If we don't know Christ, we don't know God as he has revealed himself to be known. When this is true, we must think of death as the end. Those who are able to answer, "You are the Christ! God with us!" understand life to be prelude to eternity.

Life's most important question awaits life's most important answer. Browning asks it with these words:

> What think ye of Christ, friend? when all's done and said,
> Like you this Christianity or not?
> It may be false, but will you wish it true?
> Has it your vote to be so if it can?[1]

Everything, now and forever, depends on your answer.

---

1. Browning, *Bishop Blougram's Apology.*

CHAPTER 22

ON SATAN'S SIDE

Mark 8:31-38

Do you ever find it difficult to believe in the goodness of God in a world like this? Do you ever wonder how a good God can be in charge of a deranged world like ours?

The other day I didn't find one positive piece of news in the whole first section of the morning paper. What a way to begin a day! How can we explain crime, hatred, war, poverty, segregation, broken homes, divorce, dope addiction, and adultery if there is a loving God? How can we explain selfishness, pride, dishonesty, and just plain human cussedness?

Why doesn't God do something about that? How can we say that we are his creatures if our natural bent is to resist him, hurt and condemn our brothers, thwart the causes of righteousness, and mock our potentiality with reservation and reticence? If God be God, why doesn't he change it all with a sovereign sweep of his power?

Our exposition of Mark brings us now to a passage which gives us an answer to these questions by exposing some of the most profound and penetrating truths which the Bible has to say about life. Simon's seemingly magnanimous defense of his Master against the implications of Messiahship and Jesus' sharp, telling reply lay bare four biblical truths which are absolutely essential for understanding our sick world, our ambiguous natures, and how we are to live in a time like this.

The Scripture seems to be saying: 1) that there is an objective power of evil in the world in deadly combat with God; 2) that we are the battlefield where this combat is waged; 3) that we can become an extension of evil in the world; and 4) that we are most vulnerable to be tempted at the growing edge of our character.

What a strange, almost violent reaction Jesus had to Simon's presumptuous rebuke! Jesus had just delineated the cost of his Messiahship, telling them plainly that it would mean suffering and the Cross. This was abhorrent to Simon. His preconceptions of a victorious Messiah who would lead Israel to victory were sharply contradicted. He ran out ahead of his Master, blinded by a strange mixture of protective love for Jesus and fear for himself, both intensified by his own wilfulness.

"This will never happen to you, Lord," Peter argued. He should never run ahead of his Rabbi nor dare to contradict him, much less rebuke him. It is plain that Simon was intoxicated with the heady wine of his newly assigned position as a rock upon which the Church would be built. He allowed himself an utterly unheard-of presumption of interruption, interference, and intimidation.

But note what Jesus says:

Not, "Now, now Simon, get back with the other disciples . . . poor chap, you don't understand yet."

Nor, "Poor Simon, you are more concerned with your own ambitions than the purposes of God!"

No, instead, Jesus said, "Get behind me Satan!" This seems to be a Semetic way of saying, "Out of my way Satan!"

Satan? But this was Simon Bar-Jona. How could he be called Satan? Satan was a name for the power of evil. This was the same evil power referred to throughout Scripture as adversary or accuser and confronted by Jesus throughout his ministry.

Jesus didn't believe that Simon reacted as he did simply because of misguided love or distorted ambition, but he believed that the world was at odds with God and was now using Simon as his mouthpiece to thwart Jesus' ministry. He knew Satan as the distresser who dissuaded people from knowing and doing God's will. Jesus believed that there is an objective power of evil. And he knew that this evil force had found a vulnerable pawn in volatile, vacillating Simon. Jesus exposed him for what he was, an extension of evil: "Out of my way, Satan!"

This then is Jesus' answer to our questions about a sick and suffering world. He believed that behind our misguided intentions was a personal power of evil. God's perfect creation has been deranged by a diabolical force which God has allowed to exist as a regrettable part of a free world. Jesus doesn't explain why there is evil, but he confronts its existence with deadly seriousness.

Emil Brunner suggests a vivid image. He imagines that God's creation is somewhat like a book set in type by the printer—everything is in the right place and makes good sense, and then while the typesetter is away, a scoundrel confuses the type: Everything is "deranged," whole sentences are inverted and scrambled.

Jesus put this thought in a parable. After wheat is sown in the field, the enemy comes and sows tares among the wheat. The field is almost destroyed. So it is with the world.

But this leaves us with difficult questions. Why did God allow it? Why didn't he keep his creation pure?

The only answer to be given is that he allowed it to happen because he loved his creation and wanted his creatures to love him.

What?! If he loved us, why did he allow this to happen?

We can answer our own question by looking at two kinds of fathers. One protects his children from the realities of life. He controls their environment so that germs, problems, human conflict, and anxiety of any kind can never invade the purity of their protected life. They know their father and take his love for granted, never learning to really love him because they've never known the freedom not to.

Then there is the father who allows his children to face the world as it is. He knows the potential ills which can come to them because of what life will do to them and what they will do with life. And he tries to lovingly educate them to trust in him and helps them to make their own decisions. They are strong in an evil world because in tasting life, lessons have been learned which are creative and not destructive. They choose to love him by free choice among the alternatives.

Now, which father really loves his children? The second one? Of course, because there is freedom, and in freedom love is always the result of choice and grows in the fertile soil of freedom.

So it is with God. He gave his creatures freedom and has allowed evil to exist as a part of a free world. He will not force us to love him, but waits for us to respond to his love. He gives us the awesome gift of free will and does not negate this freedom.

What man has done with this wondrous gift is the tragic story of history. He has wilfully chosen to resist God's love, and in so doing he has become an easy mark for evil. The biblical account is graphic narration of the struggle of evil against God. The havoc of history is a telling drama of man's rebellion in the sway of evil. The climax of the struggle was when Jesus came to do battle with evil and to liberate men from its clutches. Wherever he went he was confronted with evil: his own temptation, his encounter with evil in sickness, pride, selfishness and death, his confrontation of virulent evil in religious structures, and his final battle on the cross. In each case he exposed and exorcised evil from men and groups. He did not rationalize or sentimentalize evil or attempt to explain it away. When Simon rebuked him, Jesus saw again the power of evil dissuading a man at a moment of particular weakness.

This leads us to the second point: the human mind is the battle-field of conflict between this evil power and God. Simon could be an instrument of evil or a channel of God. He had tremendous potential for greatness.

With Peter's strong intellect he had sifted and sorted the Mes-sianic prophecies. He made up his mind that Jesus was the Christ. But that same mind was also made up with preconceptions. He was prejudiced by what he wanted Jesus to be and do, and found it difficult to change. His firm conviction about Messiahship put him squarely on Satan's side. In the name of what he thought was right he thwarted God's plan.

Sound familiar? How easily our thinking can go amiss. Our con-fused thinking can get us into all sorts of destructive causes. We can be so sure. Crusades, wars, prejudice, and justified hatred all come from wrong thinking used by the Satanic power. In the name of such wrong thinking men have been burned at the stake, fami-lies have been fragmented, governments destroyed and people frus-trated. "As a man thinketh so is he."

Simon was also a very strong-willed man. He was a leader of men. By power of will, he chose to follow Jesus. But Simon was still in control of Simon. He had not yet yielded the nerve center of control of his own life. He was ambitious for Jesus, the King-dom, and Israel. And down underneath he was ambitious for Simon. A cross? That was ignominious defeat, not triumph! And if Jesus followed that silly plan, they would all be in it with him. Simon wouldn't let it happen.

We all want our own way. We determine the plan of our lives and decide what we will not do. We want our own way—nothing and no one will stand in the way. We become stubborn and obstinate. We demand that Jesus help us accomplish our preconceived plans and want nothing of sacrifice or martyrdom.

A church I visited was split because of factions which wilfully demanded their own plan and wouldn't see the other point of view. The unity of the bond of Christ was broken. I spoke to people in both of the conflicting camps. Each side believed it was guided by what was "right" from their point of view. Behind it all was a power struggle of personalities which gave Satan the victory.

A young man is expelled from a family in a congregation because the parents will not forgive him and accept his failures. They cannot surrender their willful standards for the sake of family love and unity. To them principles are more important than the person. The parents have lost a son. They were "right" but their self-righteous judgmentalism made them very wrong!

Simon was also a man of passionate emotions. He loved deeply. He had given Jesus his heart; but his emotions were soft and sentimental. His love was possessive, and he couldn't bear to see Jesus hurt. How often we are like him! We find ourselves on Satan's side with this kind of inverted self-love, loving ourselves in others and not allowing them to do what they believe is right. Children are often kept from growing into strong characters because they cannot grow beyond where their parents have grown. In marriage we often keep our spouses from being obedient to Christ because we fear the challenge to us. We cripple those we love because of our own neurotic need.

Added to all this was Simon's pride. His ego was eaten up by the terrible cancer of pride. When Jesus recognized him as Peter, a rock, it went to his head. It bloated his insecurity with self-importance and arrogance. He dared to put himself in his Master's way, believing that he had to direct and take care of him. Think of the many times we have domesticated Jesus with our efforts to protect his reputation or keep his cause safe in our churches or our society.

We subtly move to Satan's side when we take the Kingdom into our hands and work for Jesus instead of allowing him to work in us. How many cause-oriented Christians fail Christ by racing ahead to save the world for him without his power.

This leads to the final thing this experience in Simon's life brings into focus for us: We are usually tempted to be on Satan's side on the frontier of our character. Satan's attack always fits the nature of the one who is tempted. Whenever Christ is at work in us in our character, that's when Satan builds up his forces of resistance. Once Christ calls us to be his person the battle begins. As Christ moves into all the areas of our lives to make us totally his and more and more like him, we can be sure that Satan will dig in and resist that invasion at those points where we are the most vulnerable. The phases of our lives which are not totally under Christ's domination are where we are likely to emerge on Satan's side. He will tempt us to do and say things which will contradict our commitment to Christ. The result is that our witness becomes ambiguous and we are thrown off balance with either defensiveness or self-condemnation.

Look at it this way. Simon had been given the gift of faith to declare that Jesus was the Christ, the Lord of his life. But that was not yet part of his character. His values, loyalties, thought patterns, and relationships were not yet infused with the implications of that confession of faith. That's also true of most of us. We are talking way beyond where we are living. Surely that's the reason "good Christians" do so many bad things. It's also the reason Christianity has had such a limited effect on history. We have been on Christ's side and Satan's all at the same time! And deadly duality results.

That's very disturbing to me. It forces me into an incisive inventory. As a man in Christ, what areas of my character really support the enemy? As a communicator, what is there in my life which contradicts my carefully honed rhetoric? As an enabler of people, when have I distorted people's ideas of the new life in Christ by the garbled vibrations of saying one thing and doing another? As a parent, what would my children discern about the power of Christ from the personal dimensions of my life style? As a churchman, is there anything about the church I lead that is counterproductive to what we preach and pray?

Our Lord is urgently concerned about the extent of the transformation of beliefs into *being his person* and our dedication to him into *doing his will*. The danger of emerging on Satan's side always is in the slippery interface between.

Paul put it flatly. "For we are not contending against flesh and blood, but against the principalities, against the powers, against the world rulers of this present darkness, against the spiritual hosts of wickedness in the heavenly places" (Eph. 6:12). He was not simplistic or sentimental when it came to calculating the strength of the enemy or his diabolical emissaries.

What can we do? Once we recognize the enemy for what he is, what hope is there? Again Paul helps us put on armor for the battle. We are to have our loins girded with truth, put on the breastplate of righteousness, have our feet shod with the gospel of peace, use the shield of faith to quench the flaming darts of evil, wear the helmet of salvation, carry the sword of the Spirit and the Word of God, and most of all, pray at all times. (Eph. 6:13–18 and 1 Thess. 5:8). This alone can keep us from being captured and ending up fighting on the wrong side.

Note how the battle armor covers and protects us. Our Lord's truth is the objective standard. His message, life, death, resurrection, and present power are the truth which must persuade our thinking. Distorted thinking or sentimentalism, unguided by what Christ said, did then and is doing now, will open us up to Satan's attack. The breastplate protects our hearts—the seat of our emotions and feelings. Righteousness is rightness with God. It is the power which comes to us when we accept our being made right with God eternally through Christ and his cross. Neither self-incrimination or self-justification has meaning for us. But our bent to condemnation of ourselves and our resistance of forgiveness often give Satan his day. He is never more victorious than when he can defeat us by catching our feelings in the whirlpool of depression and defeat. The self-justifying things we do then are on Satan's side.

The gospel of peace guides our Christian walk. Feet shod with peace equip us to walk and run with the Master as peacemakers. Christ's peace is not the easy peace at any price. Rather, it is the peace which results in the integration of our whole being around his Lordship. When that happens, we can be enablers of his peace between people and in the structures of society. But so often Christians are just the opposite. We major in the minor details of our piety or polity; we minor in affirmation and forgiveness. Satan is delighted. People are divided and Christ's cause is thwarted. But we can walk with the reconciling, healing shoes of peace.

The shield of faith protects us from the fiery darts of evil. Faith is not only the gift by which we accept and appropriate the love of God for us, it is also the vibrant hope-oriented confidence that he will intervene and give us what we need for every challenge and conflict. To live by faith is to know that we are never alone, that our Lord will give us insight and wisdom, that we will never be without his guidance and powerful presence. Satan's darts are usually sent to rip open our confidence in Christ. Without the shield of faith, we are tempted to ask, "Does our Lord know about us? Does he care? If we try to do what we believe is right, will it make any difference? Does he really interject his power in our difficult situations? Does praying really change things?" Can you feel Satan's darts in the vortex of your hopefulness? Put up the shield! Our Lord will not let us go; he is with us; his Word is reliable!

Our minds need the protection of the helmet of salvation. This helmet covers the area of our conscious thinking and of the subconscious as well. When Christ takes hold of us, he guides our thoughts about reality around us as well as our intellectual development within. His forgiveness cleans and purifies our memories. His Spirit develops a grasp of the issues in our time of history. We can think his thoughts about our life! Prolonged times of quiet with him can transform our perspective. We need not be the helpless victims of our confused, culturally developed convictions about life.

One of the Enabler's Groups in our church meets weekly in downtown Los Angeles and is made up of leading business and professional men. These men come together with the specific purpose of sharing the issues and problems they face in being faithful and obedient to Christ in the complexities of corporation life. When the current frustrations are out on the table, they study portions of Scripture and share what the Lord has put in their minds to do. Then they pray for each other. I am gratified by the many stories these men have to tell about the ways their thinking and reactions have been transformed when submitted to Christ's purification and direction. It sounds like the Book of Acts! They actually expect, anticipate, and rejoice in Christ's control of their thinking and actions. He is very alive and present not only in their meetings but on the battlefield in their offices.

These men possess the last aspect of the equipment Paul talks about: the sword of the Spirit! We are not left to battle alone. The persistent, penetrating Lord is with us.

Prayer helps us to realize this. Paul was right when he cautioned us to pray at all times. That's what unlocks the flow of the unlimited potential of the Spirit for our unceasing problems. And those problems will usually be focused around the challenge of the cross for our lives, relationships, and attitudes. Like Simon, we draw back from that. But like him we are people in process. The Lord was not finished with Peter on that particular day. He would not be on Satan's side forever. He would go through many battles until the Lord had control of his character.

What Mark wanted his readers to grapple with is now the disturbing agenda for us. In what ways, actions, unchanged convictions, unliberated attitudes, debilitating habits, and negative feelings are we still on Satan's side?

But the good news is that we need not stay there. Christ is not only on our side, he is for us and within us to win the battle. With this sure knowledge we can stand in an evil world and not break down. We have the whole armor of God for a time like this.

CHAPTER 23

GETTING THE MOUNTAIN INTO THE VALLEY

Mark 9:1–29

Life seems to be made up of two polarities: times of great triumph, success and vision . . . and times of discouragement, despair and uncertainty. Right now we are probably in the sublimity of the one or the sadness of the other. Or, worse yet, we may be stuck somewhere in between.

It's helpful to identify where we are living at this moment. It's okay to be honest with ourselves. How do you feel? Kind of valley-bound? Or are you feeling the fresh breeze of clarity and hope of the mountaintop?

The purpose of this chapter is to get the mountaintop into the valley. That's what Mark has done for us in chapter nine of his Gospel. Life without limits is living on the mountaintop in the valley.

This was a strategic time in Jesus' ministry. He had told the disciples plainly that he was the Messiah, the anointed one of God. The Spirit had revealed the assurance to Peter, and he had said, "Thou art the Christ, the Son of the Living God." There was no question now. But when Jesus spelled out the implications of Messiahship in the cross, they doubted and were afraid. They were in the valley of discouragement. What kind of Messiah was this? They needed some proof; Jesus needed the seal of God on his determined direction.

This is the reason Jesus took Peter, James, and John to the top of Mount Hermon for the confirmation of God. He knew of the immediate and repeated valleys they would pass through before the ultimate summit of Calvary and resurrection. In the valley below there would be a paralytic lad and a father paralyzed with anguish. They needed to be prepared for both.

Jesus took his disciples up this historic mountaintop filled with so many memories in Israel's life. While they were praying, a magnificent thing happened. Jesus was transfigured before his trusted disciples. Peter must have told Mark what happened. When Mark wrote it down he used a Greek word which meant that the true, essential, inner nature was radiantly shown forth outwardly—a dramatic change, a transition. An intense brightness radiated about Jesus. His face shown with a magnificent splendor, and his drab Galilean garb sparkled with a pure white flame. It was a beatific blessing from God himself.

In his baptism Jesus received the confirming assurance of God: "This is my beloved Son." Now came the same words again; this time for the disciples to hear: This is my beloved Son, my only begotten Son, my revelation in the world. Listen to him! It's difficult to imagine that the disciples would ever doubt or betray their convictions again.

What happened to Jesus is symbolic of what he wants to happen to us on the mountaintops to which he leads us. He wants us to be sure of him and sure of ourselves. It can happen when we close out the valley and intently focus on God. When we are in touch with the dynamic and creative energy which created the world and became incarnated love in Jesus, we are transfigured by the glory of God. The meaning of the word *glory* is manifestation. That happened to Paul. "We behold the glory of God in the face of Jesus Christ." We need that more than food or people or life's blessings.

Some time ago I heard this need expressed by a friend of mine in a group of pastors which had met to sort out God's direction for some aching problems in Los Angeles: "I need to be with you men. But more than that I need God! I have a longing for him that nothing I do satisfies. I can't take the pressures without him." That sent us all to our knees. We were transfigured with power.

How different my friend was from Peter. When Peter saw Jesus transfigured he had nothing to say, and he said it! He said it with religious fervor. He had seen Elijah and Moses confirming Jesus as God's Messiah. Like contemporary Christians with an edifice complex he wanted to build three tabernacles. Rather than bathing in the glory and allowing it to heal his valley scars, he wanted to do something religious.

A bishop I know counsels his clergy, "When confused, start a building program. People need something to do to galvanize and unify their differences. Get them involved in building a new sanctuary and your church will be revived!" A contemporary Peter in bishop's robes!

Peter did not realize that God was "tabernacling" before his eyes in the Messiah. There is no need to build a tabernacle for that. Peter was still smarting from the Lord's rebuke for trying to dissuade him from the cross: "Get thee behind me Satan!" Would he ever wash that out of his conscience?

Failure in the valley often keeps us from the vision of the mountaintop. Peter missed the mountain because his heart was still in the valley. The point is, he needed the same touch from God that Jesus had.

I remember a dynamic retreat I attended in the Pocono Mountains. The final challenge of the retreat leader was, "There is a valley of spiritually and physically paralytic people down there. What we have received here together is empty piosity if it doesn't work down there!" Mark shows us how Jesus did just that. He brought the transfiguration into the tragedy of the valley.

The other disciples who had been left behind were in trouble. A man had brought a young boy with multiple maladies to them with the hope that they could heal him. The scribes were there also and had undoubtedly questioned the disciples' right and power to heal. Jesus had given them that authority when he named them his disciples. But now they were frightened and cautious. The cloud of scribal reserve and negativism hung over their heads. They did not dare. The sick lad was forgotten in a heated argument that raged between them and the scribes.

Jesus strode into that hostile, confused crowd with the glory of the transfiguration still radiant on his countenance. The scribes and disciples alike were stunned and spellbound as they observed the power that he communicated. Mark says that they were greatly amazed.

But the disciples were ashamed as well as delighted to see Jesus. They had tried to heal the man's sick son without success. The disputation with the scribes had sublimated their frustration over their impotence.

Jesus looked about the crowd. Something was very wrong. Why had the disciples allowed themselves to be drawn into useless conflict?

The boy's father answered for them. "Teacher, I brought my son to you, for he has a dumb spirit; and whenever it seizes him, it dashes him down; and he foams and grinds his teeth and becomes rigid; and I asked your disciples to cast it out, and they were not able" (Mark 9:17–18).

The miscarriage of the healing power he had entrusted to the disciples brought a question of consternation from Jesus. "O faithless generation, how long am I to be with you? How long am I to bear with you? Bring him to me."

Who is there who has not felt that question? When we realize how little of Christ's power we are able to bring to our own and other people's problems, we hear it again. When we are aware of what we have done to others and to our world, it comes echoing in our hearts. How long, indeed!

The hopeful note of the story here in Mark is that Jesus does not withhold his blessing from the man and his son because of the ineptness of the disciples. That's encouraging for us, but it can never be a cop-out!

Now watch the mountain man work with valley's plight. Feel the sensitivity and compassion with which Jesus deals with the father of the boy. He may have needed healing of his sagging hope as much as the boy needed healing of his body. "How long has he been this way?" The conversation is abbreviated in Mark's account. I believe that Jesus ministered deeply in that father's heart.

Then the man expressed the creed of the valleys of life. "If you can do anything, have pity on us and help us." The man's faith had been badly diminished by the debility of the disciples. Just think of the times people's trust in what Jesus can do has been drained by what we could not or were afraid to do.

But now listen to the creed of the mountaintop for the sickness of the valley: "If you can! All things are possible to him who believes." It was as if Jesus said, "What do you mean by saying, 'If you can'? All things are possible if you believe."

The father's response is a new creed. He is honest. His hoping has been bruised by years of discouragement. He expressed what was true for him. "I believe; help my unbelief!" That's enough for Jesus—trust and a desire to grow. Confession of faith and need.

Why hadn't the disciples said that? Why was it that the boy's father had had to explain their inadequacy?

The father's words were a prayer. It's the prayer which can change a valley into a mountaintop. The humility and desire to change unlocks the power of God. He wants us to be honest about where we are spiritually and humble about what we need.

I can only imagine what that prayer meant to the troubled Christians in the valley of persecution in Rome. I know what it has meant to me in life's troubled or discouraging times. I have never prayed that prayer without liberating results. "Lord, I know you are able; forgive my doubts. I've made the first step of trusting you, but fear dogs my tracks. I know you are with me, but it's not easy to relinquish my questions. Lord, I desperately need you!" Ever pray like that? I have! And the honest confession of doubt has been the opening for the gift of faith. That prayer of the boy's father breaks the bind.

It is the prayer which needs to be prayed by the Church. We work so hard to get everything within the reach of our human capacities. We don't need the Holy Spirit because we are attempting so little which demands his power. The great need of the Church in America is to pray, "Lord we believe, but forgive our lack of daring. We have seen you do great things in history, but liberate our inflexibility. Help our lack of movement. Adventure. Joyous abandon. Keep us growing Lord!"

One of the greatest gifts our Lord can give a church is to pull the rug of security out from under us. His love is expressed when he allows us to get out on a limb where only he can help us. However much we have learned or accomplished, he has barely begun with us. To the church with the water safely up to its ankles, Jesus says, "Get out into the deep where only I can save you!"

That's what the disciples had to hear at the end of the day. After Jesus had healed the boy and they were safely out of critical earshot of the scribes, they asked the question they had been aching to ask ever since their impotence had been so embarrassingly exposed.

Jesus' answer is the power of the mountaintop available for every valley in which we find ourselves. "This kind cannot be driven out by anything but prayer." Other manuscripts of Mark say, "fasting and prayer." The two go together. Fasting was to focus the attention on God and not the bodily needs. Those who have practiced it with any duration find the total nature sensitized to God. Prayer is the dynamic of conversation with God. It is speaking and listening; telling God of our needs and receiving his direction. That's what Jesus had done on the mountaintop. The power he exercised in the valley was a result. When we wait in meditation, concentrate on God and his majestic love, we are transfigured by his assurance and hope. Our real, inner heart is manifested. The limitless power of God for our valley is never available without that. We need a mountaintop every day to survive the valley. If we come to him with honesty and humility, spread out all our needs before him and confess our need, he will answer. Be sure of that! But love yourself enough to linger in his presence. Praise him until your heart is open to receive. Then tell him all about what's distressing you. Now wait. The transformation of the mountaintop is right now!

CHAPTER 24

HOW TO BE A GREAT PERSON

Mark 9:30-50

Some years ago, my early morning walks would take me through a cemetery near my home. Often my prayers and meditation were interrupted by observation of the epitaphs on the tombstones. It made me wonder what would be placed on mine. If you could write your own, what would you like to have said about you?

One epitaph still stands out in my memory. Underneath the man's name, the date of his birth and death, was an inscription we'd all like to have. I used to try to imagine what the man had been like and what he had accomplished to deserve such an inscription. The words were deeply cut into the magnificent marble, "He was a great person!"

How would you define a great person? Halford Luccock once said, "One way of putting the question to ourselves is: are you living in B.C. or A.D.? Are the standards of greatness which you accept those that for the most part prevailed before Christ came into the world with his insistence on a new measurement of service, or are you really living in some year of our Lord?"[1] That presses our definition to stand the test of whether our conception of a great person is culturally conditioned or Christ-centered.

The remarkable thing I discern about each of us is that we would all like to be known, or at least remembered, as a great person. That means different things to each of us, but we are all alike in that underneath the surface we all have an image of what greatness is for us and are trying desperately to move toward that goal. It may

---

[1] *The Interpreter's Bible,* Commentary on Mark, Halford E. Luccock (New York, Nashville: Abingdon–Cokesbury 1951), vol. VII, p. 787.

be subliminal, but it's there! Greatness for us is a combination of our values, our hopes, our expectations, and our deepest longings. It's a blend of the dicta of what success and fulfillment are for us, shaped by the people whom we would call great persons and want to emulate. But we are to judge our ideas of greatness in the light of the Master and then to allow him to show us how to become a great person. Greatness, Jesus style, is available to all of us. We don't need to wait for an epitaph on our tombstone. As a matter of fact, in becoming great in his eyes, we may not achieve the world's final inscription of greatness. But that will matter little then; we won't be underneath the tombstone; we'll be with him!

Jesus' disciples had a hard time with greatness. They could not get it into their heads or hearts what he was talking about when it came to understanding the Kingdom he came to establish. They still thought in terms of a powerful theocracy with Israel victorious over all the nations and with Jesus the messianic king of an earthly domain. The only question which troubled them was the position which each of them would have, who would sit on his right hand of power, and who would be given the most authority and recognition. He tried to tell them that he would be most a messiah upon a cross and that his victory would be over death. The Kingdom he would establish would be in their hearts, in their midst, and through them in all of life.

Frankly, I am thankful they didn't understand because their ineptness gave rise to Jesus' richest teaching about greatness. In recording his sayings about greatness in this section of chapter nine, Mark has given us a clear picture of how to become a great person.

A great person is able to face anything because he has been given everything. That truth came from Jesus' declaration of what would happen to him. It gives us the first key to greatness on his terms. He told them plainly, "The Son of man will be delivered into the hands of men, and they will kill him; and when he is killed, after three days he will rise." The crucial issue was who would deliver him. Judas? Was Jesus a helpless victim or God's sacrifice for the sins of the world? Jesus' statement gives us his own understanding of what he came to be and do. The Son of man was to be delivered into the hands of men. The Greek word which translates Jesus' original word for "delivered" implies that it is by the Father's hand that he was being delivered. There's the secret of Jesus' greatness and ours! There is a secondary cause in all that happens to us. It is what God is allowing for what he wants to do in and through us. When we are completely surrendered to him, we know that nothing can happen which he will not use for his glory.

We belong to God! He is at work in our circumstances and challenges. But that liberating freedom issues in a bold confidence and joy which is the root of great personality. We are people who march through life having arrived! All things are ours—eternal life, salvation, the presence of the Holy Spirit, his gifts and a vibrant confidence. This confidence is also evidenced in Paul when he uses the same word for Jesus being delivered. "He did not spare his own Son but gave him up for us all, will he not also give us all things with him? Who shall bring any charge against God's elect? It is God who justifies; who is to condemn? Is it Christ Jesus, who died, yes, who was raised from the dead who is at the right hand of God, who indeed intercedes for us? Who shall separate us from the love of Christ? Shall tribulation, or distress, or persecution or famine, or nakedness, or peril, or sword? . . . No, in all these things we are more than conquerors through him who loved us" (Rom. 8:32–37).

Greatness for the Christian begins there or it has no real beginning. The resurrection is our sure sign that God is in charge and will have the final word in our difficulties. When a person knows this and lives it, there is a freedom which flowers in winsome trust and joyous affirmation of life.

Recently a friend made a telling comment about a mutual Christian friend. "I wish that guy knew that he has made it; he could stop trying so hard!" That might be said about many of us. Greatness is accepting God's greatness. A great person is never consciously striving for greatness; he is consciously dependent on God. The God who delivered Christ is the same God who delivers us. Our worries in the cult of preeminence seem rather foolish in the light of that. With an empty tomb for our symbol we can see empty jockeying for position for what it is—an uneasy state of grace. If we have been called, appointed to be saints, made a part of Christ's Body, what more do we need? We have been made great; why struggle for greatness?

But that's not enough for most of us. We are like the disciples in our lust for position and recognition. Jesus knew what was in their hearts. That's why he forced the disciples to talk about what they were discussing on the way to Capernaum. They didn't even have to tell him. He knew! That's why he punctuated his teaching about greatness with the body language exclamation point of gathering the disciples and sitting down to teach them. It was a rabbi's way of saying, "Now listen . . . this is important!"

What Jesus said gives us the second ingredient of greatness: A great person is willing to be last because he is first. The whole human parade is stopped in its tracks and sent in the opposite direction. The ones who demanded to be out front are now bringing up the rear.

What that means to me is that if we are self-appointed leaders of the parade, Jesus can't use us. Greatness is being willing to be least. Then, if in his strategy we are to lead others, he will place us where he wants to use us. There is no self-appointed grandeur for the followers of Jesus. We are to follow him and be willing to be nothing on human standards because we are everything to him. Again the same theme: If we know we are first by grace, we can be last for his glory. Greatness grows out of that!

All our standards of human greatness measured in position, power, and prestige are suddenly obsolete. We can relax and spend our energies getting to know him and his strategy. With what we believe, knowing the secret of life as we do, all we need to do is live with abandon. We will have more to do than a lifetime can contain and more people to heal than time affords. I had a pastor friend whose father kept jabbing him about his professional progress. With each visit he would say, "Are you moving up, son?" A Christian has moved up already. Now he can move out for Christ! Great people never think of themselves as great.

The second half of Jesus' statement gives us a third ingredient: A great person is a servant because he is a master. Christ has made us the master of life's situations, therefore, we can be servants. The same Greek word used for servant is also used for minister. All Christians are ministering servants. We are to serve people as if serving the Lord. That means people's needs write our life's agenda. Great persons are the Lord's foot washers. Our greatness will always be expressed in the people we care deeply about.

In our church we have hundreds of ministers and a handful of professional pastor-enablers. The New Testament concept of the church is that it is to be the equipping center for the training and deployment of nonprofessional ministers in the world. Recently

a man made a telling comment about that. "You probably wonder
why some of us resist the idea of the ministry of the laity. I bet
you think it's because we feel it's too awesome a designation. Not
so! We see what some professional ministers have to do, and we're
not sure we want to pay the price. Your schedule is not your own;
you can't reject the call of human need; your home life is often
interrupted by people's problems; you're expected to know God
better than we are; your life is not your own. I frankly don't want
any part of that kind of demanding life!" Well, that does put a
new perspective on it, doesn't it?

The real point, if we're honest, is that no one, clergy or laity,
wants to be a servant of people. Yet that's where greatness is nurtured. Our service to people is the interest we pay on the life
loaned to us. What happens to people through us is Jesus' evalua-
tion of greatness. And it's ours too, really. Think of the great people you know. They are great because of how we feel when we're
with them.

Jesus doesn't leave the conceptual statement of truth to stand
alone. He gives us an enacted parable and from it we find the
fourth aspect of greatness. A great person loves the insignificant
because he is significant. Jesus took a child and placed him in their
midst, and said, "Whoever receives one such child in my name
receives me; and whoever receives me, receives not me but him
who sent me." If we wanted to build up an entourage of significant others, we probably would not choose children. No titles, no
degrees, no clout in the world. But there the child stands in the
midst and Jesus says in effect, "What you do to whom you deem
insignificant, you do to me."

There's a penetrating, unsettling truth here. Jesus often used
children as examples of what we are to become if we want to enter
the Kingdom and what is to become of our value system if we take
on citizenship in that Kingdom seriously.

To become as a little child means that we become open and
honest, joyous and exuberant, expectant and surprisable. We are
to honor the emerging child in us and never lose the trust and dependence of childlikeness. The child of Jesus' examples is symbolic
of all the little people of life who need us and from whom we
can receive nothing but the assurance that whatever we do for
them, we have done for him. Not a bad promise!

The disciple John smarted under the incisive teaching about

greatness. He responded by trying to change the subject with a *non sequitor*. He drew attention to a man whom he had seen who was casting out demons in Jesus' name. His real concern was that he was doing this but had not joined Jesus' followers. Poor John! He wanted to regiment everything so he could control what happened. Jesus was most loving in his response: "Do not forbid him; for no one who does a mighty work in my name will be able soon after to speak evil of me. For he that is not against us is for us." A fifth dimension of greatness is implied. A great person is inclusive because he has been exclusive. Once you have gone through the narrow door of commitment to Christ, you can have an open-door policy toward others who do not do, say, or perform the way we like. Jesus knew that we would earn the right to communicate the exclusiveness of the Kingdom by a loving inclusiveness to those who differ from us. The disciples were the patron saints of narrow sectarianism. They lacked confidence in their own relationship to Jesus. Their instability was constantly equalized by judgmentalism. They were more concerned about the means of a man's ministry than the ends, and they had a forbidding fanaticism. Their own lack of purity made them purists. Most of all, they cared little for the man himself who was casting out demons in Jesus' name. Yet, he was Jesus' focus. He knew the man was on the way to salvation and did not want him excluded. Greatness will always be marked by an inclusive spirit which loves beyond theological formulations, denominations, political persuasions, and cultural habits. He affirmed David's faith, "The earth is the Lord's and the fullness thereof."

> There is a wideness in God's mercy,
> Like the wideness of the sea.
> For the love of God is broader
> Than the measure of man's mind.

It followed naturally for Jesus to give an example of greatness at this point. Note the way he turns the truth and talks not about what would be done by them but for them. Could it be that greatness meant the capacity of receiving as well as giving? Who could be a stingy receiver after a statement like this: "And whoever gives to one of these little ones even a cup of cold water because he is a disciple, truly, I say to you, he shall not lose his reward" (Matt. 10:42).

LIFE WITHOUT LIMITS

194

Thus a sixth phase of greatness is pointed out. A great person is careful because he is careless. To be filled with care for the practical needs of people can happen only when we are free of care for the false securities of possessions and material wealth. All that we have is given to us to be given away.

What are the things we could do today to meet the basic needs of prayer in our lives? What do we have that would make a difference to someone in the realm of our responsibility? What's the cup of water for us today—for our family, friends, associates? We cannot be great if we resist the impulse to do what our Lord guides as that specific act of caring.

The next aspect of Jesus' teaching on greatness is severe and demanding. But also, it's ultimately liberating. The "little ones" of whom Jesus speaks are not children but beginners in the faith. A seventh segment of greatness is given: A great person is gracious to beginners because he is always beginning. What we do to help or hinder new Christians is of utmost concern to the Master. Our greatness will be expressed in our ability to tenderly nurture those who are taking the first steps of the faith.

Lawrence Young is one of the most mature of the elders of my church. He loves Christ, knows his Bible and is a statesman of the church. He sits down toward the front of the sanctuary and is always available to help people who come forward to receive Christ or take new steps of growth in their faith. I like to watch his face as he talks to beginners. He expresses the delight and encouragement of the Savior. The secret is that his own life is kept fresh by ever-securing new beginnings.

Last summer in Edinburgh, Scotland, after a long day over the books, I would walk those history-laden streets. Often my prayers would break out almost audibly, "Lord, I love you! It's like I never knew you before. Keep me fresh like a newborn babe in Christ, forever." I find that each time I have a new blush of faith, I am very eager to care for those who are just starting to take feeble steps of faith.

To fail to encourage the beginner or to dissuade him with roadblocks of punctilious particularities has Jesus' severest judgment. It would be better to have a millstone tied around that person's neck. There were two kinds of millstones: a small one a woman could handle herself in the home and a large one which only a donkey could pull around to grind the grain. Jesus was talking about the second kind. He referred to a method of execution in his time used by the Romans. A person was tied to that kind of millstone and thrown into the sea. We catch the full impact of his message. It would be better to die a tragic death by execution than mistreat or mislead the neophytes of the faith. That should make us much more considerate of the excesses, eccentricities, and immature ineptness of new Christians! Our greatness will be decided on how we treat beginners.

Jesus presses the same point about ourselves. If there is something we place in the way of our own growth, we are to get rid of it so we can grow on to be the person He created us to be.

> "And if your hand causes you to sin, cut it off; it is better for you to enter life maimed than with two hands to go to hell, to the unquenchable fire. And if your foot causes you to sin, cut it off; it is better for you to enter life lame than with two feet to be thrown into hell. And if your eye causes you to sin, pluck it out; it is better for you to enter the kingdom of God with one eye than with two eyes to be thrown into hell, where their worm does not die, and the fire is not quenched" (Mark 9:43–48).

Greatness then is single-mindedness. It is putting our relationship with Christ above all the habits, practices and peculiarities of our lives. If there is anything that gets in the way of our effectiveness for him, we are to cut it off and be free. That forces me to make an inventory of my life. What do I insist on doing or being that makes it difficult for me to be faithful and obedient to Christ? Or what am I doing that sticks out in my personality which makes it frustrating for others to see Christ in me or find him through me?

The ninth step of greatness is couched in one of Jesus' most difficult sayings: "For everyone will be salted with fire." That's understandable only in the context that salt was required as a part of an acceptable sacrifice in Leviticus. One of the uses of the image of fire was persecution. Put together, it seems as if Jesus is saying that his followers will be persecuted and face grave trouble. Greatness is usually tempered by the fires of difficulty. Yet a great person is not troubled, because to be in Christ is often to be in trouble. Unless there is some area of resistance to what we believe and are doing in obedience to Christ, there may be some question about how much we believe. Persecution is not familiar to most of us, but trouble is. Often our troubles come from the intersection of our faithfulness to Christ and the values and standards of our culture. But our task is not to look for trouble, but to look to Christ. When we are focused on him and our life of obedience flows from doing his will, we will find resistance soon enough.

A great person is not troubled because he is in trouble! He has faced the central issue of being Christ's person. Troubles of daily living are put into the perspective of the greater trouble of persecution for his life in Christ. But isn't it exciting to be on the move with Christ with "soul-sized" issues? Check society and its practices, your church and its customs, your clubs and their regulations, your nation and its policies. Then ask Christ what he wants you to do. The legions of mediocrity as well as blatant hostility will show you what it means to be salted with fire. But what is that for one who has the fire of the Holy Spirit?

The last designation of greatness also has to do with salt. Jesus used this image frequently. In this instance it has two implications: as a preservative and a purifier. One has to do with what salt does in external things and the other with what salt does in us. In both cases salt is never noticed for itself. Its power is inadvertent. Salt seasons and preserves, but you don't necessarily have to see it. It purifies, but is never obvious for itself. "Salt is good; but if the salt has lost its saltness, how will you season it? Have salt in yourselves, and be at peace with one another" (Mark 9:50).

Finally, a great person is recognized when he is unnoticed. We are to be the seasoning for the zest and zeal we bring to the world. Greatness will be expressed in the way it brings enthusiasm and excitement to others. But the recognition will be given not to the salty Christian but to the people and institutions he enlivens.

This statement carries the same pervasive quality of salt. We are to be salted ourselves and be at peace. Peace is possible only through the purification of our motives, beliefs and purposes. Christ alone is the author of peace. He brings that through the cleansing of all secondary loyalties which keep people apart. A great person will be known for his capacity to express deep fellowship and work as a part of the group. The most significant gifts Christ has to give will be expressed in Koinonia and his most significant movements will be done by people whose love for one another empowered what they did together.

That's greatness according to Jesus. He has made us great by grace. If we believe it, we will do great things for him in the world. You are a great person! It is written on your life.

CHAPTER 25

CHRISTIAN MARRIAGE:
HOW TO DISCOVER IT;
WHAT TO DO WHEN YOU FAIL;
HOW TO FIND GOD'S STRATEGY FOR A SINGLE

Mark 10:1–16

Among those of you who read this are those who are happily married and want a deeper life together. But also there are those whose marriages are in trouble and those whose marriages have failed in divorce with all the guilt and remorse that brings. And there are those who have never married, and those who hopefully anticipate marriage someday. How can we exposit what Jesus said about marriage and divorce in a way which will be helpfully creative to all of us? So often we hear the Church talk about one or the other of these groups to the exclusion of the others.

Every time Christian communicators try to be helpful to people who are seeking to make sense of the agony and ecstasy of marriage, it sounds as if God is concerned only about those who are married. Most churches have hundreds of divorced people listening in on these zippy "How to Find a Great Marriage" messages. Also, I often wonder how divorced people feel about their sense of failure and inadequacy in the relationship which is elevated in the church to be the only way healthy people should live. Then what about all the people who are single, either at no fault of their own or by a clear choice? Are all single people simply "unclaimed blessings," as one woman was introduced by another woman?

Ever notice the way we react to a young woman who's reached twenty-five and doesn't have a diamond, or a man of any age who is not at least dating someone steadily? A modicum of insight into human personality should tell us that not all single women have a distorted feeling about men, not all unmarried men have a homosexual problem and not all young people who don't rush into marriage have some sort of hang-up. Yet the impression is created that if you love Jesus you'll get married, your marriage will be a success, and you will live happily ever after in this life and in heaven to come.

The church seldom talks honestly about marriage and the family according to the wisdom of our Lord. As a result, the church is filled with marriages made neither in heaven nor on earth; guilty divorcees; never married singles who must make some kind of self-justifying oblation for a crime they don't understand; and young people who face the frenzy to find someone so the fathers and mothers of the church can say, "Whew! They are alright . . . they are not odd . . . they got married!"

In this study of Mark 10:1–16, I want to say something about Christian marriage Jesus style. But at the same time I want to take a look through his eyes at what to do when the failure of divorce hits. Then we can develop what I want to designate as the calling to be single. I think that if we ever understood what true marriage is all about, we would know what to do with divorce and those who face that tragedy. The church as the fellowship of the bonds of Christ's love, a gracious community of saints who still know they are fallible sinners, ought to be a place where people can be honest about their needs and be Christ's remedial help to each other. We need to talk about our problems and needs, in and out of marriage. I envision the local congregation as the family of God where married couples can be helpful and supportive of singles and singles can be creatively affirming of people trying to be Christian and married at the same time.

The volatile nature of this subject of marriage and divorce is indicated in the Pharisees' attack on Jesus. They had argued with him about every other subject, and he had always won. Now they kept the most divisive subject until all others had failed. They knew that the subject of divorce would divide his ranks and confuse his listeners. The feelings of guilt, judgment and condemnation of self as well as others, were lurking just beneath the surface. In that crowd, as in any church sanctuary, there were people with problem marriages, people who loved someone other than their mates, people whose psyches were so mangled by parental distortion that they could never marry, and people who chose to remain single. Whatever Jesus said about divorce, he was in trouble! But that kind of trouble was not new for him. And he did then what he does now: he takes a trifling conflict and makes it the basis of a tremendous communication.

The Pharisees acted as if they wanted to know what Jesus believed about divorce. But their purpose was to test and trap him. "Is it lawful for a man to divorce his wife?" they asked. Jesus' retort sent them back to Moses and then to a deeper truth they had never anticipated. "What did Moses command you?" he asked with wise debater's skill. "Moses allowed a man to write a certificate of divorce and to put her away," came the response. It was then Jesus told them the profound reason for Moses' injunction as a part of God's eternal purpose: Hardness of heart, that was the reason! It was not God's intention that men should change wives like their tunics, but allowing divorce was Moses' way of dealing with their failure and sin. Jesus then goes on to tell them about God's real intention for marriage and the family and ends with a statement which must have thrown their clever devices into turmoil: "What, therefore, God has joined together, let not man put asunder."

We are left with a profound insight about life and marriage: Life is not just to get married and have children, but to be genuinely human beings. We are male and female, not just for procreation but for profession of faith in Christ and progress in personhood. We are persons, not puppets, created with the capacity to know him, love him and be filled with his life. We are to be persons before we are to be male and female. Then in fellowship with Christ we can express that personhood in the unique focus of our masculinity and femininity.

That's the key point to this first presupposition drawn from Jesus' message. Marriage is not the answer to the dilemma of life or loneliness! God did not create us to get married but to receive his mercy. If we don't know him, we will never know marriage as he intended it to be.

That's the rub! Our frenzied quest of marriage as the alternative to frustration, loneliness, and unfulfillment is inconsistent with God's intention. Yet we think a mate is supposed to do for us what only God can do. I believe the reason so many people find it difficult to be both married and Christian is that they have tried to fill the God-shaped void within with a spouse. It won't work. God created us for himself, and our hearts will be restless for him even after marriage. Unless we love God more than our mate, we can never really love our mate.

That leads to the second point. Christian marriage is for three people: a husband, a wife, and our Lord. When two people have given their lives to the Lord, then they can give themselves to each other. The sickness of so many marriages is exposed at exactly this point. A great Christian marriage is the unrestricted giving of mind, emotion, will and soul to another, as if given to Christ. A marriage is most Christian, not when it is free of any problems or difficulties, but when two persons love each other and give to each other as they have been loved and given to by Christ. Then the differences of personality can be blended, the defensiveness of our own rights can be healed, the hurts done to us can be forgiven. When two minds are yielded to the guidance of Christ, two emotional natures are surrendered to express the love of Christ, two wills are committed to discern and do the will of Christ, two souls are galvanized to seek the Kingdom of God together, and two bodies are given freely to satisfy and enjoy each other—that's the expression of God's intention for marriage. It's what Paul Tournier calls "total marriage."

Jesus reminded the people, "So they are no longer two, but one." What keeps us from oneness in marriage is sin. But what do you do with that sin of separateness and bristled individualism? Everyone who is married knows something which debilitates that oneness.

There are four things that work for Mary Jane and me: honesty, vulnerability, working contracts, and initiative love. When I begin with myself and not my wife's faults, I know what I must do. When I am honest before God, for whom I was created, and allow him to show me what I am like, then I see what I have done to break the oneness he intended for us. Often it is helpful each week or at least each month to take a clean piece of paper, and allow God to guide my writing of the things I am and do to debilitate our marriage.

But the next step is most difficult for me. Vulnerability means that the things I have confessed to God must be confessed to my wife. It's easy for me to tell God what I should have been, but to humble myself before my wife is extremely difficult. But when I do, it opens conversation and makes way for healing and new beginnings.

But suppose you are willing to do that and your mate isn't? It doesn't matter! Do it because of love for Christ, for yourself, but most of all, do it for your wife or husband. There is no greater gift than a humble and contrite "you" whatever the other person chooses to do with your gift. At least you will have gone to the uttermost in seeking a depth relationship.

A third thing which helps us is to express things we do and which no longer work for a happy relationship and work out new arrangements for behavioral change.

Marriage is more than a contract, yet a great marriage has contractual dimensions. Many people find it helpful to clarify with their mates what they need and expect from their marriages. It can be creative to write out these expectations and come to a viable agreement about them. Hidden agendas are destructive. But when two people can talk out what they want, then both need never be in the dark about what each anticipates. Often life's changing demands and the evolving of our personalities necessitate a re-negotiation of these hopes and dreams. When this happens, two people in marriage need to talk about aspects of their life together which are no longer fulfilling or satisfactory. Then a new agreement can be hammered out and tried together.

Most difficulties in marriage come from unexpressed desires and uncommunicated hopes and dreams. When these are brought out into the open, a realizable new agreement can be worked out for the future. This needs to be done repeatedly and often. We need to learn the Christian art of negotiation in marriage and to be free to express the undeniables without which we cannot live and the secondary things we are willing to do as "trade offs" for things we want. A healthy marriage is punctuated by lots of these bartering sessions! Ideals must be spelled out.

But the above three secrets are ineffective without initiative love. That's the willingness to be first in openness about your faults. Also, it is the freedom to act on what God has shown you to do to be graciously loving.

Affirmation is the composite of all this. It is the key of a creative marriage. We don't get married to straighten out another person or reshape him to our specifications, but to affirm that person's uniqueness and value. A good test of whether you should marry is if you feel you can affirm that person in his strengths and in his efforts to grow in his weaknesses. If not, don't get married.

"Wait a minute!" you say. "Does that also mean that if you

can't affirm a person you should not stay married or are justified in getting divorced?"

That leads us to the third dynamic insight we find in this passage from Mark. There is one thing Jesus accepts as the basis of divorce: hardness of heart. That happens . . . to some "good" Christians. Whatever we say about divorce must be in the context of the fact that there are many divorced people who are living together in marriage. The divorce may be spiritual or intellectual or volitional or physical or a combination of all these, but it is divorce nonetheless. It is the realization of the divorced dimensions of our marriages that makes married people tender in their judgments of people who are legally divorced.

There is no realistic, healthy way of dealing with divorce other than the blatant, bold statement of Jesus' truth: divorce is sin. He called it hardness of heart and clearly stated that Moses gave the commandment of divorce because of this rigidness of people's hearts. Divorce was a recognition of sin, not an acceptance of fickle changeability.

It's all the sentimental rationalization equaling cheap grace that makes it so difficult for divorced people in the church. There's seldom a cleansing, a confession, a contrition. We shut up a person in his or her remorse. Anyone who's honest with himself would be the first to admit failure . . . even if that failure was the inability to deal with an ex-mate's gross failure. Until people are given the freedom to admit the inadequacy, the incompatibility, the lack of communication which caused the separation, there is either facile absolution or subtle judgment, without the washing of the wound. We are too quick to sew up the gaping cut in people's psyches before the cause of the failure has been recognized and removed.

Our ministry to divorced people is to treat them not as lepers with some contagious disease, but as people whose failure is not unlike our own, though ours may be in a different realm of human experience. Remember that any unwillingness to deal graciously with human failure is a telltale sign of unforgiven regions in us. I find that people who are most severe with divorcees are those who are not making it in their own marriages or have unconfessed sins burning in the cauldrons of their own secret memories.

But what shall we do with Jesus' very incisive word about the divorcee marrying another person? It's there. We cannot tear it out of our Bibles! "Whoever divorces his wife and marries another, commits adultery against her; and if she divorces her husband and marries another, she commits adultery."

Several things must be kept clear. The Jewish law allowed a man to divorce his wife with the simple writing of a writ of divorce. Jesus' reply to the disciples makes clear that he holds men and women equally responsible. In this, as in so many other ways, he elevated women to the position of equality they held from creation. But what did Jesus mean about the divorced living in adultery?

My conclusion, after long study and prayer, is that Jesus wanted to underline what he had said about the sanctity of marriage. Divorce was an accommodation of human weakness, and it violates the divine ideal of marriage. But here Jesus is saying something more: Anyone who divorces a person with the intention of marrying another causes the person he marries to live in adultery.

I personally will never marry couples who have fallen in love while either person was married to someone else. When the precipitation of the divorce was the relationship between the two, the new union is never healthy. That's very different from facing the inability to work out a marriage, confessing it as sin, and then allowing God's grace through the Cross to do its full healing. I believe that after the healing hiatus has taken place and a person has begun a new life of dependence on the Spirit, then God can, out of sheer grace, give him a new person to marry according to the real purpose of marriage. Else what can we say about our forgiveness and new beginnings as new creatures of Christ in the new creation of grace?

If you have been divorced, the question is, "Have I faced the sin involved, confessed it to Christ, and asked him for a new life?" Or if you know people who have been divorced, "Have you been Christ's love to them, giving them freedom to admit the hurt and remorse, and then liberating them to begin again?"

This ambience of care for persons and not for categories or myths of success or failure in marriage gives us the basis of the Church's ministry to those who have what I want to designate as the calling of the single. By this I mean something more than monastic celibacy. There are those who believe they have been called to sacrifice for Christ and remain single for his glory and his ministry. But that's not what I mean. I believe that the Church must make room for those who believe they are called by Christ to be his person but, either by circumstance or situation, have never married.

Single people can be called by God! They should not be given secondary positions or prejudiced against by those who feel that there must be something wrong with a person who is not married. The issue for every single person is the degree of openness he or she has to God's guidance. We must never defend our position, married or unmarried, but be open to whatever God guides. If there is emotional sickness which causes us to be unable to marry, that should be faced and healed, not in order to be married, but because God wills wholeness for every one of his children. Often the causes of the single state are encrusted habits or deviate behavior. God wants to heal that. Others are single because of personality or physical characteristics. God wants to liberate that, but never just to get a person ready for marriage.

The questions for the single persons are, "Am I open to God's healing and growth? Am I willing to face myself as I am and allow my personality to be reformed around the person of Christ? Am I willing to remain single or be married, however God guides? Am I willing to love him more than any person I might marry and leave the results to him?"

Again, the questions for the Church are, "Do we, by attitude, program, or emphasis, make singles feel like second-class saints? Do we talk so much about the family that they feel dimensions of God's love are reserved for family life? What do we do to minister to the loneliness of singles?"

I suspect that the New Testament church did not have couples groups and singles classes! My picture of the church alive is where people are persons in a common quest for life in Christ. We "thing-it" when people are used and not loved. The fellowship of God's people is meant to be therapeutic. It is where the grace of God meets all of our needs and enables us to grow. The area where we all need help is in appreciating our sexuality as a gift from God. When Christ lives in us, we are free to affirm the masculinity and femininity of each person without the temptation to misuse that for our own ends.

In that kind of church, the fellowship can be the center in which we seek to discover, model, and encourage the best that God has for all of us. We can freely talk about marriage and help each other maximize our marriages. But we can also talk about being God's person as a single and affirm the calling of each single to be God's person. We can talk about sexual problems and get practical help. Homosexuality and lesbianism can be faced and God's healing mediated.

This presses us toward being a church where people are not only loved but also liked. One of the most touching things a friend ever said to me was, "Lloyd, I not only love you, I like you!" The true fellowship of God's people is where loving goes the second mile of liking each other, husbands and wives, married and single, children and adults. How many people in your life and mine feel liked as an extension of our love?

We are back to where we began. The essential calling of all of us, the only source of our meaning, the unique antidote to loneliness, the one basis of our satisfaction, is the Lord himself. No person, in or out of marriage, or in any of life's relationships, can or should provide the fulfillment which Christ alone can give.

That's what the Pharisees could not grasp . . . and that's what you and I need most to learn.

CHAPTER 26

WHEN YOUR HUMP IS CAUGHT IN THE EYE

Mark 10:17–31

When was the last time you had a good laugh at yourself? Jesus had a healthy sense of humor and drove home some of the most penetrating and disturbing things he had to say with side-splitting laughter. In the tensest of situations he used a comic relief to relax his listeners so they could deal with the truth he wanted to communicate. True humor is the exposure of incongruity and irrationalities. Often Jesus would get his disciples laughing at themselves and their grim grip on life. Nowhere is this more evident than in this particular passage, and in no other place does Jesus' humor shatter pomposity and pride with greater wit.

It was a very tense moment. The very issues of life had been crystallized and it was more than the disciples could handle. It was their own biography they saw dramatized before them, when the Rich Young Ruler broke his reserve and knelt before Jesus, blurting out the existential question, "What must I do to inherit eternal life?" The way Jesus dealt with the man prevented them from writing off what he said. Jesus' love carved his words on their own hearts. When he told the young man that his riches were standing in the way, the drama became painfully personal. And when the man turned away sorrowfully, and Jesus did not run after him to change the terms of commitment, the clouds of an immense seriousness gathered around them.

But Jesus knew what was happening to his dour disciples. In private he gave them a humorous saying, a pithy parable, that must have liberated them with uproarious laughter.

"Children, how hard it is for those who trust in riches to enter the Kingdom of God."

Now catch the warmth of his voice and the twinkle of his eye as he said humorously, "It is easier for a camel to go through the eye of a needle than for a rich man to enter the Kingdom of God."

Laughter relaxed them, and the laser beam of truth struck its target. They heard and understood, all too clearly. Could it be that Jesus' humor had been pent up in this whole drama with the Rich Young Ruler and now burst out on the disciples? He was not laughing at the man, to be sure, but the astounding absurdity of the situation is humorous, isn't it? What could be more ridiculous than putting more importance on riches than the richness of eternal life now and forever? The tragic and the humorous are always a razor's edge apart. We want to cry and laugh all at the same time. Jesus wants us to do both right now as we find ourselves trying to thread our own hump through the eye. This is our story! And the joke is on us. If we can laugh about it, there's a chance we can face the truth and do something about it!

How long had the urge been growing within the Rich Young Ruler? We can imagine that he had been on the circumference of the crowd which encircled the inner band of disciples around Jesus. He had heard him talk about the Kingdom of God, had seen him model the power available to its citizens, and had seen life as he hoped to live it. Then, one day the edge of the crowd was no longer a satisfactory place for him. He wanted the close communion with Jesus the disciples had; he wanted to respond; he longed to be a follower. An undeniable urgency grew within him and blossomed into an importune impetuousness. He burst through the crowd, fell at Jesus' feet and cried out the words which he had rehearsed thousands of times in his inner heart, "Good Teacher, what must I do to inherit eternal life?"

The salutation and the request expose the man! "Good Teacher," a fulsome compliment, indeed. Solicitous; manipulative; insecure. There are ways of addressing a person which immediately put him in our debt. The young man tried to take over and control the conversation and set up the basis on which Jesus would answer out of debt for the compliment. The scales of obligation are loaded and the response implied. But Jesus was neither put off nor on by these clever devices.

John Calvin's interpretation of Jesus' reply is telling: "Thou falsely callest me Good Master unless thou acknowledges that I came from God." For Jesus goodness was a quality of God and he could be called "Good" only if a person accepted that what he said and did was because God was incarnate in him and he was truly the Messiah. The man needed to understand and accept whom he was addressing before his request had any meaning.

Our egregious verbalisms in addressing God in prayer are often beyond our willingness to follow through. "Gracious Father," we say; yet we resist his grace. "Oh Lord" we pray, and are startled by the implications of his Lordship. "King of all life!" we piously intone, but who is willing to be an obedient subject? We cannot con our way into communion!

That's especially true if we dare to ask the question of the Rich Young Ruler. It is the deepest question on all our hearts. Our need for an answer is the reason we search for meaning so desperately. Many of us have seen the power, the love, the wisdom of Jesus. What must we do to make his life our own? Eternal life is not just quantity, but quality, a dynamic, not just a duration.

Note the young man's use of the word *inherit*. It implies right, deserving. Probably all his wealth was an inheritance, a legacy of his father's labor. Now he wanted to inherit something more. Did he want Jesus' gift with the same hand-me-down ease? Was eternal life to be added to his collection of valuables? Was he able to give up all he had for a true inheritance?

Jesus' attitude toward us is focused in his response to this "up and outer." Mark indicates that when Jesus looked at him, he loved him. That's how Jesus receives us as we break through our reserve and dare to ask for his gift of true life. It is sheer grace.

But that kind of grace clarifies issues. Jesus throws the whole conversation back on the young man. He quotes the ethical side of the tablet of the Ten Commandments. How gentle of Jesus! He knew the man's problem was at the heart of the first commandment—he did indeed have other gods before the Lord God. Jesus afforded him the affirmation of his positive response about his strengths. "All these I have done since childhood."

Now to the crux of the matter. Jesus strips the man of confidence in his lifelong ethical obedience. How much has he cared? How had he used his riches for human need? What he had failed to do in living out the ethical demands of the very commandments for which he had protested faithfulness, now stood between him and the life he urgently desired.

"You lack one thing." What an incisive communicator Jesus was!

The Greek verb which translates Jesus' word for lack is *husteros,* meaning behind, to be too late, to come short, to fail. There was one thing that made the young man's life a failure—one miscalculation will keep him behind, tardy for the God-appointed hour. There was one distortion in his constellation of values which kept him from realizing the reason he was born!

Jesus knew. The man's riches kept him from God. They were an extension of him. What he owned, now owned him. His possessions were inextricably intertwined in his own being—the very threads of the fiber of his nature. He did not know where his personality ended and his things began. His possessions possessed him.

Then Jesus told him he must perform a self-surgery on a gigantic malignancy within him: his love of riches. That could be healed only by a radical act. He must go and sell all that he has and give it to the poor. No wonder his countenance fell! All youthful enthusiasm to join a movement was replaced by a somber, gloomy expression. The Scripture means he had a lowering face.

The cost was too high; he did what every one of us would probably do: He turned and went away sorrowfully. He didn't want eternal life that much. How sad! How painful!

The fund raiser in all of us wants to jump into the embarrassing breach and run after the man. Change the terms! Think what a man with resources and influence like his could do for the Kingdom! "Jesus, go after him! Change the terms. Nobody's perfect. Perhaps if you let him join us, he will grow in understanding how to be a good steward of his riches."

Now Jesus' eyes turn on us. Why are we so sympathetic of this confused young man? Does he know about us too? Yes, he knows. We are the wealthy of the world. And which of us could stand the test? We, too, are part and parcel of our acquired securities. I believe that we miss the full intent of this passage unless we can cry out, "Lord, I am just like that man! I am no more ready to sell all and give it to the poor than he was!"

This is the danger point of exposition of this passage. We can easily evade this point by saying that riches here represent whatever it is that keeps us from following Christ. Anything to get the spotlight off our acquisitive materialism, our kingdom of thingdom. But it won't work! The issue here is our competing loyalty to our possessions. The acid test is whether we are willing to sell everything and give the money to the poor.

No wonder Jesus introduced a little humor to loosen up the disciples. A camel through the eye of a needle? How ludicrous! How impossible! We laugh and our laughter softens us up to hear the truth. Our love of riches could keep us out of the Kingdom; we could miss life in our lust of living; we may acquire everything and end up with nothing.

No wonder the disciples cried out, "Who then can be saved?" That's just where Jesus wanted them—and us. It's difficult for us to endure that excruciating moment of dependence, of realizing that our relationship with Jesus is not justified by something we have done or given. We dare not presume or take our salvation for granted. It's never easy to realize eternal life when our loyalty is sold out to temporal life. God alone will have to decide whether that entangling alliance will cost us our souls. "With men it is impossible, but not with God; for all things are possible with God." Grace again. Not for one moment does he allow us to believe that we could do or give enough to earn our right with him.

But like Peter we still try. "Lo, we have left everything and followed you." Sounds like our self-justifying prayers, doesn't it? We all want some end to sacrifice; some boundary line we can reach and exclaim, "Now Lord, I have deserved your love. I am worthy." But Jesus' response is not unlike the one he gave to the Rich Young Ruler. All that we have and are is Christ's gift. There's no place for boisterous pride. One final test of our life stands irreplaceably: "But many that are first will be last, and the last first."

How's your hump feel in the pressure of the eye of the needle? Again it's time to laugh, how humorous we look! The eye size is not going to change. The humps will have to go. First the love of riches and then lots more of the riches themselves.

CHAPTER 27

LOVE NEVER GIVES UP

Mark 10:32–12:11

Think of the people you find it most difficult to love. Consider the situations in which it is most painful to be a loving person. Reflect for a moment on the organizations in which you find it most problematic to discern and do what love demands. What are your honest feelings about these people and groups?

Ever want to give up? Have you ever wanted to wash your hands of them, to turn on your heel and walk away from the responsibility of loving? Is the cost ever too high, the demands too great? Are you ever tempted to say, "I've tried my best, done all I can, given all I've got, I give up"?

Now, to the most personal question. Has the most difficult person in your life ever been you, yourself? Do you ever get impatient with yourself? Have you tried to change and realized little difference? Have you started hundreds of self-improvement programs only to find out that you are back in the same old patterns? Are you ever dejected with the realization that you are just not the person you want to be? Ever tempted to give up on yourself? Could it be that our most difficult person lives inside our own skin?

If we have honestly answered these questions, we are now in touch with reality, life as it really is, not the illusion we often pretend. Now, we can go to Jerusalem with Jesus. Jerusalem was reality for him. It was the frowning fortress of his enemies, the center of resistance, the nemesis of impossible people and difficult situations. As we walk with him the last miles to Jerusalem, join in the band of pilgrims in the triumphal entry, feel his anguish over his people and share his indignation over what Israel's leaders were doing to distort God's purposes, we can learn the excruciating dimensions of true love. This is the reason I have combined the last portion of Mark's chapter ten, all of chapter eleven, and the first portion of chapter twelve into this exposition. Here is love on two legs striding into confrontation and conflict with the raw faith that God would have the final word, the ultimate victory, the eternal vindication.

We, too, have a Jerusalem. It's that person, problem, or perplexity that we would rather not face. It's the realm of resistance, hostility, conflict. We can understand what Jesus went through in those last days on the way up to and into Jerusalem only if we focus on *our* Jerusalem. As we study what happened to him, we can discover what we are to do. He comes alongside us and says, "I will go to your Jerusalem with you. We will face it together as I faced mine so long ago."

Now we can understand the Scripture: "And they were on the road, going up to Jerusalem, and Jesus was walking ahead of them; and they were amazed, and those who followed were afraid." He's out ahead of us now, beckoning us on to our Jerusalem. Here is reality—life as it is. Here are the people and problems we submerged, sublimated, struggled to forget. We feel like the disciples, amazed at his determination and afraid at what might happen. But, with him in his Jerusalem and ours, we are about to learn the dynamics of a love that never gives up.

Jesus went to Jerusalem because it was God's will for him. It was the reason he was born. He knew that it would mean the cross: "Behold, we are going up to Jerusalem; and the Son of man will be delivered to the chief priests and the scribes, and they will condemn him to death, and deliver him to the Gentiles, and they will mock him and spit upon him and scourge him, and kill him; and after three days he will rise."

Jesus' commitment to Jerusalem was based on two absolutely necessary elements of a love that never gives up. He was convinced that it was God's will for him to go and he knew that his death would be superseded by the resurrection. The worst that man would do to him would be superseded by the best that God could do. Those two ingredients must also be the basis of our commitment. Don't go into your Jerusalem until it is God's undeniable will for you! But when it is his time to face reality, face it knowing that he will validate your commitment with his victory.

We are not to go about masochistically searching for our Jeru-salems. But when they emerge on the surface of our minds and can no longer be denied, that's God's timing to set our faces to reality. Whether it's something in ourselves that must be changed, a broken relationship which must be healed, a painful problem that must be faced, a sick situation in church or society, there is a right time to move. It must be God's time. But when it's his time, we dare not turn back!

Jesus' Jerusalem was to be the site of man's salvation. All of his-tory moved toward this crucial event of reconciliation. That's why every man's Jerusalem is the commitment to face whatever in our-selves, our relationships, or our world is a denial and contradiction to Christ's plan and purpose for us.

Jesus could have turned away from his Jerusalem at the fork in the road in Peraea. He could have gone back to Nazareth and as-sumed a comfortable position of a teacher or pleasant spiritual dreamer. But he would not have been the Savior of the world! So too, we can turn away. We can refuse to obey. But what happens then? Compromise, conditional discipleship, an ineffective emo-tionalized religion. Many Christians are piously troubled people be-cause they have turned away from the Jerusalem for which they were born!

But that takes courage. That's the second dynamic for Jeru-salem. God will give us power to do the things he has willed. His Holy Spirit will be our only comfort as we face reality and dare to deal with the contradictions in ourselves and life around us.

And we must be willing to go to Jerusalem in spite of the lack of courage in the people around us. Jesus' disciples did not under-stand him. James and John were still arguing about their positions of power as they walked with Jesus on the last excruciating steps to Jerusalem. We should never go into our Jerusalem because of someone else's vision or lack of it. Intimate guidance from our Lord alone will suffice. Jesus is with us on the road. What else do we need to know? Each time we are tempted to turn back he says, "I know how you feel; they didn't understand me either."

Jesus' entry into Jerusalem was a dramatic enactment of his mes-siahship. There was no doubt in his mind. The humble riding upon an ass, the Messianic Scripture he fulfilled and the response of the people all blended into his decisive declaration that he was the Messiah. And we are most the Messiah's people when we go into our Jerusalem. The reason Jesus' love would not give up is because God had not given up. Neither can we!

That courage issues into the next aspect of the dynamics for Jerusalem: confrontation! Love that never gives up is not sloppy sentimentalism that says, "Oh well, things have always been this way. Why sweat it? You've got to learn to accept things as they are!"

Not so for Jesus. He entered Jerusalem and went into the temple; and when he looked around at everything, he saw Jerusalem in all of its sad denial of being the city of God. He observed what was being done in the temple, and felt the burning hostility of the leaders of Israel against him. Can you imagine what was in his mind and spirit that night before in Bethany? Can you feel the hurt he felt over what was being done in the name of God? To go into Jerusalem with Jesus is to see our lives and our society through his eyes. Where are the contradictions, the distortions, the injustices?

Have you ever hurt with the heart of Jesus?

Recently, I passed out cards in the worship service for people to complete the following statement, "My greatest need right now is . . ." One person's response indicated he had never gone to Jerusalem. The statement he made was, "My greatest need is for more doctrine, not all of us are hurting people." I think I know what he meant. He was trying to say that not everyone has had a painful childhood or is faced with life's difficulties. He wanted more ideas about the faith to fortify his stability. But what about the hurt in others and in the world? I wonder if that person had ever spent the night with Jesus in Bethany, aching over the hurt of the world. If he had, he would hurt over the things which hurt Jesus, and that would be the basis of his companionship with Jesus on the day of confrontation to follow.

Love that never gives up is a love that cares enough to confront things as they are. Jesus loved his people so deeply that he would not finesse them with pleasant generalities. What Jesus did that first day in Jerusalem after the triumphal entry is what he does in you and me. Any authentic encounter with Jesus means confrontation. The basic problem he faced in Jerusalem is what he confronts in us. The enacted parable of the cleansing of the temple crystallizes the issue.

What shall we do with his anger expressed in the temple? The problem was what Israel had done with God's house which was for the worship of all peoples. But be careful how you interpret what he did and why he did it! There were four courts in the temple. But it was the outer Court of the Gentiles that became the focus of his concern. This was to be the place where non-Hebrews could come to worship. The fact that this area had degenerated into a place where pigeons were sold for sacrifice and foreign money was changed to be used to pay the temple tax was a brash denial of the purpose of the Court of the Gentiles. It was to be a place for God to meet people from other races. The unholy hucksters who made this a marketplace no longer cared about the potential convert. Pilgrims who came to worship were at the mercy of their inflated exchanges and prices. What was sacred and holy to God was brashly turned into booths for bartering and stables for animals. The noise was deafening.

Many of us find it difficult to deal with Jesus' actions that day in the temple. They expose a side of him we don't want to think about and it forces us to realize a dimension of grace which we often reject. Jesus' actions were in keeping with the justice of God. All through Israel's history God had had to invade times of apostasy with punishment and retribution for his people's faithlessness and lack of obedience. God didn't get converted in the incarnation. There is not a different God exposed in Jesus. This is the same Lord of justice and righteousness we meet on every page of Scripture.

But if we follow the truth that we also are Jesus' Jerusalem, what would he find in us that would have to be driven out? What attitudes, feelings, hidden sins, practices, prejudices and customs would have to go? What about the Church? What are we doing in the Court of the Gentiles in our congregation? Are we ever so busy with our own cherished religiosity that we forget that we are blessed to be a blessing to those who come to find him?

Don't ever try to clean up someone else's temple before you have allowed Jesus to drive the distortions out of your own. We are God's temple as Paul reminds us: "Do you not know that you are God's temple and that God's spirit dwells in you? If anyone destroys God's temple, God will destroy him. For God's temple is holy, and that temple you are."

Once we have allowed Jesus to cleanse our temple and experience daily cleansing and forgiveness, then we can become constructive confronters of anything which is wrong in the life around us.

Confrontation in our Jerusalem must follow some basic guidelines:

1. Is the thing we want to change in ourselves and others motivated by forgiving love?
2. Do we will the ultimate good of everyone involved?
3. Have we established that it is God's love which has fostered our concern?

Many of us shrink from confrontation. We try to convince ourselves that toleration is an expression of love. Not so! We drift into mediocrity because we do not demand the best of ourselves and others. But Christ-centered confrontation of people or situations must be done with the gracious sharing of the concern God has put on our heart, not a petulant manipulation to control.

In my persistent search for authentic Christianity, the other day I met a man who told me about the joy and freedom he had discovered in making a commitment to Christ. At first, I groaned inwardly. The familiar language set off a charge of uneasiness within me. Was this just another wordy Christian settled in the warm bosom of Jesus? My disgust at irrelevant commitment to Christ which motivates little concern for people and the world, prompted a pointed question, "And what difference has this made in your everyday life?"

His answer was slow in coming. He thought long and hard. I respected this. Then I listened to his answer and was deeply moved: "Commitment to Christ for me means responsibility."

"And just what do you mean by that?" I asked.

"Just this. I am now becoming a responsible person. I am responsible to use the resources which God has given me to act. My church, my home, my vocation, my community, are now the realms of responsibility. I cannot rest as long as the people in my sphere of influence don't know the love and forgiveness of Christ. Before, I didn't really care about people or what happened to them! Now everything is important to me—from housing, education, integration, community needs, to personal problems. Anything which troubles people, troubles me! I often say: The task is so great, what is one man? What is one man among one hundred and ninety million Americans? . . . among three billion earth dwellers? One man on one planet in one solar system in one galaxy? But then I stop that futile line of thought. God is the Creator of all these persons and planetary systems. He has created me and given his Son to call me back to himself. If the Governor of all creation knows me, loves me, and wants me to be involved in the struggles of man, I am willing to do it. God has designed that his will on earth will always be effected through persons, and I am willing for his will to be done through me, even though I do not foresee all the meaning while I pass through my life."

How wonderful, I thought to myself. When I heard this man speak with conviction about his concern for people and the practical, specific ways he was involved with Christ in a ministry of reconciliation, I knew that I had met an authentic Christian.

I pressed him to spell out for me what had happened to him that made the difference.

"Well," he said, "my faith became real when I accepted responsibility for the world in which I live. Up to that time I was a defeated Christian. I felt guilty about my faults and anxious about our sick world. Then I realized that my feelings didn't make any difference, and each week I would make some specific effort to reproduce my faith in someone else and try to become effective for change in some social problem. What a difference this has made in the way I feel!"

This man has learned an exciting truth about confrontation in Jerusalem. Dr. William Parker, formerly of Redlands University, says, "Feelings follow behavior. What we do causes us to feel the way we feel. The only way to change our feelings is to change our behavior." This man was a frustrated Christian until his behavior was guided by his beliefs. The excitement which was so apparent in his life was that his life was now consistent with the purpose for which he had been created—to be a man for others. Dr. William Glasser, in his challenging book, *Reality Therapy*, says, "There is no mental illness, there is irresponsibility. Irresponsible persons have one thing in common: they deny the reality of the world around them." The road to emotional health is to be found taking a specific, creative step in acknowledging, facing, and changing the patterns of our life.

Irresponsibility is a mark of impotent Christianity. If we hear the imperatives of Christ without purposefully shaping our life, relationships and culture around his will and way, we will be sick.

We cannot deny our nature: We were created to produce and re-produce. When we fail to do so, we wither. The reason there is so much emotional sickness in the Church is that we have frag-mented belief from behavior. The words of Jesus, the preaching of the Bible and life together in the Church, only add to our guilt. Until we become responsible, the gospel will be a sword in our bones. Our preoccupation with the material struggle of life, the false self-assurance which comes from achievement, the distorted security which comes from respectability, all lead to the moral sclerosis of irresponsibility. The result is compromise with our ideals. It becomes easier to make peace with social wrong, racial injustices, and political ills. But, far more deadly, we give up our dreams for ourselves, family, and vocation. Life settles into com-fortable ruts. That's what Jesus said of Israel, and that's the point of the confrontation at the fig tree.

The parable of the fig tree is the parable of divine impatience with religious irresponsibility. This is another enacted parable. It is by far the most difficult of Jesus' parables. To study it carefully is to be disturbed and unsettled. This is a hard saying for our soft ears. It is not easily interpreted nor easily forgotten once it has been interpreted. This negative-sounding parable, when considered in context, proclaims five very positive truths: life is God-given for the purpose of fruitfulness; faith in God is the secret of fruitful-ness; prayer is the sustenance of fruitfulness; character is the con-tent of fruitfulness; and reproduction is the result of fruitfulness.

Jesus' actions were dramatic and his words were hyperbolic. He wanted to make a very important point in a way the disciples would never forget. Life is God-given for the purpose of fruitful-ness. Man was created to be responsible. To drive home his point, Jesus used the strongest Hebrew metaphors possible. Israel had envisioned herself as God's tree in the vineyard of the promised land. She had always thought of herself as privileged and special. Psalm 80 proclaims the truth:

> Thou didst bring a vine out of Egypt;
>   thou didst drive out the nations and plant it.
> Thou didst clear the ground for it;
>   it took deep root and filled the land.
> The mountains were covered with its shade,
>   The mighty cedars with its branches,

It sent out its branches to the sea,
and its shoots to the River.

Isaiah clarifies the same symbolism:

For the vineyard of the Lord of Hosts
Is the home of Israel,
And the men of Judah are his pleasant planting.

On that day of confrontation in Jerusalem, Jesus noticed a fig
tree with leaves. Two facts made this most unusual. Leaves on fig
trees sometimes accompany, usually follow, but never precede, the
figs. Added to this, the time of the year for figs is late May or
early June; this was Passover Week, sometime between the last of
March and the middle of April. However, this fig tree had leaves
on it. Perhaps it had been planted in an advantageous position—
sheltered from the wind, favored by moisture and sunlight, and as
the fruit of the fig tree appears before the leaves, it was natural to
expect it to have at least some fruit. But when Jesus came up to
it, he found to his surprise that it had none.

How very much like Israel! There were leaves to be observed,
but no fruit to be eaten. The disciples got the point, and so do
we. What dreadful words of commentary on the fruitlessness of
irresponsible religion: "He found nothing but leaves." The leaves
signaled the possibility of fruit for the hungry, but there was no
fruit. The leaves of religious rite, rules, and regulations suggested
the fruit of knowledge and love of God, but the hungry peoples
of the world, longing for meaning and purpose, would find only
leaves. What fruit had Jesus wanted to find from the privileged
tree of Israel? He had said it himself earlier: "The weightier matter of the law—righteousness, justice and love." Their religion had
produced leaf and not fruit. The leaves were to be a natural part
of the tree, to benefit the tree and assist in the production of fruit.
They were to be auxiliary and subsidiary to the production of
fruit. In this case, and in the case of Israel, there was such a dis-
proportionate exuberance of growth that all the life of the tree runs
to leaf, and there is no fruit to be found on it.

Think of the condition of Israel. She prided herself upon nominal, external, hereditary conviction with a system of revelation; they
trusted in mere ritualism, they had ossified faith in God to theology
and degraded morality into rules and regulations. They thought

that because they had been born Jews and because there was daily sacrifice going on in the temple, and because they had rabbis who could split hairs *ad infinitum,* they were God's chosen. There was neither character nor concern for others. Here is the same message as in the cleansing of the temple. Pride led to separatism from the world to which they were to feed the fruit of righteousness, and rigidity led to rejection of God's Son himself.

But are we any different? Our nominal Christianity, masquerading as the true thing, is nothing but leaves. We are baptized, confirmed, churched, Christianized, but there is little fruit in a hungry twentieth century! We have a church we cherish, religious formalities we favor, ideas we intellectualize, but where is the fruit of character in each of us—Christ-motivated concern? Unless all that we do together in worship, fellowship, and study produces the fruit of Christlike character in each of us, and Christ-motivated concern for people through us, we are nothing but a fig tree with misleading leaves. Life is given to each of us and to our church, as it was to ancient Israel, for fruitfulness.

Jesus had much to say about a fruitful life throughout his message. His words to the disciples near the end of the Sermon on the Mount still rang in their minds: "Beware of false prophets, who come to you in sheep's clothing but inwardly are ravenous wolves. You will know them by their fruits. Are grapes gathered from thorns, or figs from thistles? So, every sound tree bears good fruit, but the bad tree bears evil fruit. A sound tree cannot bear evil fruit, nor can a bad tree bear good fruit. Every tree that does not bear good fruit is cut down and thrown into the fire. Thus you will know them by their fruits" (Matt. 7:15–20).

The thought is clear. All that we have received from God's providence is for fruit-bearing. The challenge is also clear. If we are not fruitful, we will be cut off.

We have been placed in the world with other persons at this time for responsible management of God's world. For what are we responsible? Simply, our space, time, and resources. Space in this context refers basically to the area in which human relations occur. We have been placed in a physical body for which we are responsible and given a mind with which we are to guide our responsibilities. We live in families for which we are responsible. What happens to those around us is our responsibility. We cannot negate

it. We also work. The people around us and the conditions of
their life are our concern. We cannot escape it. We live in a community. Where there is wrong, it is our realm of involvement.

Time is also our concern. The years of our life are to be used
wisely. We cannot escape the present time, not by flight into fan-
tasy or grim rehearsal of the past. It is our inescapable responsibility to think, feel, and live out our knowledge of Jesus Christ in
every moment of time. The Bible speaks of "chronos" and "kairos"
time. One is succession of time; the other is the event-centered
right time of God's intervention. We are to live faithfully in the
succession of days and weeks, always aware of the possibility of God
breaking into this with a special opportunity to accomplish his will.

Resources are also part of responsible management. Here we
need to be honest about all that has been placed at our disposal and
see ways of using what we have for God's glory. Everything we
have is a trust. It is given us as equipment for ministry with Christ
in the world. It is not ours! It belongs to him. We are only man-
agers of what is God's. Responsible management is the fruit of the
gift of life. We are alive now in time and space. We cannot escape.
We are to bear fruit.

Jesus cursed the fig tree. "May no one ever eat fruit from you
again." This was not just petulant anger, this was a statement of
fact. There was no fruit to be eaten. The tree no longer fulfilled
its purpose for being.

Does God ever lose patience with us? Is he ever done with any
of us? Is there no second chance?

Jesus' dialogue with the disciples about this points us to an answer and a hope. Faith in God is the secret of fruitfulness. When
the disciples and Jesus passed by the fig tree the next morning,
they saw it had withered away to the roots. Peter was astonished
. . . and frightened: "Master, look! The fig tree you cursed has
withered!"

Jesus answered simply, "Have faith in God!" What did that have
to do with a withered fig tree? Everything. They too would wither
in fruitlessness. The only hope was to have faith in God. Faith is
response to God's love. It opens the self to God's Spirit in thankful
response. This kind of openness would produce in them the kind
of fruit God had ordained for man. Israel had become self-assertive
and self-dependent. The disciples, by faith, could become self-

surrendered and transformed. Through faith they would find freedom to see themselves and seek forgiveness. God's love would then
produce in them the fruit of Christlike character.

Later, at the Passover, the fruit of faithful abiding in Christ was
explained: "I am the true vine, and my Father is the vinedresser.
Every branch of mine that bears no fruit, he takes away, and every
branch that does bear fruit he prunes, that it may bear more fruit.
You are already made clean by the word which I have spoken to
you. Abide in me, and I in you. As the branch cannot bear fruit
by itself, unless it abides in the vine, neither can you, unless you
abide in me. I am the vine, you are the branches. He who abides
in me, and I in him, he it is that bears much fruit, for apart from
me you can do nothing" (John 15:1-5).

Paul caught the significance of this in his letter to the Galatians.
The fruit of Christian character was the gift of the Spirit. When
we respond by faith, we experience the fruit of his indwelling
Spirit: "But the fruit of the Spirit is love, joy, peace, patience,
kindness, goodness, faithfulness, gentleness, self-control; against
such there is no law" (Gal. 5:22-23).

The fruit of our Christian character is not only God's demand,
it is his gift. We can receive by faith. Faith is the secret of fruitfulness.

But prayer is its sustenance. Strange that Jesus should talk about
removing mountains at a time like that. Yet the truth is inseparable
from the parable. In prayer the disciples would be given the power
to remove the mountainous obstacles which hindered them from
being fruitful. In Jesus' time, teachers were often called, "Mountain removers" because they could remove the mountains of ignorance and confusion from men's minds. Here Jesus shifts the
metaphor. In their conversations with God in prayer the disciples
could confess whatever impediments they had to fruitfulness. The
mountains of personality and habit which produced pretentious
leaves and no plentiful fruit could be removed. The pruning of their
lives could be accomplished if they would pray honestly. The promise is for a prayer for fruitfulness: "Therefore I tell you, whatever you ask in prayer, believe that you receive it, and you will"
(Mark 11:24).

The Christian character is the content of fruitfulness. God's will
is to make us like Jesus in thought, action, and reaction. This is
the essential fruit of the tree of life. This is not the result of self-

reformation efforts; it is the result of abiding in prayer and of removing the mountains by the power of God.

But the Christlike character results in concern for others and the world in which we live. Reproduction is the result of fruitfulness. The fruit of one Christian is another. We exist to reproduce. God communicates through people. He reaches those whom he wishes to know him through you and me. The Israelites failed to be communicators of God's grace. They wanted political power and prestige instead. We, too, like the privilege of being Christians without the cost of caring for people in order to communicate God's love, help them to know Christ, and stand with them as they grow. What do you communicate to people? Has anyone ever found the love of Christ through you? This is not the task of clergy alone . . . this is the legacy of the laity. Jesus goes on with pointed words about our relationships: "And whenever you stand praying, forgive, if you have anything against any one; so that your Father also who is in heaven may forgive you your trespasses" (Mark 11:25).

In essence it tells us that we are to be to others what Christ has been to us. We are to be forgiving, approachable people. This produces a permissive openness which attracts people and welcomes them into dialogue. When we are free of judgments and negative opinions about people, we can be used by the Spirit to love needy people. Genuine interest and concern for people grow when we let go of our plans and images and dare to love. We can ask questions, penetrate into values, exchange needs, and affirm life with people when this quality of forgiving freedom is ours. The Spirit is at work. All we need to do is get involved with people. He will show the way and give us the words to speak. Trust him! The fruit will flow.

The parable of divine discontent with human irresponsibility can never be completely understood without some thought given to its twin in Luke. Here the setting is different. The message is the same, but a tremendous hope is added. Here the fig tree is planted in a vineyard. The owner came to check the tree for three years and found no fruit. He ordered the vinedresser to cut it down, but the vinedresser pleaded with the owner: "And he answered him, 'Let it alone, sir, this year also, till I dig about it and put on manure. And if it bears fruit next year, well and good; but if not, you can cut it down' " (Luke 13:8-9).

There is the hopeful note. Perhaps we, too, have been unfruit-ful. But now we have a second chance. The bad ground around our lives can be loosened and fertilized and we can begin to fulfill our destiny to be fruitful.

The last dynamic for our Jerusalem is confidence in God's final victory. The last chapter always will be written by him. The para-ble of the wicked vinedressers has a bold truth to sustain us. It is Jesus' autobiographical parable. The owner of the vineyard was God; the vineyard was Israel; the vinedresser, the leaders of the people; the emissaries sent to collect the fruit of the vineyard, the prophets; the son, Jesus himself. The despicable behavior of the vinedressers is expressed by their assumption that the vineyard is theirs. What Israel did to the prophets and would soon do to the Messiah is clearly exposed. No scribe or Pharisee who heard the parable could have missed the point. But the ultimate truth of the parable which they did miss and which we dare not miss is found in Jesus' quotation of the passage from Psalm 118:22–23, which had clear Messianic implications: "The stone which the builders rejected has become the head of the corner; This is the Lord's doing; it is marvelous in our eyes."

The confidence which Jesus had in his Jerusalem and the hope for us in ours, is that though they destroyed the Son of the parable, he came back! The resurrection was God's final word. Here is love that never gives up! God is never finished. Nor are we. What hap-pens to us, whatever difficulties we face, God is not through with us. Out of our failures and frustrations he will bring resurrection. And we will be able to say, "This is the Lord's doing, and it is marvelous in our eyes."

CHAPTER 28

THE EXTRAVAGANCE OF LOVE

Mark 12:13-44

Strange, isn't it, how a little event in the seemingly insignificant daily round of life will suddenly bring into focus what has been churning under the surface of our consciousness for a long time. An incident which would hardly have meaning in the crucial demands of life quickly clarifies our thinking and we see things as they are.

It happens with people. We watch, listen, try to relate. Often what people do and say is an enigma to us. "Who are they really? What makes them tick?" Then in a simple act or expression, they play their trump card, and we know what's truly motivating, driving, or confusing them. We say, "That single thing tells me volumes. Now I see what was only a nebulous suspicion."

It happens with ourselves. As we try to understand ourselves with creative introspection, we often are an uncertain mixture of conflicting values and purposes. Then in some crisis or opportunity, we act or react, speak or are silent, and we see what we are really like. We say to ourselves, "Ah, that specific event, thought, or action truly shows what I am feeling down underneath. That reveals what kind of person I am!"

It happens with situations. We gather into our feelings and thoughts what is happening—not really clear as to what it all means. And then, without expecting it, something happens and we see the whole thing clearly as never before. Our thinking is crystallized, and we realize the situations for what they are.

This is what happened to Jesus in the seemingly insignificant event of the widow contributing her mite. Why was the contribution of one little, old widow so important? Others had given much more! Why did Jesus single her out and immortalize her so that the very words "widow's mite" should carry such profound meaning down two thousand years of history?

Jesus had been through days of grueling disputation with the legalistic Pharisees, the sly, compromising Herodians, the this-worldly Sadducees, the nit-picking, uncommitted scribes. At every turn he had been confronted with resistance, reticence, and reservation. Why did he have to convince people who should know and understand the very basics of the law of love and sacrifice? Why was it necessary for him to absorb their hostility? What was wrong? Why did the leaders react the way they did? Essentially, they believed many of the same things he did; they had the same heritage and history he had! Why did they react so violently?

Jesus wanted to be quiet. He found a place in one of the courts of the temple. He sat down across from the large metal boxes which collected the contributions for the upkeep and sacrifices. In a cherished moment of anonymity, a quiet eddy in the raging tumult of the storm of conflict, he sat down to think and pray.

But Jesus could not easily wash out the painful conflicts from his thoughts. They were on his mind and ached in his psyche. The argument and the tension in the Court of the Gentiles was not easily forgotten. Even for the divine Son of God the hostility of "good" religious Hebrew leaders had taken a profound toll.

As Jesus sat musing on all that had happened to him, he was barely aware of the stream of people who passed by, flinging their tithes, offerings, and temple taxes into the contribution boxes. These were called "trumpets" because of their trumpetlike shape. People would throw their contributions in with force in order to make a loud noise and attract the attention of those around them. The larger the coin, the bigger and better the sound.

Then there occurred an incident which focused all that Jesus had been through that week and vividly clarified its meaning. The frail, little, old widow unpretentiously approached one of the trum-pets and quietly slipped in her contribution of two mites. The coin she contributed was called a lepton, which literally means "the thin one." It was the smallest of all coins and was worth about one-sixteenth of a penny.

The little tinkle of the lepton sliding down the throat of the trumpet resounded within Jesus. He had a way of hearing what

was insignificant to others. In the milling crowds, he could hear
the frail cry of the little people in need. When the loud barking
of the marketplace deafened others' ears, he could hear the sound
of human need. Remember how he sensed the need of the woman
with the hemorrhage in the milling crowd and responded to her
need for healing; think of how he heard Bartimaeus' cry for mercy,
sight, and hope. Everywhere Jesus went the heaven-exposing, love-
delineating truth of personal care was given. Now again, here in
this situation, Jesus was true to his concern for the seemingly insignificant. In the stream of ostentatious, loud contributing by
prosperous, affluent people Jesus heard a slight tinkle of a little
coin. How amazing!

Jesus called his disciples to him and said, "Truly, I say to you,
this poor widow has put in more than all those who are contributing to the treasury. For they all contributed out of their abundance,
but she out of her poverty has put in everything she had, her whole
living." In substance he was saying, "Listen, did you hear that
blessed sound? There is a sound that declares gratitude, sacrifice,
love!" The widow's mite slipping into the trumpet drew Jesus'
attention in a way that the pretentious flinging of expensive contributions had not done. Suddenly Jesus was on his feet, alert to
the tremendous parable of truth which had been enacted before
them. He made so much of it that the event was indelibly imprinted on the minds of the disciples. People had been streaming
past him for some time making contributions out of their abundance. Now the widow had given what little she had, perhaps the
cost of her next meal, and Jesus honored her sacrifice.

Here was a bold contrast to what Jesus had experienced throughout that day in Jerusalem in his disputation with the officials of
Israel. This woman exemplified the wholeheartedness Jesus longed
to find in the negative leaders. In each encounter he had met a
fateful fragmentation of reality, a devastating division, a tearing
asunder of wholeness, a separation of inseparable truths God had
joined together. The poor widow caught Jesus' attention because
she had it all together; she expressed a wholeness of gratitude and
giving; she realized her blessings and gave everything she had. Note
the contrast of the extravagance of the widow with the equivocation of the leaders of Israel Jesus had faced that day.

The widow believed that all she had was a gift from God and
belonged to him. The Pharisees and the Herodians haggled over

what belonged to God and what belonged to Caesar. Jesus clearly declared that everything was God's. He is the Lord of all life. What we render to Caesar is as much God's as what we render to him. Life cannot be compartmentalized into the sacred and secular. We are as accountable for what we do in society as in the church. Giving our tithes and offerings to God does not relieve us of the necessity of seeking his guidance as stewards in everything we spend or save. The image of Caesar may be on the coin, but God's image is on our souls. We belong to him! The extravagance of true love begins there.

Now, compare the widow who gave everything she had with the Sadducees who refused to realize the gift of eternal life they had been given. They contended that there was no resurrection— no life after death. They tried to entangle Jesus in their conflict with the Pharisees over the resurrection, presenting a silly situation of a woman who had survived as the widow of seven brothers. Each had married her in keeping with the Jewish law of levirate marriage which stated that if a man died without a child, his brother must marry his widow. The irrelevant and irreverent question on the Sadducees' minds was, "In the resurrection whose wife will she be?" Jesus' answer cuts to the core of their resistance to receive all that God offers in life now and forever. "Is not this why you are wrong, that you know neither the Scriptures nor the power of God?" He then interpreted the Scriptures to show that the power of God has made this life but a small part of eternity. The resurrection and life forever are God's gift. This life, therefore, cannot be separated from life in eternity. Jesus was not satisfied with preoccupation either with temporal life or immortal life. Worldly immersion was no better than other-worldly evasion. His concern was that by misinterpreting the Scriptures and misusing the power of God, the Sadducees were missing eternal life in this world and the next. We are alive forever! Death is defeated. Nothing can separate us from the love of God! The extravagance of love is motivated by that.

Next, see the widow in comparison with the scribe who was described as not being far from the Kingdom. He is the most confounding of our comparative characters in this section of Mark. His division of life was more subtle. "Which is the most important commandment?" he asked. Why would he ask Jesus a question like that? He knew that the *Shema* every pious Jew repeated every day was only a summary of the 613 obligatory commandments taught by the rabbis and scrupulously maintained by the scribes. Did he protest too much? Was his own weakness exposed by his question and the affirmation of Jesus' answer? He complimented Jesus and agreed that to love God and your neighbor as yourself was much more important than burnt offerings and sacrifices.

When Jesus told him that he was not far from the Kingdom of God, did he discern that the man's last step into the Kingdom would be the longest? I suspect that Jesus realized that this self-justifying scribe didn't love himself very much and, therefore, had little love for his neighbor. But the real issue was: who was his neighbor? For the Jew, the neighbor was a fellow Jew. For Jesus, there was no division between love for God and love for all men. He had made this painfully clear in the parable of the Good Samaritan.

The same question rings down through the ages: "Who is my neighbor?" What a great gift God has given us in neighbors—the people of life! Inclusive love for them can never be separated from the love of God. How we love them is the telling way we love God.

The argument over who is the Messiah exposed a further lack of gratitude in comparison with the widow and the sacrificial giving of her mite. Here we meet the division of traditional beliefs and realized truth. The leaders Jesus confronted that day were so intent on interpreting the Messianic Scriptures that they failed to recognize the Messiah! I am alarmed at how often our squabbles over scriptural interpretations keep us from realizing the amazing promises the Word of God offers. Think of the ways we twist Scripture into the shape of our presuppositions! The scribes taught that the Messiah was to be the son of David. They used Psalm 110 to funnel the Messiah into the limited ministry of reestablishing the theocracy of Israel in the line of the Davidic kingdom. They wanted nothing more than for the Messiah to establish a kingdom of political and military might. Jesus was up to something much more profound than that!

Once again the distortion of Scripture and the lack of intimate guidance through the power of God led to a terrible inability to grasp the gift of life Jesus, the Messiah, offered. Jesus deliberately clarified the true message of the Psalm. David called the Messiah his Lord. Jesus was unquestionably and incomparably greater than just one leader in the succession of David.

What about us? When has our commitment to a prejudiced scriptural position kept us from realizing the power of God? Have we ever domesticated the dynamic of Christ into an emasculated, safe religion? Think of the joy of the abundant life we miss! The extravagance of love is guided by the forgiveness and grace we have received from his life, death, and resurrection. Take what is yours!

Lastly, the widow's mite is in convicting contrast to the proud, self-glorification of the scribes. Jesus was direct in his warning, "Beware of the scribes, who like to go about in long robes, and to have salutations in the market places and the best seats in the synagogues and the places of honor at feasts, who devour widows' houses and for a pretense make long prayers. They will receive the greater condemnation" (Mark 12:38–40).

No wonder Jesus was impressed with the poor widow. Instead of seeking the honor of people, here was the honoring of God; instead of using position for self-esteem, here was self-respect expressing thanksgiving; instead of outward display, here was the inner disposition of love leading to a discreet offering of a costly gift. The widow's mite shows the shallowness of the division between privilege and responsibility. An amateur exposed the professionals! The extravagance of love is always spelled out in humble gratitude.

In this event of the widow's gift, Jesus saw what he had been through and what he knew was ahead of him in a new light. He saw the pride of the leaders against the humble gratitude of this woman. They wanted recognition, the chief seats in the synagogue, honor among the people. The woman wanted nothing other than to express her thanksgiving. The antidote for pride is not humility, it's gratitude. They wanted to be seen by men; this woman wanted to be seen by God. The Pharisees resisted Jesus' message and life because it resounded with the "Go and do likewise" admonition. They could not accept his giving and forgiving life because it meant that they too would be engulfed in the same kind of unreservedness.

I believe that Jesus was profoundly comforted by what he saw in the woman's gift of self. Could it be that for a moment, in a split-second of inspired insight, he saw the sacrificial gift of his own life? The shadow of the Cross loomed over him. Golgotha was only hours away. Would God care? Would this death be the means of the forgiveness and salvation of the world? Could God take one execution in the maze of a cruel world where life counted for little and death was cheap? Would God honor his faithfulness and raise him up and clear the air with the triumphant trumpet blast of the Resurrection? Yes, Jesus honored the widow's mite as he knew God would honor and vindicate him on Resurrection morning. To give your mite when you don't know where your next meal will come from, to give your life in an angry world, that takes courage. Only the gift that costs ultimately counts!

Jesus wanted his disciples never to forget that, and they didn't. The "widow's mite" became part of their parlance and what she did also became a part of their memory of what was important to Jesus. The disciples must have retold the incident over and over to one another through the early years of the Church because it became part of the composite source of authentic sayings of Jesus from which Mark wrote his Gospel. Peter must have reminded him about it when he recalled the last days of our Lord in Jerusalem. Since then, this little gift has accrued in amazing dividends. We cannot give of our gifts or ourselves without wondering if we have in any way approached the sacrifices of her gift.

We can only speculate as to why Mark chose to include this story in his Gospel which was written for the persecuted Christians shivering under the horrendous, cruel blows of the Roman Empire in Rome. Why tell this story? What good could this serve for these frightened, haunted, misunderstood people in the capital of the world? Simply this: *they* were the little people—the offcast of society, suffering because they believed Jesus was the resurrected, living Savior.

What did the sacrifice of their safety, peace, and life mean to God? What difference did their faithfulness and obedience to the truth make to him? Mark quoted this little event to remind them that their "mite of commitment" to Jesus, slipped ever so quietly into the "trumpet" of life as they knew it, meant everything to God. The trumpets of Roman military might were blaring everywhere announcing the horrid orgies at which the Christians were fed to lions, but God heard the trumpet call of their obedience and some day the whole world would know!

The story lingers and penetrates. What does it mean for you and me? That depends! Only as we answer where life counts can we say where giving will cost. Life is given for giving. What we have, have experienced, and have become is all a trust for giving. We can never say, "That's mine!" We must say, "That's my trust— how shall I use it?"

This is illustrated by a famous doctor who had little time for his family. He would appear at meals, pay allowances, and give advice, often without really listening to the problems of his family before he spoke. One afternoon as he was preparing an article for a respected journal of medicine, his little son crept into the forbidden sanctuary of his study.

"Daddy," he appealed.

Without speaking, the doctor opened his desk drawer and handed the boy a box of candy.

"Daddy," the boy persisted!

To this the doctor responded with a grunt, indicating he knew the boy was there but didn't really acknowledge his presence personally.

"Daddy!" the boy called out again.

With this the busy doctor swung around in his chair and said, "What on earth is so important that you insist on interrupting me? Can't you see I'm busy? I have given you candy and a pencil. Now what do you want?"

"Daddy, I don't want any of those things. I want you! I just want to be with you!"

Has that ever happened to you? Have you ever come home and wanted to mend the wounds of a busy schedule, criticism, overwork, or exhaustion, by being by yourself, only to find spouse, roommate, children, mail, calls staring you in the face? Have you ever looked forward to an evening fulfilling your own plans, only to find the demanding needs of the people around you at home, apartment, or dormitory so great that there is no retreat? To give of yourself then is a gift that costs—and counts to God. Psychologists suggest that people need a reentry period when they come home from shop, office, or activities like astronauts returning to earth, where they can adjust to a new environment before giving themselves to their family group. Doesn't this point up the fact that we are centered in on ourselves and our careers too much so that we have to make an adjustment? But, that's what we are for! If we are never interrupted, never stretched, never contradicted in our careful plans, we are never giving to the point of cost to ourselves.

The other evening, I heard Yager Cantwell, a famous trial lawyer, tell about his conversion experience. Three people spent an immense amount of time with him during the period in which he was struggling as a brilliant intellectual agnostic to discover the new life in Christ. He used every argument and cross-examination technique he could muster. A lovely blond whom he was dating at the time, who knew Christ and would not compromise her convictions in a romantic relationship, persisted in sharing with him what Christ could mean for him. Her father, a clergyman, gave him countless hours in point by point exposure of viable Christianity. An old friend who had once shared Yager's scoffing ridicule of Christ was inexhaustible in intellectual confrontation about Christ as the truth. The result was that my friend was deeply converted and has been used immeasurably in both his law practice and in personal counseling to help others find the reality of Christ. As I heard him tell his story I was reaffirmed in my deep conviction that there is no alternative to personal caring.

We all have people outside our families who demand and need our care. A life of caring for people is not extraordinary, it is everyday Christianity. We hold the secret of life! Our experience of God's love carries with it the tremendous demand that we turn our time over to God so that he can send needy people to us to know what we know.

The secret of a great church as a caring community is not in multiplying the number of clergy to care for people. The alive church is not a place where people stand in endless lines to get a moment with the pastor, but rather a place where people learn to care for each other and people in the world. Most clergy are overloaded with the impossible task of being available to hundreds of people who grasp for a relationship with the pastor. Psychiatrists would never dare to carry as many people as many clergy try to help one-to-one. The only hope is for people who cling to the clergy to discover the adventure of multiplying his ministry by being to others what they want him to be to them. That's when the church starts to move and the pastor can regain not only his essential calling as a coach, but his sanity!

Another area where the gift costs and therefore counts is in the

area of our privacy. Most of us can sing the old ballad with conviction, "We'll build a little nest, way out in the West, and let the
rest of the world go by."

We all like our privacy. There is a fortress of privacy within all
of us which is impregnable, our own private possession. It is difficult to venture out of the fortress because we are forced to face
new experiences and problems. Our inner selves are considered
our own for us to invite whom we wish and whom we love. It
costs when our private lives, so carefully defended, become a
thoroughfare for others. We fear being used and misused by others.
What we think is our own business, what we want to do, is no one
else's business. We have lost a sense of the corporateness of being
the people of God. Rampant individualism has pushed back the
frontiers of thought and civilization as we have pushed out ahead
of the masses, but it has had its terrible result in irresponsibility
for others.

There are times when we must be alone to gain perspective and
insight as well as wisdom and strength, but this is always for the
purpose of involvement with others. The "leave me alone" attitude
of contemporary life is dangerous because it contradicts the essential
nature of the Christian as a man for others. When we begin to
care about people, we sacrifice a private life, the fortress is im-
pregnated, and we no longer belong only to ourselves. Beware, that
will cost. But we are not our own—we have been bought with a
price, we belong to God. When is the last time you allowed your
privacy to be invaded to care for at least one other person?

The last gift which costs, closely related to the above, I have
kept until the end because I want it to be understood in the light
of the whole exposition of this passage. It can be misunderstood,
misused, and misdirected. The gift which costs most of all is the
gift of being personal with another. Note that I did not use the
word *personable*, which means pleasant and happy. The personal
. . . this costly gift of self-exposure must be given with utmost
care and with God's guidance. Jesus gave us a clear warning, "Do
not cast your pearls before swine." By this I don't think he meant
your intellectual treasures or spiritual insights. I believe he meant
those experiences in which we have learned the true meaning of
life through some deep, personal pain, tragedy, failure, or experience, which to share with another would make us vulnerable. It
is a costly gift to give to another—to let down the mask and allow

another person to know us as we are. When we share with another what we have been through, we give him a valued gift. Jesus warns that this is not for swine—the casual observer or the seeker after the spectacular. When, in the context of trust, we share how we have found the secret of God's power in weakness or difficulty, we open ourselves to two frightening possibilities: we may be misused and exposed; and we can never again live on a superficial level of life with that person. We must trust that we will be respected and loved as fallible persons who have found life out of weakness. That's difficult! How much easier it would be to share our victories, our truisms, and our accomplishments. These build us up but do not build up relationship with another person.

How do you suppose the disciples ever learned about Jesus' dark night of the soul in Gethsemane? The garden was not wired for sound. They had not surreptitiously slipped a Sony tape recorder in his bag to hear what he said to God in his anguish of soul. No! He told them! Jesus confessed the whole, painful thing to them. Not very pious, is it? The Son of God in anguish, asking God if it were possible to take the cup of suffering away from him. But he told them, and they loved him for it! When they met trials and temptations, they knew Jesus had been through them too.

"As one tempted like as we are . . ." Read the Scriptures—if you wanted to write hero stories about God's great men and women, you would never have exposed their weakness the way the Scripture stories do. Abraham should never have told about how hard it was to offer Isaac; Jacob should never have been so personal as to expose his wrestle with the angel; David should never have let the publishers have Psalm 51; Peter should never have confessed his denial; Paul should never have admitted his feelings about Peter or that he stopped and healed a frantic woman just because she begged him to the point of distraction. But also read history. If the personal is to be hugged to ourselves as our possession, Luther was very unwise in his self-disclosure; Calvin went too far in telling about his own fears; Wesley should never have confessed his doubts; Kierkegaard was foolish in telling history his conflict with his father and his unfulfillment in romance. Read the great men of our own time. Listen to Paul Tournier tell about his struggles; to Helmut Thielicke confess his conflicts; to Catherine Marshall, after all she had been through, sharing the growth in faith with the death of Peter Marshall III, her grandson; to Norman Vincent Peale, expressing the ache of criticism for simplifying the truths so people could at least begin a life of faith; to William Stringfellow, sick to death of the racial crisis; to pastors and church officers telling of the heartbreaks of renewing the Church. Do we come away from reading or conversation with these people ready to write them off as weak people? No! Instead, they are real people who have dared to be personal about what the faith has meant in the crises of life.

But this is a costly gift to offer to another in Christ's name. We dare to trust God by trusting another when our experience will help him to know how much we love him and when the gift of the personal will illuminate what God can do in a life. Classical examples of faith alive in people of literature or history are often helpful, but never as powerful as when we dare to say, "I know what you are going through; let me tell you how I know from my own experience." This is not public exposure or washing of dirty linen; it is profound love expressing personal concern for another —enough to let him know us.

Every time I talk with someone in need or uncertainty, I find there is a God-given moment of empathy and identification. I have not had all of the problems which are shared with me, of course. But my right to help a person find God's solution and hope for his life usually is qualified by my willingness to expose my own personal pilgrimage. This is not only true for helping people with problems. It is God's strategy for deep relationships.

The other day I had coffee with a friend whom I love and respect very much. Often our conversation is preoccupied with church business. That morning, it seemed right to share with him a difficult discovery about myself I had made in a relationship with one of my children. The result was amazing. He shared some problems he was facing and we established a new bond of closeness.

The same thing happened at a breakfast meeting I had with a church member recently. The man confessed that he was in love with another man's wife. I have had many problems as a growing Christian, but that was one I could not identify with directly. But I was able to share with him the discoveries my wife, Mary Jane, and I have made about establishing profound relationships with fellow Christians of the opposite sex. Our struggle to be gracious and warm without misusing or negating other people's sexuality, was the point of contact with this man. By sharing our journey into the personal, I think I was able to help this man find an alternative direction.

These are widow's mites, not because they are small, but because they cost us something of ourselves. They are gifts that count because they cost. What have we got to lose? Our life? Well yes, that's true, but that's what Christianity is all about anyway, isn't it?

"By him, actions are weighed," said the psalmist.

When God weighs, the important thing is what weight he puts on the scale for us to balance. We look closely: his side is weighted with the Cross. How shall we balance it off? Nothing we can give, only our own cross—the giving of ourselves. He sits in the temple of life today . . . watching, listening! What sound will you make in the trumpet box?

CHAPTER 29

A CLEAR WORD ABOUT THE END OF THE WORLD

Mark 13

One of my most vivid boyhood memories is of a group of Christians whose leader pronounced with undeniable authority when Jesus was to return and the world was to come to an end. The newspapers picked up the story and made much of the sect's summit gathering to wait for the appointed hour of the Lord's arrival. There was to be terrible travail, punishment of unbelievers, and mass destruction of man's kingdoms. Only the small number of believers in this sect were to be saved. So, in obedience to their leader's commands they gave away all they had and huddled together singing hymns to greet the Lord's return.

I can remember the awaited day. Publicity had made the exact time a subject of everyone's conversation. When I got up that morning, I wondered if it would really happen. My family's breakfast conversation was focused on the morning radio accounts of the sect's activities of what it believed to be the last day of history. My parents tried to allay my concerns, but what if the prophet of doom was right? The predicted happening was clearly set to the moment. I had calculated ahead that it was going to be during my math class. Since that was my most difficult and least enjoyable subject, I gained some comfort in the fact that I might not have to worry about the results of the exam to be taken on that day.

Even now, over thirty years later, I can recapture the feeling I had as I watched the classroom clock tick away to the fateful moment. Then it came. Nothing happened. The world did not end, but the period of the exam did! The excuse of my distraction over the demise of the world didn't impress my teacher. Life went on;

the exam had to be retaken; the end of the world had been miscalculated.

Since that time, I can think of at least twenty times I have read about or actually heard predictions of exactly when the world would end or when the Lord was to return. Presently, there is a great preoccupation about the end times. Hundreds of books are being written and avidly read on the subject. Interpretations of current events point to the shortness of time. Some people today are planning their lives around the belief that the Lord's return will be any moment. Recently I talked to a student who left college because he was sure the Lord would return before graduation the next June. So why waste time studying? An evangelist told me recently that the reason we should spread the gospel is because there is so little time left.

Coupled with a growing emphasis on the end times is a deepening despair over the present times. The frustration of many Christians over evil and suffering has grown into an immense discouragement. Hopelessness is rampant. Questions which lurked beneath the surface are now out in the open. Is God in charge? Does he care? How long will he wait to intervene with judgment?

The international situation doesn't help. How long will détente last? Where will war break out next? Which raw nerve will be touched next by the world-grasping fingers of communism? Can we keep the balance of atomic power much longer?

But all this becomes very personal in our own struggle to be authentic Christians in a secular culture. Many of us face problems in our relationships which seem insurmountable. Others suffer physical pain or emotional uncertainty. Some who are relatively free of difficulties still feel the anguish of people around them and wonder why God lets it happen.

No wonder there are those who say these are the end times! There are moments when we all question where the sorry mess of history is leading and when Christ will come to center stage for the last act of the drama of humanity.

Mark 13 was written for times like ours and for people like us. It is one of the most difficult passages to interpret and one of the most crucial to understand. A thoughtful penetration of the chapter is necessary. We must consider the people for whom Mark recorded Jesus' message, what that message really means, and what it

says to us today. The Roman Christians were faced with persecution and suffering. They were also beset with false prophets who
predicted the end of the world and were preoccupied with, when
Jesus would return. Some actually claimed to be the Christ. What
Jesus said during the last week of his ministry about the end times
was essential for them to comprehend and believe. This same
message is the only source of our hope today. Jesus gives us a
clear word about the end of the world and how to live in it in
the meantime. There are two major facets which, guide our understanding and summarize this powerful chapter.

The first is: What we might consider the end is often God's
new beginning. What we discern as death throes may be the
birth pangs of a new creation. In the midst of personal or social
tragedy or difficulty, we are not to speculate that this may be the
end of the world but to anticipate and enter into what God is
about to do despite the worst that man has done.

This is the thrust of Jesus' message at the end of the second day
of conflict and confrontation in Jerusalem. He offers this as an
alternative to either human optimism or fatalistic despair. It was
the first which prompted an ill-timed ebullient remark about the
magnificence of the temple. It was the second which urged an
explanation of Jesus' response.

"Look, Teacher, what wonderful stones and what wonderful
buildings!" Jesus brushed aside the reverence for man's artistic
achievement and its permanence with a blatant prediction: "Do
you see these great buildings? There will not be left one stone
upon another that will not be thrown down." Quite a prophecy!
Some of those stones weighed one hundred tons, and others were
plated with gold and jewels which reflected opulantly in the sun.
No wonder four of Jesus' intimate disciples found it difficult to
hold back expressing their despair.

Late in the afternoon, seated on the Mount of Olives across
the Kidron Valley with the majestic grandeur of the temple in full
view, they blurted out the question, "When will this be, and what
will be the sign when these things are all to be accomplished?"
Jesus' answer is realistic and honest, but hope breaks through.
There will be wars and rumors of wars; nations will rise up against
nations, kingdom against kingdom; famine and earthquakes will
come. But the key words for our understanding are, "Do not be
alarmed; this must take place, but the end is not yet. . . . this is

but the beginning of the birth-pangs." There it is! A clear prediction of the destruction of Jerusalem, not the end of the world. It is as if Jesus were saying, "The worst possible thing you can imagine will happen and will be repeated many times. But when it happens, don't be troubled and don't assume that it's the end and don't follow false prophets who say it is. The total depravity of man makes it so, but God will not be finished!"

What Jesus predicted in 30 A.D. and Mark recorded in Rome about 65 A.D., actually happened in 70 A.D. Anyone in or near Jerusalem when Titus swept down on the city, razing the buildings to the ground and slaughtering millions of Jews, would have thought that the end of the world had come. Josephus, a contemporary Jewish historian, wrote, "No one visiting the city would believe it had ever been inhabited."

But the world went on. And the tragedy of Jerusalem became the turning point of the expansion of the Church. Nestled in Jesus' prediction is a triumphant assurance: "For in those days there will be such tribulation as has not been from the beginning of the creation which God created, until now, and never will be." But now note the hope. "And if the Lord had not shortened the days, no human being would be saved; but for the sake of the elect, whom he chose, he shortened the days." The period of divine judgment will be shortened so that God's chosen, the Church, might be saved. This actually happened. The Christians were warned by Jesus' words. Many of them fled their city at the onslaught of Titus. The destruction of Jerusalem marked the end of what would be called the Jewish period in which the Kingdom of God was identified solely with Jewish nationalism. The great obstacle to the expansion of the Kingdom Jesus proclaimed was removed. The Church was liberated from being an appendage of Judaism.

If we follow the line of thought that Jesus' prediction was of the fall of Jerusalem and not only the end of the world, what he says next brightens our hopefulness. Two things he said proclaim the beginning of a new age: "And they will see the Son of man coming in clouds with great power and glory" and "Truly, I say to you, this generation will not pass away before all these things take place." It is my conviction that this was the promise of the Lord's coming in power for the expansion of his Church to the far corners of the earth and not just the prediction of his final coming at the end time. The crucial question revolves around the word *genera-tion*. Does this mean the generation of people at that time or the lineage or race of God's elect at the end? I choose the former, but also affirm the implications of the latter. Jesus predicted both. He would come in power as Lord of the Church. The destruction of Jerusalem marked the beginning of that period. The liberated Church now spread to the Gentile world—the Roman Empire, then Europe, then the Americas, Africa, and now to the uttermost parts of the earth. We are now living in the later days of the period of world-wide expansion. During this time there have been tragic periods of history which have caused Christians to identify with Jesus' explanation of what would happen to Jerusalem.

Some have felt in each crisis that the end was near, but at the same time they gained confidence from Jesus' authority that God would bring good out of the worst of man's evil. And he has never failed . . . in Rome or London or Berlin. Across the sweep of 1900 years of history, Jesus has pressed on with the expansion of his Church. Today a revival is breaking out in Africa; modern transportation and communication enable the spread of the gospel to every kingdom and tribe. Jesus' words are coming true: "And the gospel must be preached to all nations." That is our agenda. Our concern is not when the end will be but the communication of the good news so that the end will be. We are not to take our readings from the tragedies of life but from the Lord of life!

Our calculations about the end of the world must always be corrected by Jesus, our counsel: "But of that day or hour no one knows, not even the angels in heaven, nor the Son, but only the Father." Mark's anxious readers in Rome needed to know that, and so do we. They had false prophets of the end even as we have today. But only the Father knows. And that's enough for me.

But in the meantime, I see a second thing Jesus is telling us in this passage. Preparation for the last things is to concentrate on the first things. Concern over setting the date of the end must be replaced by being faithful to the end. Any study of the last days should sensitize our present days. An alert Christian realizes this in three ways: in the daily interventions of Christ, in his own physical death, and in the return of Christ in the glory of the second coming.

For us Jesus Christ is the Lord who came, who comes, and who is coming. That threefold assurance makes for a triumphant faith.

Jesus said, "Take heed, watch, for you do not know when the time will come." We do not know when Christ will break through either our dull or our disastrous affairs and give us new power and hope. But do we expect him? Do we recognize him when he comes daily? Jesus told the disciples that in this world they would have tribulations, but they were to be of good cheer for he would be with them.

And what about our death? Are we ready for him to come as the resurrected Lord to make of our death a transition in living? What if this were to be our last day of physical life? Do we have an assurance that eternal life has begun for us and death has no power to separate us from Christ's love? The people who know they are alive forever are the people who are able to live, really, right now. Watch!

And then, how ready are we for Christ's return in glory? Do we have the assurance that if that were to be today we would be among the elect to reign with him? We believe that history will come to an end, but we don't know when. Richard Trent said, "The Second Advent is possible any day, impossible no day." The Lord who intervenes in our daily life and who has invaded the worst periods of history with hope will come finally to reign victorious upon the earth. We long for the day. Alexander Maclarin caught the spirit of the early Church which ought to be everyday Christianity for us: "The primitive Church thought more about the second coming of Jesus Christ than about death or heaven. The early Christians were looking not for a cleft in the ground called a grave, but for a cleavage in the sky called glory."

What then are the first things we are to be doing in preparation for the last times? Jesus was very clear. We are to seek first the Kingdom of God and his righteousness. That means his Lordship in all things: every relationship, responsibility, and realm of our existence. That should keep us occupied for all the days of our life! Add to that the challenge to do what he did, for he said, "These things which I have done, you shall do also." That should reorient our priorities and involvements. Living is for loving— Jesus style. But he goes on to remind us of the greater things, greater than he could do: We are to communicate his love and enable people to know him personally. There's a purpose to stretch us every moment of our days.

The unsettling thing is that our readiness to meet the coming

Christ in daily living, our death, or in his second advent will be based on what we have done with the gift of life. That prompts an incisive inventory.

Jesus' clear word about the end of the world is concluded by an all too clear word about our preparedness. He told a parable about a man who went on a journey. When the man left home, he put his servants in charge, each with his work, and the doorkeeper was commanded to be on the watch.

The parable is clearly autobiographical. Jesus told this just before his crucifixion. What confidence he had. He would be back! The resurrection, his return in the power of the Holy Spirit, his return as triumphant Lord of the expanding Church, and finally, his return as glorious king of creation. His words ring with assurance which should alert us to wake up and live the rest of our life: "Watch therefore—for you do not know when the Master of the house will come, in the evening, or at midnight, or at cockcrow, or in the morning—lest he come suddenly and find you asleep. And what I say to you I say to all: Watch!"

That leaves us a disturbing question. Am I ready? How can I know? How can I be sure? Here's my test. It may work for you: Preparation for the last days is to live today as if it were my last day. Preparation for the Second Coming is to receive the Lord who came and comes right now.

The New Testament ends with an affirmation and an assurance. The Lord says, "Surely I am coming soon." And with the Church of all ages, claiming our hope for the frustrating present and the future promise, we say, "Amen, come, Lord Jesus!"

But for today, and all our days until he comes, "The grace of the Lord Jesus be with all the saints. Amen."

CHAPTER 30

BROKEN OPEN AND POURED OUT

Mark 14:1–9

We've all been invited to a party, a very special gathering at Simon's home in Bethany. It's a time of tremendous celebration, and we are invited to share in the excitement. Use your gifts of imagination and let Mark's account come alive for you in all of its beauty and tenderness. We are there! Jesus said the Kingdom of God is to be like a joyous feast. So come to the party!

Picture this scene in Simon's home. Catch the gaiety, the warmth, the love, the sheer joy of it. Here is Christian fellowship as it was meant to be! Do you sense the depth of love being expressed by this strange and unlikely gathering? Do you feel it? Surely you can see it in the faces and hear it in the conversation!

Our host, Simon, is enjoying the party most of all. He seems like a guest, he is enjoying it so much. But, then, he is sort of a guest in his own house. It was only recently that he was allowed to come back to his own home. You see, Simon was a leper and it was only a short time ago that he was given permission by the rabbis to return to society. He had been healed by Jesus of Nazareth. You can be sure that he had some difficulty explaining his healing to the rabbis! Many people didn't believe it and kept the strict Levitical law forbidding association with the unclean. But the guests who came to help him celebrate knew that it was true! They could believe because of the miraculous things which also had happened to them.

Take Lazarus for example. He can share Simon's delight for he is alive because of Jesus. He died and had been shut up in the tomb when Jesus answered Mary and Martha's plea for help and comfort and had come and called him out of the tomb.

Is it any wonder that Mary and Martha still look at Jesus with amazed eyes of overwhelming gratitude? They watch his every movement with praise and thanksgiving. Their brother whom they loved so much has been given a few more years with them!

Martha now is busy preparing the last details of the meal. How very gracious of her to have the humility to bring the meal to Simon's house and serve it there rather than insisting on her own more pretentious home. Her very presence indicates that she believes Simon is well.

Our eyes quickly dart about the room. We look into the faces of the disciples. They too have caught the spirit of the occasion and share the enthusiasm of the celebration. There are dark lines upon their faces, though. We can readily see that the recent days of conflict have had their toll on them. One in particular seems a bit grim for such an occasion. We are told that his name is Judas.

The whole gathering has gravitated about Jesus, the guest of honor, the One who has made it all possible. He is seated, listening to the joyous reflections of the guests and enjoying the respite in the turbulent days of the last week in Jerusalem. Now for a brief time he thoroughly enjoys the comfort and encouragement of dear friends who love him because he has so generously loved them. We are taken by the vivid picture of mutual acceptance and concern displayed by these people and hardly notice that Mary has left the room.

When she returns, we are immediately struck by the deep emotion written upon her face. She is trembling a bit, indicating that she must be about to do or say something which comes from the depth of her being. Our eyes focus on a cruse she is holding in her hand. She holds it with tender care, indicating its value and preciousness. Walking directly to Jesus, she kneels beside him. There is a moment of indecision, and then, with an irresistible burst of eagerness, she breaks off the narrow neck of the cruse and uses the entire contents to anoint Jesus' head and feet. The rest of the guests look on, spellbound by her movements.

What does this mean? Was this an anointing for Jesus' comfort? Was it an act of honor—did she recognize that he was King or Messiah, or could she have meant the anointing for death? Does Mary know something of which the rest know nothing? Has she listened more intently to Jesus' words?

The gracious fragrance of the unguent amazes us. Why that's spikenard from far-off India! Do you realize what she has done? This is a highly valued anointing oil used very sparingly in hot Eastern countries. And she has used the whole cruse! That must be worth 300 denarii, almost as much as a daily laborer makes in a year! Why that is more than $400 worth of dollar buying power![1]

The guests look on—some with loving appreciation, almost feeling the tender anointing strokes of Mary; some with quizzical looks of wonderment; some with affirmation and encouragement, feeling that Mary has done what they wished they had had the means and boldness to do. But some look on with consternation. Judas is the spokesman for them. His short-fused temper had been ignited by what he judged was an outrageous act of extravagance. When he speaks, his voice is staccato, and we wonder what's behind the words he's saying: "Why was the ointment thus wasted? For this ointment might have been sold for more than three hundred denarii, and given to the poor!"

The mood of the party is immediately changed. The others pick up the negative mood and join in the consternation: "Why?"

Jesus, who had thoroughly enjoyed and appreciated this act of tender love, is obviously now filled with grief. Again Judas did not understand. Jesus knew! We can tell that. He knew about this ambivalent man with an ambiguous nature; he saw through his pious externalism. As he speaks we can feel the pathos and pity mingled with love: "Let her alone; why do you trouble her? She has done a beautiful thing to me. For you always have the poor with you, and whenever you will, you can do good to them; but you will not always have me. She has done what she could; she has anointed my body beforehand for burying. And truly, I say to you, wherever the gospel is preached in the whole world, what she has done will be told in memory of her."

We realize that we have witnessed one of the tenderest moments of history, blighted in the end by the harshness of resistance and reserve. The guests are quiet now. No one dares speak a word. Judas is restless, smarting under the Master's rebuke. Suddenly he leaps to his feet, looks around the room in anger, and

---

[1] There have been varying estimates of the value. Frederick C. Grant, in his exegesis of Mark in the *Interpreter's Bible*, VII, p. 868, suggests $240; Major, Manson, and Wright in *The Mission and Message of Jesus*, p. 165, estimate $500.

then stomps out of the house. Where is he going? Jesus knows where! And so do we.

We, too, must leave for it is late and we have a great deal of thinking to do. What did all this mean? What does it reveal, motivate, challenge? We have witnessed the exuberance of love, and we can never be the same again. We've seen life polarized between Mary and Judas, and we must search deeply to discern how we would have reacted in this same situation. Where did you find your sympathies, with Mary or Judas?

Being at Simon's party moves me profoundly. I have witnessed an example of unrestrained response to the Master at a difficult time of uncertainty and transition in the lives of the followers of Jesus. It speaks to my deepest need; I too, once again, need to break open the cruse of my life and pour out all that I have and am in grateful response. I have great expectations for the future which now must be matched with a broken and a poured-out life. I have expectations for myself, for the future of the church in America which I believe is about to begin its most dynamic decade, for our life together across the country as part of the adventure, and for new effectiveness in ministry for life-changing in society. My greatest concern is that our expectations may be too small! That's the reason this story is so crucial to me.

In Mary we see the gaiety of abandoned praise. With glorious imprudence she broke the container and with loving care used the whole contents. She was liberated out of herself in a dramatic devotion. Her unimpaired impulses moved her to give a great gift. The serendipity of love had a free agent. It was not smothered with caution and prejudice. She was lifted out of arithmetic calculation to abandoned compassion.

She did not allow reserve to keep her from the moment which would never come again. Unlike most of us who hear life's glorious opportunities knock at the door of our lives only to go away unwelcomed and unentertained, she grasped the moment and expressed her love. There is a time, this account tells us, when people should be careful, but there is also a time when they ought not to be cautious. There is something to be said for careful saving of our resources in order to make possible a great moment of unrestrained thanksgiving. Mary let herself go and taught us the basic essential of response to Christ's love and forgiveness. The Christian is not a tight-fisted, clenched-teeth, grim-faced person. Rather, he is one who loves and laughs and gives himself to Christ lavishly. In Mary we are challenged by extravagant love. And I believe Professor Whitehead was right when he said, "A certain excessiveness is an important ingredient of greatness."

Jesus' response to Mary agrees. That's why he said that wherever the gospel was preached, what Mary did would be remembered. In this passage he seems to be saying: "This is what I want! This is true self-abandonment, responsive self-giving, which I have been talking about and trying to help you understand. This is the way I want you to live the abundant life." Jesus' defense of Mary is one of his most misinterpreted, misunderstood statements: "The poor you always have with you, and whenever you will, you can do good to them."

This statement has been misused to justify the social syndrome of poverty: "And after all, it's their own fault. If they would get up and exercise their energies, pull their own weight, they wouldn't have to live off the hard work of other people!" But note, Jesus used the present tense of "to have," not the future, and we have not listened to the second half of Jesus' statement, "If you will, you can do good to them." What he meant was that there are the continuing problems of life which are with us always in which we are to invest ourselves. The freedom of Mary's love for Jesus would be the motive and driving power for these problems. Jesus knew that once a person was creatively related to him, he would be adventuresomely invested in the wounds of the world. He did not want people to serve the world for him, but *with* him and by his power. What Mary had done was absolutely essential as the basic ingredient of a mature Christian life which would overflow in costly caring for the poor—in body or in spirit.

Perhaps Jesus' reaction would have been tempered if he had seen genuine concern for the poor in Judas. He knew that his statement was a deflecting action, a divide and conquer mechanism, and not concern for the poor. Judas knew only too well the source of Jesus' statement. It was based squarely on the Old Testament passage in Deuteronomy 15:11: "The poor will never cease out of the land; therefore I command you, You shall open wide your hand to your brother, to the needy and to the poor, in the land."

Hadn't Jesus told them that he would meet them in the poor? "When did we see you poor?" His answer is telling: "Even as you have done it to the least of these, my brothers, you have done it unto me!" In this context Jesus seems to be saying, "You will have abundant opportunity to serve me by being unreserved in the same way with the economically and spiritually poor of the world." The thing Mary did was exactly what he wanted them to do for the poor after his death. They would have ample opportunity to express the same quality of love.

I will never forget what a friend said to me one time when I faced a difficult situation with equally challenging alternatives. He blasted open the horizon for me when he asked, "What would you do if you threw away your reservations?" That changed everything! I got a picture of the potential that had escaped me.

Our Lord meets us in the "least and the lost" inside ourselves, in the people of our lives, in our churches, and in the world. What does love for Christ require in those quadrilateral dimensions? What would it mean to love lavishly in each area?

I believe that the Lord guides us with what I call sanctified imagination. He gives us the gift of forming an image in our minds of what the shape of love is in these areas. He gives us a dream, an expectation of what he is able and ready to do. Praying begins with him. He plants in our minds the picture of what is needed and then releases us to pray for the very thing which he is often more ready to give than we are to receive. It is in quiet, receptive listening that we discern the marching orders of the Master as to how most effectively to break open our cruses and love him in ourselves, in people, and in the sickness of our society. Let's consider first breaking the cruse for the Christ in ourselves.

I remember talking to a woman who had been in a horrendous auto accident. Her body was mangled and for a time her memory was impaired. She is a brilliant intellectual and one of the truly original scholars and teachers in her field. After the accident she found lecturing quite difficult. Despair and hopelessness possessed her.

We took a long walk to discuss her determination to end her own life. She confided that prior to the accident her intellect had become her security and her reason for being. Though she was a Christian, her scholarship had become a diminutive god and now she no longer found prayer or Christian fellowship helpful in her desperation. I felt like I was reaching out to a life held by a thin thread which was about to break.

We talked for hours. Her self-deprecation was so intense that there seemed to be no breakthrough to hope. As we talked, I asked our Lord to give me a special word for this troubled child of his. Then an idea formed in my mind. I said to her, "Imagine a woman in late middle age sitting over there. Her body is shattered by an accident of human fallibility. Her mind is temporarily impaired and she has difficulty remembering. Now, would you go over and take her by the neck and murder her and put her out of her misery?" "Oh God, no!" she said. "I would not do that. I would try to love her and nurse her back to some patient hope for the future." "Then, should you do less for yourself?" I asked. Suddenly she could see her lack of love for herself, and we could talk about what the shape of love would be for her—for herself as loved by Christ.

Often I ask groups at conferences: "If you loved yourself as much as Christ loves you, what would you do as a creative expression of love's challenge for yourself? Listen carefully to what your body, your emotions, are trying to tell you about your needs."

What would it mean for you to break open the cruse and give Christ a chance in you?

I am convinced that the reason we have so little to give others is that we have never experienced what I call Christ-centered self-love and Christ-guided self-interest.

Recently, I have been trying an exciting experiment with people. As I continue to be released from self-negation and self-deprecation myself, I am increasingly enjoying being me. I have taken seriously the Scripture that God is not against us—he's for us. Our greatest need is to catch a vision of his dream for us. What a liberating thing it is to exchange my meager expectation fraught with problems for his mighty expectation filled with potential. In this ambience of freedom, I have found great delight in asking people, "What is your dream for yourself?" Believing that we become what we envision, I want to know a person's most abandoned hope and expectation for the future. Then I covenant with them to pray daily for three things: one, that God will clarify and affirm that dream as a part of his plan for them; two, that they will claim the guided dream as his gift for them; and three, that they will break open their lives to realize the dream.

Fantastic things have happened. People who would have resisted evangelism of any kind find that they become open to God and begin to seek his will for their lives as never before. It isn't long before the excitement of what they are discovering spills over to others and their environment.

Next, let's consider breaking open our cruses for the Christ in the people in our lives. Remember Joe Saul, John Steinbeck's character in *Burning Bright*? He was past middle age and his great fear was that he would die without an offspring to bear his name. When his wife shared the news of an expected child, he became delirious with joy: "I want to bring a present to her . . . something like a ceremony, something like a golden sacrament, some pearl like a prayer of a red flaming ruby of thanks. That's the compulsion on me . . . I must get this thing. My joy requires a symbol."

That's how we feel at times, isn't it? But why is it so difficult for us to express love in the language others can understand?

Mary's gift of extravagant love reminds us of life's lost opportunities. What false trust we put in the future! "Tomorrow and tomorrow" we say. We put off what is today's opportunity and priority. We may never have another chance! Jesus honored Mary's exuberant lack of moderation and prudence. He found her spontaneous expression of life to be symbolic of the kind of response which he desired for all people. The Christian life is not striving after moral perfection (that's a by-product); it is a continual prodigality of heart as we give ourselves to Christ by breaking ourselves open to others.

I recall one couple at a marriage conference who were able to break open their cruses to each other in a new way. They had been living in a dutiful but dull marriage. Life had settled down into the ruts of routine. All through that particular weekend we talked about what it means to love in the language and action that the other person can understand and appreciate. Then one evening the couples were sent to their rooms to be alone. Each person was given an uninterrupted half hour to talk about what his dream had been for his marriage and what had happened to that dream through the years. Neither was allowed to interrupt the other. Each had the task of enabling the other nonverbally and only an enabling "Aha" or an encouraging "I hear you" was allowed. It was amazing what tumbled out of the recesses of memory and inner feelings.

This particular couple heard each other for the first time in years. A pattern of withholding denial and demand had developed and they exposed ways they were debilitating each other. Hostile memories which had been crammed down inside were opened to the healing love of Jesus Christ. As the conference proceeded, each couple was paired off with another couple to talk about what they could do for their spouses if they did the things love demanded.

In the closing communion service an informal format was used. The couples gathered in groups of eight around the room. Bread and wine were provided for each group. At the conclusion of the service, each couple was asked to give the communion to each other. The memory of this particular couple is indelibly printed on my mind. They broke bread that night saying, "This is Christ's body broken for you and I am willing to be broken open for you. This is Christ's blood for a new relationship, and I am willing to be poured out for you."

The real question for us now is—how can Christ get through us to other people most effectively? If we are to be agents or channels through whom Christ manifests himself to the people of our lives, then surely sin is anything which blocks that love from flowing through us to others. Our habitual reaction patterns, our unresolved tensions, our schedules, our judgments, our impatience, our preconceptions or prejudices—anything which keeps love from being mediated is blasphemy!

Picture the people of your life. Allow each one to pause there in your vision for a moment. Consider each one carefully, thoughtfully, prayerfully. Then pray, "Lord, thank you for the gift of yourself wrapped up so graciously in this person and given to me. What do you want me to be, say, and do to incarnate your love? What's the one thing I can do today which will incarnate your love for him or her?"

We hear a lot about ecology these days. The word means the interdependence of all species and the natural world upon each other. God has made us interdependent for the experience of his love. We are responsible for the lives of the people he gives us. We are to be with people in such a way that they can catch God's dream for them and dare to experiment adventuresomely in whatever is the first step of that unfolding dream.

But what of the Church, the Body of Christ? What would it mean to break open our cruses and love lavishly there? All too often this passage about Mary's "beautiful act" is used to motivate people to give to some beautification project in the church building. Not so! Jesus honored the giving of self expressed by Mary. There is a freshness, a freedom, a flexibility, in people who have broken out of traditionalism, convention, and reserve. These are the people our Lord needs in his Church today.

Lastly, let's consider what breaking our cruse means for society. What is Christ's motivated dream for society which prompts you to want to love Christ by loving the world?

We have given that question a great deal of thought and planning at the First Presbyterian Church of Hollywood. Our evangelism program has been developed to help our members care deeply about the people in the world around them. Specialized training is offered repeatedly to give specific training. Our local mission program has offered organized efforts to discern and do something about the social problems which grip our city. I am delighted by the large number of our members who are involved in such efforts as the Laubach Reading Program; the Hot Lunch Program for senior citizens; the Life Line Telephone Ministry to the disturbed and distressed; the Singles' Ministry; the broad, inclusive youth program; group activities for social justice; and the Deputation Team working in areas of human need. There are many others, but they are not the most exciting things I see. Our involvement in the crucial crises of our city brings joy to me. The emphasis of our church on the ministry of the laity has prompted hundreds of our people to take seriously their responsibility to become effective for Christ in some area of human need as a part of responsible discipleship. There can be no healthy, lasting relationship to Christ without it.

But we cannot find God's guidance for others. That's why we try to help people ask the Lord for his particularized guidance for each of them. When a person finds the social problem or need which the Lord places on his heart, then the challenge is to break open the cruse and pour out the resources which he has given us.

As I consider the brokenness of our society, I am grateful that I can also see people deployed who dare to follow the drumbeat of the Master's dream for what they can do to bring love and justice, coupled with practical caring and involvement, to a particular situation.

Faced with that kind of challenge, we wonder if we are not more like Judas than Mary. He did not like what he saw during that last week. The cleansing of the temple was great, but what was all of this talk about a cross and sacrificial death? This scene at Simon's home only watered and nurtured the growth of the thought of defection. Judas was obviously a nationalistic zealot who wanted, not God's new creation, but a return to the days of Israel's past glory. Increasingly, Jesus did not fulfill his image, his dream. He could not see that Jesus' revolution of love would bring his understanding of the Kingdom. Finally, it dawned on Judas that in this act of unreserved love he could see what Jesus wanted from him and he knew that he didn't have it. He just did not love Jesus that much. And what he could not give himself, he had to ridicule and criticize in Mary.

On the other hand, Mary experienced just the opposite. She saw the shortness of time and the length of eternity. Jesus' words after the raising of Lazarus had shocked her into a new dimension of living and giving: "I am the resurrection and the life . . . he who believes in me shall never die." She discovered that this life is but a small part of our eternal existence, a parenthesis in forever. The "you only live once" attitude was maximized with a "We are alive forever" conviction. So why not give ourselves away now? Why not live to the hilt in the now?

It is a disturbing insight that Judas sold Jesus to the enemy for thirty pieces of silver, the price paid for a slave. And slave he became . . . of his own criticisms, ego, and distorted motives.

While I was working on this passage of Scripture one night, I had a dream of Simon's party. The attention of the dream was on two men—one knelt before Jesus and offered his whole life, the other stood off and criticized the unreservedness of the other. I awoke from the dream with a disturbed spirit. As I lay awake in the dark quiet of early morning, I reflected on the dream, trying to recapture its meaning. I was astounded to remember the faces of both men in the dream. They were both mine! The painful truth is obvious: there is both response and reserve in my being when it comes to the Master. Like most of you, there is a part of me which says boldly, "Yes!" and a part of me that says, "Be careful; count the cost!" We are all a mixture of the impulse to let go and follow Christ as the Lord of our life and love others with extravagance and a repulsion at the price of costly involvement. There are opposing forces tugging at our souls right now. But Christ will win, be sure of that!

What shall we do with a love like that? What does a love like that motivate? Simply this: we break off the top of our cruses and let the hoarded ointments of ourselves flow out in unreserved praise! If you love someone, tell them so, for Christ's sake. If there is something you must do to express love, do it now for his glory. If you are disturbed by conditions in society, get involved out of love for Christ.

Sense for a moment how you would feel if you were completely open to Jesus Christ's strategy for you. Picture yourself filled with his love and freedom. Get the picture? What would you do with today if you were? This could be the most glorious day of our lives!

CHAPTER 31

WELL, WHAT WOULD YOU HAVE DONE?

Mark 14:10–15:21

The last day in Jesus' life is everyday. What happened that day exposes the issues of everyday of life. The same power play we see dramatized on that historic day when Jesus was betrayed, denied, tried, punished, and crucified is being played out in our lives right now. The people of the passion of our Lord are with us still . . . we are among them. The question is first, "What would we have done if we had been there in Jerusalem?" And then, "What are we doing right now as Christ is crucified anew in our personal, interpersonal, institutional, and social life?"

The answers depend on the level of depth with which we experience the traumatic account of Jesus' last day in Jerusalem. We can read it with historical interest to observe the treacherous events which led to Golgotha. We can look from a distance and see what men did with Jesus Christ. Then too, we can observe from the safe perspective of theological ideas and words. The events of those hours move swiftly to the conclusion of what God did for the world on the cross. We can theorize on the spiritual truths of a suffering Savior misjudged, misunderstood, and shamefully mistreated for sinful humanity. We can accept the fact of his substitutionary sacrifice for the sins of the whole world; once, never to be repeated. If we go deeper, we are immediately drawn into more than just a theory of the atonement, but an experience of Calvary today.

We believe that God was in Christ. Therefore the incarnation is our exposure to the heart of God. Blaise Pascal was right. "Christ has been in agony from the foundation of the world." But go one step further: not only from the foundation of the world, but right now! Calvary is the ultimate intersection of history. All of God's encounters with his people before it were a foreshadow; everything which has happened since then is a reflection and extension of it. What this means for us is that the Cross is now. In this moment of our lives, in this day of history, the Cross must be rediscovered as our hope of forgiveness, as the basis of our living, and as the strategy of God in our evil, sick world. Suddenly we realize that what Jesus did on the last day of his earthly ministry, he must do again right now. The issues which gripped his world grip ours; the same evil incarnate in man which resisted him resists him still; the same injustice in society which broke his heart persists virulently today; the same uncertain vacillation he found in his disciples, he anguishes over in his Church. John Ruskin was too close to the truth for comfort when he wrote, "There are a great many things Jesus will put up with in the human heart; but there is one thing he will not put up with . . . second place."

Let me put it bluntly. If Christ were to come to our city, our society, our nation, what would we do with him? But he has come; he is here right now! What shall we do with his ultimate demands, his priority-delineating challenge, his unsettling urgency for personal and social righteousness? The Cross is erected again on the Golgotha of our hearts and in the offices, shops, and homes of our city. Whenever we destroy ourselves with self-justification or self-aggrandizement, we need the Cross. When we need to be forgiven, but will not forgive ourselves or another, the Cross impinges. When the Church becomes inverted upon itself in private, formalized religion, the Christ is crucified but upon the altar of our religious hypocrisy. When a city or nation will not order its life around the Kingdom of God, Christ suffers the Cross again. We put him there.

Find yourself in the passion narrative recorded in Mark, if you dare! We are all there. As we study the events of those last hours, we see each one of us. That's the reason we will approach this portion of Mark 14 and 15 through personality studies of the people surrounding the death of our Lord. In examining each person let's think about what we would have done, how we would have reacted, what we would have said.

The first person is never mentioned by name. He is the eyewitness of all that happened in Jerusalem. He was a member of Jesus' secret followers who formed an underground network in Jerusalem. He was the host of the Upper Room where the Last Supper was held. The home belonged to his mother, and he had made all of the preparations for Jesus' Passover feast with the disciples. He had deployed a sentry with a jar of water near his home. This was the prearranged signal. His servant led the disciples to his home. On the edge of the band of disciples, he observed Jesus as he celebrated the Passover. He watched Jesus with love and admiration, and then listened with sadness mingled with anger when he heard Jesus say that someone would betray him. He saw Judas leave the room in anger and discouragement. And then he followed at a distance when Jesus went to Gethsemane to pray. He saw Jesus' anguished hours of prayer and was close at hand to see Judas return with the soldiers to arrest Jesus.

This was none other than Mark, the author of the Gospel we have been studying. I am convinced that he gave us an autobiographical self-identification when he wrote, "And a young man followed him, with nothing but a linen cloth about his body; and they seized him, but he left the linen cloth and ran away naked" (Mark 14:51). Who but Mark would either know about this young man or think it important to refer to this near capture?

Mark was hovering about the tragic events of that night. He was a secret follower, a disciple at a distance. Why did he run away? What would you have done?

Mark's relationship with the Savior that night is like that of many of us today. We are spiritual entrepreneurs who want to help the Master's ministry, but always at a distance. We are sure that Mark contributed his home and his resources to Jesus, but not his heart. Like him at that stage of his life, many of us are secret disciples. We have heard the message, recognized the truth, given our money, but we're not able to take the confrontation of declaring what we believe. Why didn't Mark identify himself as a follower, fight for Jesus when he was arrested, and go with him to face the terrible hours of the night which was ahead? He was afraid, unsure of himself and the Master.

But do we do differently in our own witness or our own faithfulness when Christ or his message is being ridiculed by people around us at home or at work whose approval we need and whose rejection or categorizing we cannot take?

In Simon Peter many of us find ourselves in the events leading up to the Cross. We personally identify with his humanity and fallibility. But on that last night, especially, we empathize with his feelings and failure.

I can feel with Peter his shock and consternation when the Lord said that someone would deny him. But it was personal hurt and indignation which burned in his loyal heart. When, later, on the Mount of Olives, Jesus said, "You will all fall away . . ." he impetuously blurted out his courageous reply, "Even though they all fall away, I will not." Then his eyes met the Master's. "Truly I say to you, this very night, before the cock crows twice, you will deny me three times." Nothing could have been worse for Peter to hear. He envisioned himself the most loyal of the disciples. It was as if Jesus had said, "You are going to let me down!"

The bugle was sounded from the Tower of Antonio at six, nine, twelve, and three A.M. This was called a gallus or cock. The trumpet sounding at twelve and three were called gallicinia or cock-crowing. This must have been what Jesus meant by the twice crowing. But the word for three times, or thrice, is a Greek idiom which means "repeatedly." Jesus' declaration then was, "Before morning you will deny me over and over again."

And that's just what happened: the denial of his anguish in Gethsemane when Peter went to sleep, the denial when he fled at Jesus' arrest, his denial in the courtyard outside Herod's palace when a young woman recognized his Galilean accent, and then repeatedly when he watched helplessly as his Lord was crucified.

What was it? Fear, uncertainty, cowardice? In the same circumstances would we have done differently?

I am disturbed by the realization of the ways I deny my Lord—in my life, my relationships, my world! I would die before I would say that Jesus is not my Lord. I would take persecution, but what of prosperity? We all deny our Lord in thousands of ways in resistance to his will by settling for less than his maximum for us, by closing him out of our future plans. Every time we say "No!" to his Spirit by not being faithful, we deny him. Think for a moment what our lives would be like if they were completely yielded to him, if our speech were filled with his love, and our lives were obedient to do the things he would do in our society.

Denial is one thing; betrayal quite another. What shall we do with the Judas of Mark's account? I think Judas has been badly treated by history. When we learn more of him, we discover we're more like him than we would want to admit at first.

Judas was the only disciple who was not a Galilean. He was from Kerioth, a town in the south of Judea. Could this have given him the insecure feeling of never really belonging? We wonder what it was in this man that caused Jesus to be attracted to him? Historical study reveals that Judas was probably a member of an insurrectionary band of Jews who smarted under the irritating dominance of Rome. He was a fanatical nationalist motivated by a "liberation now" urgency. I am convinced he joined Jesus' disciples first because he was attracted by Jesus' message and personal power. Then as Jesus exposed his true Messiahship, Judas probably became excited by the possibility that Jesus would fulfill the Messianic expectations of Israel: When the Messiah came, he was to raise the forces of God's people and lead them to victory over all the invading armies and set Jerusalem free forever. But then he became very disillusioned and disappointed when Jesus talked of a cross and the Kingdom of God in men's hearts and their relationships and not of a victorious theocracy on earth with him as king.

Judas loved Jesus. He was loyal and passionately committed to him. But his impatience gave illegitimate birth to insurrection as the only way. He had to force Jesus' hand! That's why he acted as he did. Judas truly believed that if he forced Jesus into confrontation with the leaders of Israel and the authorities of Rome, he would declare war and galvanize the restless pilgrims and hostile insurrectionists deployed everywhere in Jerusalem, calling forth the legions of heaven and doing final battle with the occupation troops of Rome. And from that victory, there would be a mopping up action until Israel was again supreme among the nations of the world. Judas had a "man of the hour" complex and believed that he was acting decisively for God!

Have you ever felt that way? Is the Lord ever too slow for you? Have you ever felt that you needed to step in to force him to act the way you wanted him to according to your plan?

Judas' sin is the sin of taking things into our own hands. I am sure that in Judas' confused mind he believed Jesus was the Messiah and nothing could hurt him. If he forced him to act, God would sustain his insurrectionary invasion. On the other hand, I think he entertained the possibility that perhaps Jesus was not his kind of Messiah. If that were true, it would be better for all that the whole world know it. He loved Jesus as a man enough to want to save him from the cross he had told the disciples so much about.

If he drew the lines of conflict sharply, the leaders of both Rome and Israel would soon know whether he was Messiah or not. This Judas did because he loved Jesus!

Judas' true nature and the depth of his affection for Jesus is exposed by what he did when he saw the results of his betrayal. He realized that he had not helped his Master but had led him into the unrelinquishing trap of the enemy. When he saw what he had done and Jesus did not meet his militaristic expectations, Judas was engulfed in excruciating, pathetic remorse and self-incrimination. He ran to the leaders of Israel to try to intercede to save the friend he had sold for thirty pieces of silver: the price of a slave. Now Judas was the slave of a new master: his own self-willed manipulation and clever cunning. What does a man like that do with failure? He desperately needed Jesus' forgiving love, but it was too late! He had taken Jesus' destiny into his own hands. Now he must do the same with himself. The same hands which had clutched the pieces of silver in a clever scheme now twisted his mantle into a ropelike noose to hang himself. But the rope broke, and he fell on the rocks beneath splattering open the tissues of his guilt-ridden, tension-infected anatomy.

Now look at the contrast of what Judas did with his betrayal and Peter did with his denial. One committed suicide; the other wept bitter tears of failure. One determined his own judgment; the other accepted the judgment of God. One put an end to himself; the other experienced what God did to put an end to self-atonement. For one, failure was the ultimate hopelessness; for the other, failure was fertile soil of ultimate hopefulness.

How should we handle our mistakes and errors today? Like Judas or like Peter? The Cross which was the essence of one's denial and the other's betrayal now looms as our only hope. Christ died for both Judas and Peter. Only Peter realized the gift and went on to become a flaming preacher and a mediator of the grace he had experienced. For today, and all my days, I want to choose Peter's confession, tears, and the joy of new beginnings.

As we follow Mark's account of Jesus' trial, we are faced with a struggle for power which reads like this morning's newspaper. In Caiaphas we meet ecclesiastical power in gross distortion. He was the chief priest and had watched Jesus' growing popularity for a long time. He was a Sadducee and the leader of the Sanhedrin. His role was to be the leader of the spiritual life of Israel. In him we see religious authority focused. All leaders should empathize and walk in his shoes. We cannot read the account of what the chief priests did to Jesus without bearing the shame of what organized religion has done to him and in the distortion of his purpose in his name all through history.

For Caiaphas, Jesus was a threat both theologically and politically. He asserted the resurrection which, as a good Sadducee, Caiaphas denied. He claimed to be the Messiah, which Caiaphas abhorred. But most of all, Jesus had thousands of followers. That Caiaphas feared! Something had to be done. The intrigue thickens as we see the power-greedy ecclesiastic weave the plot to destroy Jesus. The high priest sent emissaries to expose him, but with little success. When Jesus came to Jerusalem and Caiaphas observed the welcome and adoration given him in the triumphal entry, he was sealed in his determination to manipulate everyone around him to effect his will.

Caiaphas was one of those people to whom everyone owes something. He engineered everyone to be in his debt. His ledger sheet was always filled with people's indebtedness to him out of fear or obligation. Now he decided that it was time for everyone in power in Jerusalem to pay up.

His relationship with Pilate had been stormy and hostile. He had beaten the young procurator at the game of power several times. The first was when Pilate foolishly placed images of Caesar on the Temple of Antonia. Caiaphas had marshaled thousands of the people to surround his palace in Caesarea praying to God to have the Roman yield and remove the images. Pilate surrounded the people with his throngs and could easily have massacred them all. But he knew how that report would read in Rome. After six days he reluctantly and angrily removed the images.

The second move on the chessboard by Caiaphas put Pilate in further jeopardy. He proposed to build an aqueduct from the pools of Solomon to the interior of Jerusalem. But the mistake was his plan to use the sacred temple funds without the private connivance with Caiaphas. Once again Caiaphas raised a multitude of demonstrators. This time Pilate had his soldiers dress as civilians and infiltrate the crowd. They beat and killed many of the Jews. It was Caiaphas who filtered the information back to Rome. The result was that the young governor was severely rebuked by Rome for having legionnaires dress as civilians and beat and kill helpless people including women and children. No wonder Pilate hated the Jews!

Caiaphas won a third time when Pilate put shields bearing images to foreign gods on Herod's palace in Jerusalem. Once again pressure was brought and Pilate had to yield. His activities as a leader were constantly under pressure from Rome because of the clever power pressure applied by Caiaphas.

A final defeat came when Pilate executed some Galileans in the temple courts "mingling their blood with the sacrifices." Jerusalem was in a political uproar; the ire of the Jews was inflamed and the fire was fanned by Caiaphas. This accounts for Pilate's presence in Jerusalem at the time of the Passover. An uprising was expected, so grudgingly he had come to the city with his wife Claudia to personally supervise the maintenance of order.

He might better have stayed in Caesarea. For on that fateful day he was to have every sinew of his being stretched on the rack by Caiaphas. We suspect that he came to Pilate sometime during that night to pull the puppet strings on the man he had prepared for the checkmate so long.

In Pilate we see a man not unlike many of us who was unable to discern the right and do it. He had pressure from Caiaphas to execute Jesus on the trumped-up charge that he claimed to be a king. But he also had pressure from his spiritually sensitive wife who had had a dream about Jesus and warned him to have nothing to do with the conflict over the Galilean preacher.

Mark's account of Jesus' arraignment before Pilate exposes Pilate's pressure. He immediately asks Jesus if he is the king of the Jews. How could he have known that was the charge unless Caiaphas had prearranged the charge? The composure and confidence of Jesus are a bold contrast to Pilate's uneasy vacillation. "You have said so," was his only reply. Then the chief priests interposed their fake charges. Pilate could not comprehend that Jesus made no defense for himself. "Have you no answer to make? See how many charges they bring against you," Pilate asserted, incredulous at Jesus' silence. When Jesus made no further answer, Mark summarized that Pilate *wondered*. Indeed he wondered! All of the Gospel accounts of that trial bring one thing out clearly: Pilate was profoundly impressed by Jesus and moved by his kingly power. But the power of Caiaphas' prior maneuvering kept him checkmated. We feel as if Pilate is pathetically reaching out to Jesus in a desperate hope that the would-be king will help him!

Caiaphas had created Pilate's only way of retreat long before. The week before he had used his office as chief priest to prophesy what he had devised would be the only way to destroy Jesus. The eleventh chapter of John gives the account of the clever preparation he had made to destroy Jesus. He knew the way things would go during that week. He also knew that there would be a desperate moment when he would have Pilate like a trapped animal. So he set it up long before that trial on Friday. In response to the frenzied Pharisees and the council who feared Jesus' growing power, he said, "You know nothing at all; you do not understand that it is expedient for you that one man should die for the people, and that the whole nation should not perish."

Caiaphas used the ancient prophecy to fit cleverly into Pilate's custom to release one prisoner at the Passover feast. He banked on the hope that his quislings could infect the crowds against Jesus to demand Barabbas, an insurrectionist who was in prison for murder, instead of Jesus. Mark leaves nothing to imagination: "The chief priests stirred up the crowd to have him release Barabbas instead."

But Pilate's checkmated defeat was not without final galantry. Was he convinced that Jesus was the king of the Jews in some strange messianic way he could not comprehend or did he want the final word to ridicule Caiaphas? Perhaps a bit of both. When Pilate appeared on the balcony before the angry mob, his hatred of Caiaphas and the hostile Jews was expressed: "Do you want me to release for you the king of the Jews?" The manipulated crowd cried for Barabbas. Then a second time Pilate queried, this time asking a question which has haunted all men ever since: "Then what shall I do with the man you call the king of the Jews?" The emphasis, I imagine, was forcefully, unmistakably on the pronoun "you." Had some in that crowd called him king? Indeed they had. Pilate knew the fickle heart of that crowd. Its vacillation was like his own pressured heart.

What Pilate did that day earned him a place in history and a line in the affirmation of the early Christians which we know as the Apostles' Creed: "Suffered under Pontius Pilate"—the preposition is wrong! Jesus suffered *with* Pontius Pilate and *for* him! Pilate was a victim as much as the one he victimized.

And so the Pilate in all of us knows. We get trapped in our own divided loyalties and bungled compromises. The Caiaphases of life are always lurking about to entangle us in failures which hang like millstones around our necks and alliances which sink us into the morass of immobility when it comes time to move out for what we believe.

Pilate leaves us with a question every person has been forced to ask since that fateful Friday: "Have I made promises; have I tried to cover my failures with promises and deals; have I allowed myself to be cornered by people, possessions, or prosperity; so that when Jesus is on trial before me in the courts of my daily living and business, I cannot see what love and truth require and do it regardless of cost?"

But in Barabbas we come closer to the heart of the meaning of the Cross for us. The bizarre intrigue of Caiaphas and Pilate may seem distant from our experiences, but Barabbas is "Every Man" when it comes to the Cross. We can feel with him what it must have been like to have someone go to death for us.

Like Judas, Barabbas was a Zealot and a fierce insurrectionist. His stature and bearing portray aristocratic birth and culture. He was Jerusalem's Robin Hood. But his unbending nationalism had led to murder, and however justified he might have been in the defense of Israel's cause, he was sentenced for his crime. Did he know of Jesus? We cannot be sure. What we can assume is that he was probably incarcerated with Jesus. Imagine what communication went on between them. They had the same love for Israel, but their ends and means could not have been further apart. But I can feel what he must have felt when he heard his name shouted by the crowd. He knew what that meant! Had Caiaphas groomed him for the part? We do not know, but we do know that Jesus took the cross that was meant for Barabbas' execution that day.

Jesus did the same for us. We have been set free because he went to Calvary for us. He took our place. He suffered for us. He died for our sins. He opened eternal life for us. He absorbs the blame, takes the guilt, answers the sentence. By God's grace Christ has taken our place! What he did then, he does right now if we will only realize it.

In the soldiers we find ourselves again. They had a duty to perform. But why did pent-up anger at all authority find such a rampant revenge? They were ordered to scourge Jesus, that was all. That meant beating him with leather thongs with pieces of metal and bone interwoven in them. Instead they took the punishment into their own hands and added insult to the scourging injury. The kingly purple robe or the crown of thorns had not been instructed by Pilate. Nor had the beating, kicking, and spitting. Jesus became the victim of their rebellion and self-hatred.

Are we any different in what we do to people who have failed —are broken or condemned? Think of the distortion of religious people who focus their anger and hostility on others, never fitting the punishment to the crime. In those people I see the criticism, gossip, and judgmentalism of any of us who play the judge and take the punishment of others into our own hands.

Returning to our Scripture, we see that the scourging and cruel treatment of the soldiers left Jesus half dead. Bleeding and exhausted by both the emotional trauma and the physical torture, Jesus was forced to carry his own cross to the place of execution. It was the heavy portabellum, the crossbar; the *stipes crucis,* the vertical portion of the cross, awaited him on Calvary. The weight was unbearable. He could barely put one foot in front of the other as he made his way through the jeering crowd. On the way, he fell in the dung and dirt of the street, the crossbar leveling a further blow on his already beaten body. The soldiers whipped him like an animal to rouse him to his feet. When this failed, they commandeered a by-stander to carry the cross.

His name was Simon of Cyrene, a Jewish pilgrim from North Africa who had come to Jerusalem for the Passover. He had been watching the cruel procession from a safe position of observation. Now he was a participant in the passion! Can you feel what he felt when he lifted the cross off Jesus and he struggled to his feet? What must it have been like to look into the face of the Savior stained with blood and the smarting wounds of the thorns? What was in Jesus' eye? What did Simon feel when his eyes met his?

Whatever it was that passed between them in that moment must have drawn Simon to watch Jesus die on Calvary. But further, it must have drawn him into the fellowship of the disciples and later into the early Church. Mark's reference to his sons Alexander and Rufus tells volumes in one almost parenthetical reference. That, and Paul's reference to these sons in his letters, indicates that Simon became a leader and influenced his family to follow the risen Christ. I like to imagine this man sharing the story of what happened to him with his family. I can picture his boys listening in rapt attention and then giving their lives to the one whose cross their father carried.

In Simon of Cyrene we experience the implication of the Cross for our lives today. We, too, must carry Jesus' cross. We stand on the sideline today watching the cruelty and sickness of the world. Then Jesus' words break into our consciousness: "If any man would follow me he must take up his cross." Suddenly we are Simon. Only now Christ's cross is spelled out in human need. Denial of our own interests and desires makes way for our involvement in wherever the Lord is being crucified anew in our time. That's why we were born. We are not to repeat the atonement but to accept it and then live it in our relationships.

And the Alexanders and Rufuses of our lives will be blessed. They symbolize not only our families but our friends and people whom we want to know the love of Christ.

In this sweeping summary of Mark's account of the last day and the events leading up to Calvary we stop short of the crucifixion itself. That we will see through the eyes of the centurion who said what God wants us to say, "Truly, this man was the Son of God." But linger for a moment before we go on to Calvary and ask this question, "Where would I have been on that day? What would I have done?" The painful truth is that what we would have done then is probably what we are doing right now. But the liberating truth that touches us all whether we are a frightened Mark, a denying Peter, an impatient Judas, a conniving Caiaphas, a vacillating Pilate, a vicariously liberated Barabbas, an angry soldier, or a commandeered Cyrene, is the knowledge that Jesus went to the cross for all of us. And that means we don't have to remain what we are. The Cross is for now! Forgiveness, the defeat of death, eternal life, a life of crossroads, and an assurance that Christ's victory is ours!

CHAPTER 32

THE GIFT

Mark 15:21–47

It is impossible to comprehend the Cross. Human intellect alone cannot fathom the depths of what happened on Calvary. No amount of study or contemplation will unlock its truth to us. Our human capacities can only touch the outer periphery of its meaning. We may reflect on its historical significance and still not experience its reality. We can theorize about its theological import and be untouched by its power. Christians and nonbelievers alike can evaluate the symbolism of the Cross and be moved by the idea of vicarious suffering of a man because of love for his friends, but miss the cosmic implications of what happened at Golgotha.

Surely that's the reason that we talk so much about the Cross, but experience little more than faithless familiarity. It's now very fashionable to wear costume jewelry crosses around our necks. I was at a formal party the other evening at which I overheard a group of ladies discussing the crosses their fashion designers had found for them. The status symbol was the value of the jewels which were inlaid in the gold or silver. I wondered how much these people knew or cared about the sacrifice and cruel agony of the cross when it was roughhewn wood. There were no rubies on the Cross which executed the Son of God. We place magnificent crosses on church steeples and yet the life of the church beneath is often not motivated by the inclusive, humble love of the Cross or the Lord of the Church. We are fastidious about the carving or metal work of the delicate liturgical crosses we place in our chancels, but seldom is either pulpit or pew centered in obedience to take up the Cross.

One year during Lent, I surveyed one hundred members of various Christian churches about the difference the Cross made to them. The question I asked was, "Would it have made any difference to your life as you are now living it if Christ had not died on the Cross?" Forty-five said they didn't think so! Twenty-five said that they thought so but did not understand what difference it made from the theological explanation they had heard. Twenty indicated that it made all the difference both in what they believed and how they lived, and ten said they just didn't know because they had never comprehended what the Cross was all about.

How would you have answered? Does it make any difference to us? I mean in our inner being, so the fact that Christ died for us is the basis of our security and hope? Do we feel forgiveness and have we become forgiving people of ourselves and others? Has the Cross liberated us from self-justification or defensive patterns in our relationships? Have we ever realized that the Cross is not only the message of our faith, but also the mandate of our style of life? Many of us would have to say, "No, sorry, but after all I've heard, sung, and repeated about the Cross, its real meaning is still elusive to me!" Still others ask honestly, "How could the death of a man so long ago be the basis of forgiveness, reconciliation, and new life for me now?"

The crucial issue is: Who was it that died on that Cross of Calvary? Was he the Messiah, the Son of God? That was the issue for Mark. He believed that Jesus was truly God's Messiah and that he had gone to the Cross in fulfillment of Isaiah 53. After the resurrection, the early Church looked back on the Cross and understood what Jesus had tried to communicate throughout his ministry. He had gone to the Cross as God's sacrifice for the sins of the whole world. He was the Lamb of God. Now they could put Jesus' name in the pronouns of Isaiah's prophecy: "Surely he has borne our griefs and carried our sorrows; yet we esteemed him stricken, smitten by God, and afflicted. But he was wounded for our transgressions, he was bruised for our iniquities; upon him was the chastisement that made us whole, and with his stripes we are healed" (Isa. 53:4–5).

Throughout his Gospel Mark has been trying to tell us what Paul articulated: "God was in Christ reconciling the world to himself." That's what he wanted his readers in the early church at Rome to understand with undeniable clarity. Having made clear that Jesus was God with us, loving, forgiving, atoning, he described the details of his death on the Cross with vivid clarity. Mark knew that the experience and acceptance of the Cross is a gift. It is supremely a gift of the Holy Spirit. We cannot break through the barrier of our limited reason and insight unless God himself breaks through to us. It is by the gift of faith alone that we can know the meaning of the Cross, realize its implications for us personally, and begin to live in its power. But the gift cannot be earned. God wants to give it. When he does, one of the greatest miracles of all creation occurs. Then we are able to express the profound reality of the Cross and say, "He died for me! I am forgiven! I am loved! Now that's the way I want to live with and for others!"

That's the magnificent meaning of what happened to the centurion at the foot of the Cross. Mark has given us a personalized example of the transforming miracle of what happens when the Cross happens to a person. Only the Holy Spirit could have enabled this rough, uncultured soldier to say, "Truly this man was the Son of God!" I personally believe that Mark included his exclamation not just because it was a part of the collected oral tradition of the crucifixion, but because the centurion exemplified and personified the miracle of what he wanted to happen in all his readers. The vivid details of Jesus' suffering and death should bring forth nothing less from us. The same Spirit which enabled the centurion to comprehend what was taking place in this One he crucified is available to us: "Truly the man is who Mark has been telling us he was. He is none other than the Son of God, my Savior!"

Let's penetrate the mind and heart of the centurion. We can imagine that he groaned and grumbled when he received his orders in the early dawn of that Friday. The crucifixion detail was an unpleasant, brutal duty. He had been assigned to that before. It was a dirty business. Prisoners shrieking in pain, writhing in agony, struggling wildly to escape. Often it took all the strength of his soldiers to hold prisoners down on the crossbar while the hands were nailed to the rough, splintery wood. Then like a worm on a fisherman's hook they would squirm and twist as they were lifted up and the crossbar was put into the socket of the vertical stake where the cross was formed. Next, the feet were nailed one over the other with just enough bend in the knee to allow the prisoner to desperately lift himself up to breathe. Death would

come slowly but surely from suffocation. Usually the process was
hurried some by a severe scourging before the actual crucifixion.
Most prisoners were half dead before they reached the cross.

The centurion had doubtless seen thousands of men die, many
at his own sword in more battles than he wanted to remember.
Crucifixion was different for him, somehow. It took so long, the
sun would be blistering, and the waiting for the victim to die could
be tedious and boring. When he learned that those to be crucified
that day included insurrectionists like Barabbas, he feared an uprising of the unpredictable mobs of Jerusalem. He knew that the
political unrest was at a turbulent high pitch over issues which he
neither cared about nor understood. All he knew was that the Jews
hated all their Roman occupiers. To be ordered to serve Caesar in
Palestine was considered one of the worst assignments for a Roman
legionnaire. Now to oversee an execution was one more event in
a bad tour of duty that he hoped would end soon so he could return home to Rome. He wondered why he had worked so hard to
rise to the ranks of the sought-after position of commander of a
hundred men.

Little did the centurion know that he was to be a participant in
the event which would change the course of history and would
transform his own life.

When he arrived at the maximum security cells to pick up his
prisoners, he was surprised that only two were turned over to him.
One had been released by a strange order of Pilate in response to
the persistent appeals of the Jews. Little matter, he thought. He
was told that the third prisoner was to be apprehended from the
praetorium inside the palace. So he started his grim crucifixion
march, his two prisoners carefully bound and guarded by his men.

As he reached the praetorium, he heard loud, jeering laughter
and mocking shouts from the soldiers within. It was obvious that
the scourging of the prisoner had gotten out of hand. When they
finally led the prisoner out, he was a sorry, bleeding, beaten man.
The soldiers, howling with laughter, had placed a royal looking
robe over him and had mercilessly crushed a crown of thorns onto
his head—the thorns cutting deep into his flesh causing blood to
flow down his face.

The centurion looked at him carefully with the discernment
that comes from years of leading men. "What has he done?" he
asked.

Then one final burst of anger and ridicule came from the soldiers as they pushed him into the crucifixion procession, crying, "What did he do? He claimed he was a king! Hail, king of the Jews!"

A placard was given the centurion by Pilate's order to place on the cross over the head of this prisoner. The inscription on it was in Latin, Greek, and Hebrew. The centurion could make out the Latin. "This is the King of the Jews!" it proclaimed boldly. "What a strange charge," the centurion thought. "The Jews have no king!" Then he began to piece together the rumors he had heard about a Nazarene rabbi who had been welcomed to Jerusalem with such triumph a few days before. He had heard talk about his popularity and the hatred of the Jewish leaders for him. "So this is Jesus of Nazareth," he mused to himself. "We will soon see what he's made of!"

The centurion knew from the first that this prisoner would never make it carrying the heavy crossbar. He was too badly beaten for that. The centurion watched him struggle to put one foot in front of the other as they made their way through the narrow city streets, the crowds pressing in upon them, some jeering, others laughing, still others anguishing with the prisoner's pitiful plight. He was not surprised when Jesus stumbled and fell. He felt a strange mixture of pity and impatience for him. Then he reached out and grasped the shoulder of a strong young African who had been following the procession for some time. "You carry the man's cross!" he commanded with a centurion's undeniable authority.

As they approached Golgotha, so named because of the skull-like shape of the cragged rock on the hillside, the centurion thought, "How appropriate for a crucifixion place." But it was another face that magnetically drew his attention. It was the calm countenance that baffled him. Several times on the road he had felt the prisoner looking at him with warm affirmation. Now as they began the crucifixion procedures, he seemed to be more concerned about the anguish of the other two than himself. When they got to him there was a display of courage the centurion had never witnessed. He admired valor, endurance, and fortitude in a man more than anything else. But he had never seen anything like this.

He offered Jesus a drink of the wine mixed with myrrh, a narcotic. It was prepared by benevolent women and meant to have a dulling, pain-deadening effect on those being crucified. Once again the centurion's eyes met Jesus! There was appreciation for the kindness, but he refused the drink. "Take it; it will help!" Still, he refused. "Does this man know what he's in for?" the centurion wondered, "Or was this sheer tenacity, bravery? What kind of man is this?"

Now a soldier roughly threw Jesus down on the crossbar that the Cyrene had carried to the place where the permanent vertical bar stood ominously under the hot Palestinian sun. The centurion had to supervise the dirty work closely to be sure it was done right. Again, that face! Through the blood and sweat, Jesus' piercing eyes caught his. Still that amazing courage! He did not resist. No struggle. No shrieking cries for mercy or release.

One of the soldiers sat on his chest as another stretched out his arms on the crossbar and drove the nails, blood squirting out on all of them. "What was it about this fellow?" the centurion thought. "Was he too weak to resist, or was there something else?" Whatever, here was raw physical courage that he admired.

Now several soldiers lifted his body with outstretched arms on the crossbar. There was an ominous thud when they finally got the crossbar into the socket of the vertical pole. They nailed his feet flat against the wood. The crucifixion process was now begun and Jesus struggled to lift himself up for breath. Then, when the pain in his nailed feet became too excruciating, he slumped down and the throbbing, piercing pain shifted to his hands.

It was then that Jesus spoke words that shocked the centurion: "Father, forgive them, for they know not what they do!" The soldier turned to one of his men and blurted, "Did you hear what he said? Who's his father? He forgives us! What do you think of that!" The soldiers laughed. But the centurion didn't think it was funny, somehow.

Off to one side of Golgotha four soldiers now turned their attention to dividing Jesus' garments among them which they had stripped from his body. The tunic was strangely woven from top to bottom and without seams. One said, "Let's not tear it, but cast lots for it to see whose it shall be." And so they gambled for the robe, happy to have some distraction from the grim business at hand.

The centurion carefully watched the strange crowd that had

gathered on Golgotha. Chief priests from the temple were intermingled with a strange mixture of scribes and the street rabble.
He was particularly surprised by the hate they expressed toward
Jesus. It was obvious to him that the chief priests were the jeer
leaders of the crowd. He could see them telling the people what
to shout at Jesus. At their signal the crowd began to parade beneath the cross, fiercely wagging their heads and spewing vitriolic
jibes.

"Aha! You would destroy the temple and build it in three days,
save yourself and come down from the cross!" The chief priests
inflamed the crowd further when they threw caution and reserve
aside and entered into the deriding themselves. "He saved others;
he cannot save himself. Let the Christ, the King of Israel, come
down from the cross, that we may see and believe."

Curiosity was fired by genuine interest in the centurion. He
drew one of the chief priests aside. "Look here, why do you hate
this man? What did he do to you that you should carry on like
this?"

"He claimed to be our Messiah, the Son of God," was the anger-
infected response.

The centurion looked up at Jesus' face again. "What was going
on here?" he thought. He didn't think of himself as a religious
man. As a Roman he believed in many gods, each with a different
name—Mars, Jupiter, and all the rest. He was unashamedly su-
perstitious about getting help from the gods in battle, and he had
to admit that he was strangely attracted to the Jew's belief in one
God, Yahweh. Now here was the one that claimed to be the Messiah, the Son of God, that the Jews talked so much about and
expected so feverishly. Why wouldn't these people take the man
at his word? Could it be that he was the Son of God? The centurion was surprised that he felt sympathy for the man on the
cross.

But it was what Jesus said as the crucifixion hours dragged
by that stirred something within him. The other two being crucified with him picked up the derision of the crowd and they, too,
began to mock him. One said, "Are you not the Christ? Save
yourself and us!" But the other one made a strange reversal in
the mocking. He shouted out to the other, "Do you not fear God,
since you are under the same sentence of condemnation? And we
indeed justly; for we are receiving the due reward of our deeds;

but this man has done nothing wrong. Jesus, remember me when you come into your kingdom." Did this man know about Jesus? Had he followed the events of that last week in Jerusalem? Was he partially convinced that Jesus was what he claimed to be? The centurion didn't know. But Jesus' response shook him: "Truly, I say to you, today you will be with me in Paradise." Even though he was racked with pain, his words had authority. Paradise? He spoke like a king!

There were others in the crowd that now attracted the centurion's attention. They were weeping, holding on to each other for assurance and comfort. Two in particular caught his eye. A young man and a woman. Grief was written on both their faces. He was told that one was Jesus' disciple; the other his mother.

The tender sensitivity hidden beneath the centurion's gruff exterior was deeply moved by what he heard Jesus say to them. In spite of his own anguish he was concerned for his disciple and his mother. Strange, loving words came from the center cross: "Woman, behold, your son! Behold, your mother!" He gave them to each other. The centurion felt the closeness these two seemed to have for each other. He had seen all too little of that as he had marched and battled for Caesar throughout the Empire.

At the sixth hour the sky was strangely dark. It produced an eery feeling in the centurion. "Why was it so dark at this hour of the day?" he wondered. Then Jesus' suffering was growing more intense. The centurion could not make out the meaning of the words he cried out. The Jews off to the side of Golgotha heard it: "Eloi, Eloi, lama sabachthani!" Some recognized it as the first lines of Psalm 22. It sounded like a cry of dereliction, "My God, my God! Why hast thou forsaken me?" We are sure that Jesus continued the prayer to the end of the Psalm: "For he has not despised or abhorred the affliction of the afflicted; and he has not hid his face from him, but has heard, when he cried to him." And then I believe Jesus found comfort in the sovereignty of his Father over the worst that could happen: "All the ends of the earth shall remember and turn to the Lord, and all the families of the nations shall worship before him. For dominion belongs to the Lord, and he rules over the nations" (Ps. 22:27). It is my conviction that Jesus drew assurance that his suffering and death would be used by God for the ultimate fulfillment of his purpose.

Mark's account has a strange twist. He records that the by-standers completely misunderstood and used even his prayer in the familiar words of the Psalm to ridicule him. The words for Eloi and Elijah sound very much alike, especially under the duress of suffering. It is revealing that the Jews immediately thought that Jesus was calling for help from Elijah rather than from God. That could be taken in two ways. There was a belief that Elijah would come to help at a particularly difficult time in a Jew's life. There was also a belief that Elijah would precede the coming of the Messiah. Perhaps all of these things were discussed among them within the centurion's hearing.

Then they played with Jesus' plight. One of the crowd put vinegar on the end of a reed. The Jews wanted to keep Jesus alive to see if Elijah would come. What a revealing thought Mark has given us. Whether to help or precede the Messiah, it reveals that the people were not so sure that their judgment about Jesus was altogether right. Would Elijah come to one who blasphemed as they said he had? Or could it be that some of them wondered about his claim to be Messiah? Whatever, their offer of the vinegar was not out of pity.

The final moments of Jesus' dying drew the centurion irresistibly to him. He heard Jesus pray again to his Father, the same Father from whom he had asked for the centurion's and the soldier's forgiveness. "Father, into thy hands I commit my Spirit"—a childhood prayer known to every Jew from his mother's knee. But now for Jesus it was a trusting commitment of himself to his loving Father whom he trusted unreservedly.

One thing the centurion knew now was that this man believed he was a Son of God. God was his Father and the centurion could see superhuman endurance as a result. He could not deny that now, and the strange thing which amazed him was that he didn't want to deny it. In fact, he felt a growing conviction within him that this man was authentic.

Then the end came: "It is finished!" In one final gasp for breath, Jesus died finally of suffocation—his being collapsed, his human heart beat a final beat of total exhaustion.

Now the centurion found himself fixated as he looked at Jesus' face. Through the blood and sweat now caked on his face, he could see a serenity and peace that he had always longed for, but never had known.

As he stood there watching, the centurion felt a tremendous flush of emotion growing within him. His mind was gripped by an undeniable conviction. "This man really believed that he was the Son of God. And now, I believe it too! I don't know all that means, but whatever it meant to him, it means to me!"

Then the centurion shouted out what had grown within him: "Truly this man was the Son of God!" He surprised himself. He didn't care what his soldiers, the Jews, or the officials of the temple said. As for him, this man was a true Son of his Father, and he believed it.

There are several interpretations of the centurion's confession of belief in Jesus. Some have said that he observed Jesus to be the best of good men and that he simply admired his courage. His statement, according to this view, is an affirmation of the manly way in which Jesus died. Others have said that the statement attests to the centurion's belief that Jesus was innocent. This would be consistent with Luke's record, in which the centurion said, "Surely this man was innocent!" Some others have said that the correct translation of the statement is, "Truly this man was a son of God!" That would be consistent with his religious background, even if he had been affected by the Jewish monotheism of the city in which he served.

None of these satisfy me. "Son of God" was a Hebrew expression which would not be common to this centurion. I believe that he picked up the phrase from the accusation of the Jews that day. The expression of the man Jesus as he watched him suffer and die led him to believe in him and the claim he had made.

But we will have come far from the truth unless we include in our consideration that the Spirit of God was particularly active on Calvary that day. If we accept that as basic to our interpretation and couple it with the Church's later conviction that "No one says that Jesus is Lord except by the Holy Spirit," then we have more clearly exposed what happened to the centurion. It was by the gift of faith through the Holy Spirit that he spoke that tremendous, life-reorienting conviction.

That's the response I feel Mark wanted from his readers. Any consideration of what Christ did for us and the whole world that day on Calvary should bring forth the same response. What we cannot achieve by reason or contemplation the Holy Spirit gives as a gift. There is a magnificent unity in the way God both accomplishes our reconciliation through Jesus and works to liberate us to believe it is true for us and is the basis of our hope and joy.

If we accept the gift, it will transform our lives. We are loved to the uttermost. A sacrifice has been made for all our sins, failures, and distortions of life. We are now free to accept ourselves as loved. That will spill over in a new affirmation of other people. There's no need for defensiveness now! Self-justification is a habitual pattern which is now broken when we accept that we are justified by Christ's death. More than that, by his death, fear of death is gone and we can live the days of our life fully.

But is that the most stable and indestructible reality of your life? If not, ask God to give you the gift he gave to the centurion. From the deepest reservoir of your being you will be able to say, "Truly, this was the Son of God! He is my Savior and Lord!"

CHAPTER 33

LIFE WITHOUT LIMITS

Mark 16

May I ask you a very personal question? What is it that limits your life? What sets the seemingly immovable boundaries of life's limitations on you? What is it that keeps you from being the person you had hoped to become and doing what you long to accomplish? Who or what is it for you: the people in your life, burdensome handicaps, or the circumstances in which you find yourself? What debilitates your dreams, discourages your daring, drags you down?

Focus on that for just a moment of honest introspection. Perhaps the limitations are self-imposed. Does the memory of previous failure ever immobilize you with a fear of trying again? Are you frustrated with a feeling of inadequacy, a lack of energy, strength, or intellect to face life's problems? Do you ever feel an insufficiency of inner resources to tackle the challenges and opportunities life offers? Do you have too little time, patience, and will to do what love demands? Then, too, the limitations may have come through no fault of your own in ill health or disability. Do you ever feel resentful and disturbed that life has dealt you a cruel blow? Are you tempted to give up the possibility that you will ever be liberated? Do you wish you could say with Robert Louis Stevenson, "I will not allow the medicine bottles on my mantelpiece to be the limits of my horizon"? Or perhaps the limitations are imposed by other people. Are you frustrated by the resistance or negativism of others? Do they stand in your way? Ever want to give up on changing human nature? And what about the world around you? Do you feel like you are caught in the web of society's insolvable problems? Have you felt the overwhelming inability to change the complexities which hold a death grip on the jugular vein of your happiness?

Now let me ask you an even deeper question. Do you think it will ever be any different? Is there any hope for these hindrances; any opening through these obstacles? Must you live a limited life forever?

These questions help us to empathize with the followers of Jesus after the crucifixion. They were painfully aware of the limitations of life. The cruel and excruciating cross had ended the most abundant life that they had ever seen. Death had conspired with the complex collusion of evil men to extinguish the most winsomely loving person whom they had ever met. If that could happen to their Master, what hope was there for them but to merely endure their remaining days? Anger over what men had done to him, coupled with remorse over their own cowardice to help him, mingled with consternation at God that he had allowed it to happen, pounded relentlessly in their minds. They had loved and lost. All the old doubts and fears rushed back into their lives to fill the void left by their crucified Lord. Their hearts ached with grief and their bodies were racked with anguish. Life did have limits after all! Now there was nothing to do but give Jesus a proper burial and remember what might have been.

Some of the women who followed Jesus made their way through the dim dawn of the first day of the week. As they trudged wearily toward Joseph of Arimathea's garden where they had hurriedly placed Jesus' body after the crucifixion, they asked one another a question which further intensified their feelings of futility: "Who will roll away the stone for us from the door of the tomb?" Who indeed? The soldiers? The frightened disciples?

How like our questions in response to life's amazing possibilities and astounding potentials! What hope is there? Do I have what it takes? Should I even try?

That stone over the tomb reminds us of life's insurmountable barriers. We all have them. What's yours? Is it a situation you would rather not face, a person who's difficult to love, a problem that resists solving? Unless I miss my guess, most of us are more aware of the things we can't do than those we are willing to boldly try. "There are limits you know! There are some things that just can't be done. We will be happier if we settle with life's impossibilities." Sound familiar? For most of us life is defined by the boundaries of limitation. That's the way the women felt when they finally reached the garden, eyes downcast with infeasibility. But when they came to the tomb, they looked up with startled wonderment. The stone had been rolled away! Awful fear gripped them. Who had rolled the stone away? They rushed into the tomb. Jesus was not there! Their minds leaped to a further evidence of life's tragic eventualities. Had someone stolen the body? Would they not even have the opportunity of expressing their grief by anointing his body? Mark tells us that they were amazed. They were completely undone!

Then a young man sitting on the right side of the tomb dressed in a white robe proclaimed the good news of Jesus' resurrection: "Do not be amazed; you seek Jesus of Nazareth, who was crucified. He has risen, he is not here; see the place where they laid him. But go, tell his disciples and Peter that he is going before you to Galilee; there you will see him as he told you."

There's the trumpet blast announcing a life without limits! In that joyous proclamation we find three great truths which break the boundaries of life's limitations: He is risen; he goes before you; his promises are true—he told you it would happen. That's what we all desperately need to hear and realize today.

There's nothing too big for God! Death is defeated. Christ is alive. The resurrection is now the basis of our hope: If God could do that, is there anything which limits us that is impossible for him?

But recognizing the fact of the resurrection is one thing; realizing the power of the resurrection is quite another. Mark's account shows us that the followers of Jesus had difficulty with both. Fear seized the women who first heard the limitation-liberating news. It's difficult for us to imagine. They said nothing to anyone. Why? They could not put their minds around the limitless power of God. After Jesus appeared to Mary Magdalene and she told the disciples, they would not believe it. Then he appeared to two of his grief-stricken followers on the road to Emmaus. They realized that he was alive and tried to convince the disciples. But they hurt too much to hope again. "They did not believe them," Mark records with flat finality. They just were not open to daring to believe again.

Disappointment and discouragement do that to all of us. That's why we can feel how the disciples felt. We too have heard the good news of the resurrection. Why do we continue living debilitated lives with that dynamic available? Like the disciples our greatest need is to have the resurrection happen to us.

Look at what happened! The resurrected Lord persists. He presents himself alive to the disciples and penetrates their lives with the undeniable truth of his living presence. He upbraided them for their unbelief and hardness of heart. That means he confronted them with their galvanized resistance to new possibilities. He blasted open the tomb of their own hopelessness, rolled away the stone of their resistance, and made it possible for them to realize that he was alive. Then he told them the startling news that he would continue his ministry through them. They were to go into all the world and preach the gospel. Then he exposed the unlimited power over life's limitations they would have. What oxygen is to the lungs, the resurrection was to become for the disciples.

Surely the most powerful historical proof of the resurrection is the "resurrected" disciples. Dull, defeated people became fearless, adventuresome leaders. Cowards became courageous; the timid became triumphant; the inept did the impossible. "He is risen!" became the joyous chant of a new life without limits. On the pages of the Book of Acts and the history of the early Church we meet the vibrant Easter people for whom the word impossible no longer had any meaning. The Lord whom they loved and followed in his ministry was now alive and his post-resurrection home was in their hearts.

But now look more closely. In the days following the resurrection we find the secret of the same quality of life for us. The transforming experience for the disciples was that they were filled with the same power that had raised Jesus from the dead. Jesus' promise became true: "I am the resurrection and the life."

The two must be kept together. And that's exactly what happened during the days following the resurrection. The life they had seen modeled and mediated by Jesus during his ministry now became theirs. His words, "Because I live you shall live also," became a reality. They, too, were resurrected into a new quality of life. The resurrection afforded them not just a duration of eternal life but the dynamic of the abundant life—not only the promise of infinity, but the power to live an infinitely different life. More than the fact that fear of the end was over; now the end of fear was theirs. All things were possible. Life without limits had begun. That alone accounts for the contagious love and power that we see in the disciples because of the resurrection. Mark tells us plainly what happened, "And they went forth and preached everywhere, while the Lord worked with them and confirmed the message by signs that attended it."

That's the exhilarating message of Easter! Not only that Christ is risen, but that the resurrection can happen to you and me right now. The resurrected Lord works in us what he wants to communicate through us. What does that do to the limitations we talked about earlier? What would we dare to do and be if we knew that the Lord was working with us? What would be within the range of possibility if the only concern was to follow his guidance and live by his indwelling power?

When most of us are faced with challenges and opportunities, we ask questions like these: Is it possible? Will it work? Are we able? One is the question of human potential, the next of human opinion, the last of human capacity. But now, in the context of the resurrection, there is only one authentic question: Does the Lord will it? That sends us back to prayer and the realization of the resources of the resurrection.

Recently I spoke at a church in a large city called The Church of the Resurrection. What a glorious name! But I wondered if the people who worship and study there realized the power available to them. When I met and talked with them, I sensed the same reservation and limitations I find contradicting so many Christians today. They had the right name for their church but the possibilities for them as individuals and for their life together were all determined on the basis of human adequacy. They desperately needed what happened to the disciples after Jesus rose. They needed to know that the same power which raised Jesus from the dead was available to them.

And so do we. A defeated, debilitated Christian is a contradiction of terms! To join the Easter chorus and sing "He is risen!" without being able to shout, "I am risen! I am alive forever! Death for me has no power! Now I can live without limits," is to miss Easter.

The Apostle Paul spells out how this can happen to all of us. In Romans 6 he identifies us with the cycle of death, resurrection, and new life revealed in the Savior's life: "For if we have been united with him in a death like his, we shall certainly be united with him in a resurrection like his. We know that our old self was crucified with him so that the sinful body might be destroyed, and we might no longer be enslaved to sin. For he who has died is freed from sin. But if we have died with Christ, we believe that we shall also live with him. For we know that Christ being raised from the dead will never die again; death no longer has dominion over him. The death he died he died to sin, once for all, but the life he lives he lives to God. So you also must consider yourselves dead to sin and alive to God in Christ Jesus" (Rom. 6:5–11).

Did you catch the liberating power of what Paul said? Here are the basic steps we can take to begin a life without limits right now.

The first step is to become united with him in a death like his. Our old self is to be crucified with Christ, our sinful body is to be destroyed, and we are no longer to be enslaved to sin. It is crucial that we understand what sin is in that context. We were created to know God, be filled with his Spirit, and live dependently on his power and guidance. Sin is just the opposite of that. It is more than wrong things we do; it is the independent, self-sufficient person we are. Sinfulness is estrangement and separation from him. The original Greek word meant to miss the mark. We sin when the arrow of our life misses the target of the reason we are alive: to know God, love him, and serve him, utilizing his unlimited resources. We become sinners when we struggle to go it alone, to run our own lives, and try to determine our own destiny. It becomes habitual, and that's what Paul means about enslavement to sin. We all know what that's like—loveless, lonely, limited. But Christ died on the cross so that we might know that God loves us with unlimited grace just as we are.

We are crucified with Christ when we die to ourselves. We give up the management of our own lives. The secret is surrender. That means total commitment of all that we have and are and acceptance of the Lord's complete control over our lives. Our cruxifixion with Christ means death to our plans, our will, our self-justification, our cleverness. There is no resurrection without crucifixion. We cannot by-pass the Cross—Christ's or ours!

The second step is realizing our own resurrection. When we die to ourselves, that's the only real death we will know. Physical death will be a transition in living. Following the crucifixion of our old self-centered nature, there is an actual resurrection to a new life which takes place in us. We are lifted out of the cycle of trial and error, discouragement and despair, to a new quality of living. The power of Christ comes within us to guide and direct us. We experience the transformation of the transferred life. Our hearts become the container and transmitter of the living Lord!

The final step is resurrection living. This is life without limits, indeed! Instead of prohibitions, we are given a life of possibilities. Surrendered to Christ, filled with Christ, we are now able to walk in what Paul calls newness of life: "We are dead to sin and alive to God in Christ." The vicious pattern of self-propelled adequacy of trying to live by our own wit and will is replaced by a wide-openness to the Lord's intervention and surprising infusion of power in our daily living.

In Romans 8 Paul marshals all the enemies of life and parades them before us to expose their impotence: "Who shall separate us from the love of Christ? Shall tribulation, or distress, or persecution, or famine, or nakedness, or peril of sword?" These are the environmental circumstances which no longer have power over us. Can anything limit Christ's life in us? Listen to Paul's answer. "No, in all these things we are more than conquerors through him who loved us." Next Paul parades all of the fears which frustrate us: "For I am sure that neither death, nor life, nor angels, nor principalities, nor things present, nor things to come, nor powers, nor height, nor depth, nor anything else in all creation, will be able to separate us from the love of God in Christ Jesus our Lord." Think of it! Death is finished and we can live every day to the fullest. None of the dimensions of time—memories of the past, fear of the future, worry over the present—can limit us. Forgiveness is given for what has been, guidance for what shall be, power for what is now. No evil power can possess the person who is sealed in Christ.

That's the resurrection—the limitless life God offers. Now what can we do to receive it? Paul teaches us the prayer which unlocks this life without limits: "That I may know him and the power of the resurrection" (Phil. 3:10). Another translation puts it, "All I want is to know Christ and experience the power of his resurrection" (TEV). The quality of life we have been talking about is a profound, penetrating, personal relationship with Christ himself. The power of the resurrection is his own power in us. He infuses our minds to think his thoughts, indwells in our emotions to express his love and forgiveness, and he inspires our wills to discern and do his will. That's why living in the power of the resurrection is so exciting and unpredictably interesting. No drab creed, it is moment by moment surprisability. We are constantly amazed by the insight and wisdom he gives us, the doors of unexpected opportunity he opens, and the raw courage and physical strength he pulsates through us.

Carl Sandburg said, "Woe to him who believes in nothing. Always the impossible happens." When we believe in Someone whose track record includes the crucifixion, resurrection, and present power, the impossible becomes the anticipated and expected.

Recently, I drove behind a VW which had a sticker on the fender which read, "Honk if you believe in anything." We've all seen stickers which ask that we blow our horns in esoteric identification. This one was a very broad, inclusive plea: Honk if there's anything you believe. So I honked vigorously. At a stop sign I pulled up beside the VW and shouted out to the man behind the wheel: "Not anything . . . Someone! His name is Jesus. Happy Easter!" The young man smiled in appreciation and shouted back, "Right on, man!"

We live in a world which has run the course of human potential. Our time is marked by a pervading hopelessness. I say shout if you believe in the only One who can give us hope that lasts. We need a hope which is not circumstantial or dependent on the conditions in which we find ourselves. No human being however gifted or wise can be an authentic source of hope. I am not willing to put my hope in anyone or anything which is not ultimately reliable. Christ and the power of his resurrection alone can be that. Who else covers all the dimensions of our need for forgiveness and love; who else can solve the problem of me in my complex self-centeredness and liberate me to give myself away in caring concern; who else can push back the boundaries of my negativeness about life and show me a way to live expectantly; who else can liberate me from the fear of dying and free me to live unreservedly?

In the ancient Roman cemeteries there can be found tombstones on which are written the mood, not only of ancient Rome, but of our time, *"non fui, fui, non sum, non curo."* That translated into English is, "I was not; I was; I am not; I do not care." Have you ever felt that way? Do you feel that way now? How very different in contrast to Martin Luther who wrote with his finger in the accumulated dust on his desk, almost symbolic of the besetting problems which had accumulated in his life. *"Vivit, vivit!"* "He lives! He lives!" That's what I need to know for my life today. In the words of a motto of Edinburgh, *"Nisi Dominus frustra,"* "Without the Lord, everything fails."

The resurrected Lord not only dwells within; he leads out ahead. Just as he was always ahead of the disciples leading the way during his ministry, and then as the victorious frontiersman of the early Church, so, too, he's way out ahead of us. There is nothing to fear now. He will lead us through all the problems of every tomorrow and all the impossibilities of today. The Scottish proverb is right, "Whom God will help no man can hinder."

Now look again at the limitations with which we began. With honesty we can admit that we are not able. But with the confidence of the resurrection we can know that he is able. Listen to the undaunted faith of those early Christians in whom the resurrection was more sure than their own pulse beat: "He is able to strengthen those who are tempted" (Heb. 2:18); "He is able to save those who draw near to God through him" (Heb. 7:25); "He is able to keep you from falling" (Jude 24); "He is able to subdue all things unto himself" (Phil. 3:21); "He is able to keep that which I have committed unto him against that day" (2 Tim. 1:12); "He is able to do exceedingly abundantly above all that we ask or think" (Eph. 3:20).

That's the explanation of the unconquerable gusto of the early Church. They had tapped the unlimited, enabling power of the only One who is consistently able. I feel it; don't you? But there are times we all lapse back into our own capacities and must cry out with the final chorus in T. S. Eliot's *Murder in the Cathedral:*

> Forgive us, O Lord, we acknowledge ourselves as
> type of the common man
> Of men and women who shut the door and
> sit by the fire;
> Who fear the blessing of God, the loveliness
> of the might of God, the surrender required.[1]

The words bite and wound. There are times when we fear the blessing of God and would rather shut the door and live a limited

[1] Reprinted by permission of the publisher, Harcourt Brace Jovanovich, Inc.

life. But I agree with Evelyn Underhill, "If Christianity sometimes seems hard, it is the hardness of a great enterprise in which we get great support."

I know that to be true for me. Christ is alive for me and I believe that by his grace the resurrection has and continues to happen to me. I have felt his intrusion on my own self-centeredness. I have known his infusion of power into my own insufficiency. I have experienced his intervention into my problems. I have felt his incisive direction in my life. I have sensed his uplifting strength when I am weak. I have realized his inclusive love pulsating through me.

What I have tried to say about life without limits comes direct and flaming out of my own heart! I dare to say with Paul, "I can do all things through Christ who strengthens me." I know that as a man, a husband, a father, a leader, and most of all an indomitable adventurer in the new life in Christ. It's not always easy, it often demands the raw courage of trust, but it is never dull! To know Christ and the power of his resurrection is unashamedly exciting. I cannot subdue the joy which breaks through all my limitations and I want to sing:

> Because He lives I can face tomorrow,
> Because He lives all Fear is gone.
> Because I know, I know He holds the future,
> And life is worth living, just because He lives.[2]

Do you know that? Can you join the Easter chorus and sing that? Death could not hold him; he arose! Our reservations cannot resist him; he is here. Our negation about life and ourselves cannot defeat him. He comes to each of us: "Behold, I stand at the door and knock. If any man will open the door I will come in to him." If we open the door of our hearts and invite the living Lord to come in, the resurrection will happen to us. We will be new people; shaped in his image. And then we will become participants in his unlimited power. If you want to know Christ and the true life without limits he makes possible, will you pray with me the following prayer?

"Living Lord Jesus, I want to know you and your life without limits. Thank you for dying for me. Your love for me right now melts the cold resistance of my heart. By faith I accept your forgiveness for the sin of running my own life and limiting the immense possibilities of joy, of peace and love you offer. I want to know you and experience life through the power of your resurrection. I surrender myself to you. Here is my mind, think through it; here is my will, guide and direct all my decisions; here is my heart, come and live in me. Make me your Easter miracle right now. Thank you Lord, that with this commitment, I have died to myself and am alive forever. All things are possible now. Hallelujah and Amen."

FOR FURTHER READING

By Lloyd John Ogilvie . . .

Let God Love You. In 38 devotional messages,   **$3.95**
the author takes the struggles of life seriously
and turns them into stepping stones to Christian
growth. The riches of Paul's Epistle to the Philippians is the basis for these refreshing messages. In Quality Paperback (#2831–1).

Drumbeat of Love. Lloyd Ogilvie's fresh, chal-   **$7.95**
lenging studies in Acts offer the secret of an
exciting life in which "you and I are to be the
subjects of the new Chapter God wants to write
today." Hardcover (#80483).

When God First Thought of You: The Full Mea-   **$6.95**
sure of Love As Found in 1, 2, 3 John. In Lloyd
Ogilvie's lucid and sensitive style, these small
books of the New Testament become a vast resource for the recovery of an intimate relationship to Christ. Hardcover (#0102–2).

. . . and Others!

Matthew and Mark: A Relational Paraphrase,   **$6.95**
by Ben Campbell Johnson. Ben Johnson's
astute relational paraphrase of the books of
Matthew and Mark. These two books are illuminated as never before in modern language,
using contemporary relational concepts. Hardcover (#0093-X).

The Intimate Gospel: Studies in the Book of John, by Earl Palmer. An often neglected side of Jesus emerges from this incisive study of the Gospel of John by one of the more popular commentators writing today. Here, says the author, is a Gospel writer who gives us an intimate "behind-the-scenes" narrative of the life of Jesus. Hardcover (#0101–4). **$6.95**

Salvation by Surprise: Studies in the Book of Romans, by Earl Palmer. A moving new Bible study, now in quality paperback. Paul is seen as the prosecutor of mankind offering history's first genuine, whole view of man. The prosecutor then moves across the courtroom and offers a defense, a strong word of hope. And finally, Paul's words become pastoral and supportively personal. Brings sure counsel to believe in God's faithfulness. (#2842–7). **$3.95**

Women Like Us: Learn More About Yourself Through Studies of Bible Women, by Maggie Mason. The stories of ten of the most interesting female figures of the Bible—like Hagar, Leah, Elizabeth, and Mary Magdalene. A capable study guide which includes probing questions into the reader's thoughts and opinions on the actions and fates of these women, both noble and besieged. Great for study groups. Quality Paperback (#2835–4). **$3.95**

Survey of the New Testament, by Ronald Ward. The ideal overview of the New Testament for the new Christian or experienced believer. Included is an inspiring discourse on the certainty of the gospel, its reality and effectiveness in the lives of so many today. Hardcover (0069–7). **$7.95**